When Consumers Complain

ARTHUR BEST

WHEN CONSUMERS COMPLAIN

New York Columbia University Press

Library of Congress Cataloging in Publication Data

Best, Arthur.
When consumers complain.

Includes bibliographical references and index.
1. Consumer protection—United States.
I. Title.
HC110.C63B47   381'.34'0973   80-21789
ISBN 0-231-05124-7

Columbia University Press
New York   Guildford, Surrey

To my parents

Contents

Acknowledgments

THIS STUDY is based on research supported by a generous grant from the Carnegie Corporation of New York to the Center for Study of Responsive Law's Consumer Complaint Project. Case studies were made of 132 consumer problems, by interviewing the buyers, sellers, and third parties involved in each disputed complaint. A national survey of responses to unsatisfactory purchases was conducted in thirty-four cities, with 2,419 respondents. Substantial thanks are owed to consumers and business people who contributed thousands of hours of time in interviews, thus making the study possible.

The project's primary advisor was Laura Nader, Professor of Anthropology at the University of California. She showed a clear understanding of the difficulties inherent in exploring so broad a subject as consumer complaints, and inspired everyone to undertake the exploration optimistically, and with a keen eye for new theories, ways of testing theories, and ways of understanding our subject. The advisory panel included Judge George Brunn, Municipal Court Judge in Berkeley, California; David Caplovitz, Professor of Sociology at the City University of New York Graduate Center; Dr. Albert Hirschman, fellow at the Institute for Advanced Study at Princeton; Ralph Nader; and Gordon Sherman, former president of Midas Muffler Corporation. The advisors provided highly useful criticism, advice, and support, both to the Center for Study of Responsive Law's work and to concomitant work carried out at the University of California at Berkeley. Much of the work centered in Berkeley is published in *No Access to Law* (New York: Academic Press, 1980), edited by Laura Nader. On several occasions, meetings were held in Washington to discuss working papers. We are grateful to members of the project's advisory panel and to William L. F. Felstiner, Marc Galanter, Klaus-Friedrich Koch, and Michael Maccoby for participation in such meetings.

The case studies were supervised by Dr. Christopher Wheeler, who designed the case study methodology and directed the Consumer Complaint Project from January 1974 until the spring of 1976. The methods of inquiry he developed were highly effective; he elicited a high degree of care and enthusiasm from the entire staff. The case researchers, who participated in the project for periods of time ranging from several months to two years, were: Penny Addiss, Janice Lowen Agee, Robert Byron, Carol M. Dana, Steven Everly, Michael Ford, Joanne Horvitz, Deborah Leff, Pilar Markley, Joyce Munns, Susan Rasky, Nancy Sachs, Andrew Sharpless, and Cheryl Wyman.

Some of the case researchers did other research in addition to case studies. Also, the following individuals participated in the noncasework research of the project: Bernard L. Brown, Daniel Clearfield, Ruth Darmstadter, Marion Eaton, and David I. Greenberg.

The survey was conducted under my direction, with the help of Call For Action, a national voluntary organization that operates referral and assistance programs in many cities. Ellen S. Straus, the group's chairperson when the survey was carried out, was instrumental in its success. David Caplovitz recognized that the combined resources of the Consumer Complaint Project and Call For Action could produce an accurate and significant survey, and he helped liberally in developing the questionnaire and analyzing the data. Seymour Sudman, Professor of Business Administration at the University of Illinois, gave valuable help in the design of the questionnaire and the survey's sampling techniques. Alan R. Andreasen, Professor of Business Administration at the University of Illinois, collaborated in analysis of the data, and in reports of the survey published in *Law & Society Review* and *Harvard Business Review*. The University of Illinois College of Commerce and Business Administration generously permitted use of its computer. Painstaking coding was performed by Jane Batt and David F. Sand.

The title of my book refers, with high regard, to *When Americans Complain: Governmental Grievance Procedures* by Walter Gellhorn (Cambridge, Mass.: Harvard University Press, 1966). Nearly fifteen years ago, that classic work on problems with government services first raised many of the issues the present study deals with in the context of purchases. The manuscript was reviewed by Laura Nader, Ralph Nader, Penny Addiss, Andrew Sharpless, Christopher Shugart, and Thomas Stanton. Their comments are appreciated. The influence of Ralph Nader, in particular, should be credited for any benefits this research may produce.

Following my work at the Center for Study of Responsive Law, I was a member of the faculty of Western New England College School of Law, in Springfield, Massachusetts, from 1976 to 1978, and have since served as Deputy Commissioner of the New York City Department of Consumer Affairs. Work on this book was completed at Western New England College School of Law, where Paul McCary, of the class of 1979, gave me the benefit of research and editorial assistance. The manuscript was typed by Mary Omartian, Jean W. Tremblay, and Diane Cicchetti; it is a pleasure to thank them for their fine work.

Arthur Best

New York City
February 1980

When Consumers Complain

PART ONE

Introduction

One

The Universe of Consumer Troubles

DO AMERICANS get fair value in the marketplace? Sometimes. But when we get less than we pay for there are complicated and serious consequences. Breakdowns in dealings between buyers and sellers affect the quality of life, the quantity of life, the reality of justice, and the credibility of government. A fair and efficient consumer complaint process can compensate for losses that occur when purchases have deficiencies, and can prevent those losses from leading to a range of adverse effects on society as a whole. If consumers are encouraged to speak up about problems, and if careful use is made of the information they provide by complaining, the quality of products and services will improve and there will thus be fewer occasions for buyers to register complaints.

We make millions of purchases every day, from chewing gum to film developing; TV sets to appliance repairs; automobiles to home improvements. When things go wrong with these purchases, we deserve to have the products repaired or replaced, the services performed again, or our payments refunded. This would be fair, since we suffer losses from products that do not perform properly or services that fail to accomplish their purposes, but the usual occurrence is not fair. The vast majority of purchase shortcomings are never rectified. We bear the losses, and sellers keep payments worth far more than the products and services they provide.

Except where health and safety are concerned, no one expects every product or service to be flawless. But when for any reason a seller does fail to provide fair value in exchange for a buyer's money, it is reasonable to expect that seller to encourage the buyer to complain about the problem and to treat the buyer's complaint quickly and equitably. Nowadays, this expectation is unfulfilled.

Buyers sometimes do not—or cannot—notice the shortcomings in their purchases. Even when buyers are aware of problems, they often choose to avoid complaining, and to absorb their losses. And finally, when they do complain, businesses often reject their requests. When this happens, buyers usually cannot secure effective help.

Complaints can serve two functions: compensating individual buyers, and collecting information valuable to all buyers. If complaints are properly solicited and fairly treated, they will direct compensation for deficient products and services to the buyers who deserve it. Properly monitored consumer complaints, collectively, can serve as a fund of information to help businesses improve service to customers, to help government improve law enforcement and other regulatory actions, and to help consumers plan purchases to avoid sellers or particular products and services with poor records of problem occurrence or complaint resolution.

It would be pointless to analyze the complaint process if consumer problems were rare, but as most people know intuitively, such problems are widespread. For example, when researchers meet consumers, business people, or government officials to conduct interviews on the general topic of complaint handling, each interview seems to include an obligatory discussion of the individual's *own* most recent consumer problem. When top executives of three automobile companies appeared before a Senate committee to comment on proposed taxes for cars with poor fuel economy, two of the senators began the session by presenting their own complaints about cost, workmanship, and design in cars they had recently purchased.[1] These personal stories may seem irrelevant to the subjects being discussed, yet they are not disgressions at all. They show that everyone suffers from consumer troubles, and are examples of the widespread annoyance, inconvenience, unhappiness, and economic loss inflicted on people when purchases fail and complaining is difficult and often fruitless.

The incidence of consumer problems has been measured in a number of surveys, including one conducted for the present study. Quantitative data are reported in chapter 6, but a description of the kinds of problems buyers face can provide a context for discussion of the implications of the current failure to treat consumer complaints properly. Some of the problems people notice frequently (and may or may not complain about to sellers or other complaint handlers) are: high cost, breakage, poor design, poor workmanship, insufficient durability, failure of a service to accomplish its purpose in a single attempt, failure to deliver a product or delay in delivering a product, and misrepresentation.

In our survey, some typical responses indicate the variety and importance of consumer troubles:

Battery operated toys use the batteries up too fast.

The doll's hair fell out four days after Christmas.

I bought a hearing aid for $350. They told me it was new. Then I found out it was secondhand.

They cut the legs off my new sofa when they came to deliver it. They should have measured the front door better.

The turntable cover is too flimsy. It should be stronger, or it should have instructions that you have to handle it very gently.

Radial tires were expensive, and then when they wore out within the 40,000-mile guarantee time, the company didn't honor the promise.

[Car] seats are uncomfortable, light switch is hard to use, battery wore out after six months, thin paint, springs are starting to poke through the seats.

Bought outside antenna for TV set. The display in the store isn't like the the real unit. They installed it sloppily. Might be a fire hazard.

Doctor took X-rays in his office and said I was all right. Then he called me up and told me to go over to the hospital for more X-rays. I went, but never found out if anything is wrong.

Brought an iron home after the cord was replaced. When I plugged it in, the lights blew out. The repair shop said that if they looked at it again, they would charge me again.

They didn't fix my car right the first time.

Explicit product and service failures penalize consumers several ways. The value of the purchase is decreased, or its purpose may be thwarted. If a consumer decides to seek redress he or she must devote additional resources to that effort. To some degree, confidence in our economic system and method of producing and marketing goods and services is diminished.

Consumers can see these explicit problems, but many other problems are nearly impossible to perceive. Thus, the perceived problems are in fact a subset of all the problems consumers experience. Many times products or services do not live up to the claims sellers make about them, but consumers lack the expertise or resources to discover the deficiencies. Furthermore, there are products and services which do live up to sellers' claims, but which ought to be better and would probably be rejected by many buyers if practical alternatives were publicized or made available. To purchase any of these products is to become, in a sense, a comsumer with a problem.

All products sold to consumers explicitly or implicitly claim to be safe for their intended uses. Yet the Consumer Product Safety Commission has found that many products are unsafe in ways that consumers cannot recognize. Every user of such an unsafe product is an unwitting victim of a consumer problem; it is primarily when injuries occur that ignorance is transformed into knowledge of the dangers.

Toys injure about 700,000 children each year. A terrifying catalog can be written of the undiscernible dangers that account for many of these injuries. For example, manufacturers have designed and marketed flammable dolls, spring-loaded toy rifles, and hobby kits with irritation-causing ingredients. All parents who give hazardous toys to their children are, along with the children, victims of serious consumer problems.[2]

Buyers of mobile homes have been injured when formaldehyde used in adhesives in some plywood and chipboard flooring vaporized to form an odorless gas irritating the eyes and the upper respiratory passages. These adhesives are used much more frequently in mobile homes than in conventional homes. The homeowner is hurt by gas that cannot be seen or smelled, and that comes from adhesives used in construction materials that he or she had no power to select or reject.[3] Such a homeowner suffers serious problems, but is often incapable of perceiving or articulating them.

There are problems of possible long-term toxicity of hair dyes, and with radiation from microwave ovens and other consumer electronic products. But information on these known or suspected hazards is often withheld from buyers by manufacturers and retailers.

In commonly purchased foods, too, undiscernible hazards have often been present. For a long time before the Food and Drug Administration acted to remove Red Dye Number 2 from its list of approved food colors, manufacturers had known of the controversy over its safety. Yet people who consumed billions of food products each year were generally ignorant of the danger of Red Dye Number 2, and were totally unable to ascertain from product labels whether any particular food, beverage, candy, or medicine was colored with it.[4]

Inherent safety defects exist in millions of automobiles. During the early years of the automobile recall era from 1966 to 1972, 25 million automobiles were subject to recalls for safety defects. Many other cars had similar serious defects but were not recalled due to oversight by the National Highway Traffic Safety Administration. Some owners of 1965–1969 Chevrolets had to wait seven years to discover, in a 6-million car recall agreed to by General Motors in December 1971, that their cars had been designed and manufactured with engine mounts that might fail and send their cars almost out of control. In 1977, Ford Motor Company announced a recall that by its own admission should have been carried out four years earlier.[5] In 1978, there were 270 recall campaigns, covering 9.1 million vehicles with safety defects.[6]

In addition to design defects which affect all cars of a particular make and model, individual manufacturing errors abound in new automobiles. Consumers Union (CU) found 826 defects in the 36 cars it tested in one year. This finding, an average of 23 defects per car, *excluded* hundreds of cosmetic flaws found in paint, trim, and upholstery. The defects were related to the cars' functioning and included an average of 5 defects per car that were considered serious by CU engineers. Many of the serious problems are, according to CU, hard for consumers to ascertain. For example, loose or missing body parts, often difficult to detect, in association with exhaust leaks which CU found to be prevalent, can kill.[7]

In the health field, consumers are victims of an estimated 2.5 million unnecessary operations each year. Each operation harms a consumer financially (either directly or through an effect on insurance rates) and exposes the patient to a variety of risks including, in many cases, possible loss of life. But the consumers who bear these burdens ordinarily have no way of knowing that they have been victims of such poor performance.[8]

To round out the discussion of product and service flaws that are difficult or impossible for buyers to discern, two important kinds of economic information must be considered. Ordinarily, consumers assume that a product will be reasonably durable or that the effects of a service will endure for an appropriate length of time. Another common assumption is that the costs of operating a particular product will be similar to the costs of operating other similar products. In fact, to make decisions based on durability and cost of operation, consumers must usually rely on such assumptions, even though they are often unwarranted. Thus, buyers of inefficient refrigerators that use much more electricity than is used by otherwise comparable but efficient refrigerators are burdened with a severe consumer problem but cannot judge their full economic injury.

Similarly, buyers of poor durability toys or appliances are victims of inherent but nondiscernible problems. When the seemingly premature breakdown occurs, they know they have a problem, but they cannot compare beforehand the durability of the toys or appliances they buy with that of rival products. There is usually no way consumers can determine durability or cost of operation of a product for themselves. Test reports by consumer organizations and a few legal requirements for operating cost disclosures at present provide only slight help to the majority of buyers. Low durability and energy inefficient products still find buyers, and then penalize those buyers with their inherent disadvantages.

Another economic issue relates to the cost of virtually everything that is sold, and yet is invisible to buyers: the impact of price-fixing and other business practices that distort the market process. Enforcement of antitrust laws has never adequately protected consumers against artificially high prices.[9] The largest corporations are able, even without collusive arrangements with rivals, to produce and market products with gross disregard for the ultimate interest of consumers. Yet no single buyer can be aware, for example, that buying a particular brand of detergent might contribute to maintaining unfair employment practices or policies that take too little account of environmental risks.

On a smaller scale, the housing market places buyers at a similar disadvantage. To judge the fairness of rent increases, for example, tenants would need to know a variety of operating costs and other management details. House buyers are typically unable to evaluate the long-range operating costs of particular houses, or to know whether mortgages are offered on an equitable basis.

The chronicle of consumer problems is incomplete with a review of only the perceived and unperceived problems in products or services. Consumers suffer yet another category of problems with products and services that are indeed what they claim to be, but would probably be rejected by consumers if alternatives were freely available, and if the attributes of the alternatives and the currently purchased products and services were all well known.

Many car buyers do not give careful consideration to the lack of passive restraint systems in automobiles. No one would buy a car with a wheel or a driver's seat missing, but cars that are not equipped with air bags or other passive restraint systems are, in the opinion of a number of automobile experts, just as incomplete.[10] Still, people buy and ride in cars that are far more dangerous to their passengers than they should be. Because they do not have adequate information, or because they have been misinformed, many buyers do not consider the lack of safety features a shortcoming in new cars.

In another way, cars cause problems for consumers by doing what their sellers say they will do. Millions of cars are sold that pollute the atmosphere far more heavily than need be, given the current state of automobile engineering knowledge. Consumers buy them out of ignorance of the dangers of such pollution, and without being aware of the possibility that a particular manufacturer's cars may be significantly less polluting than those produced by the largest companies, or that even the largest companies could be influenced to produce cleaner running cars if they felt more pressure from the marketplace.[11]

Some additional examples demonstrate how a product that does what it is supposed to do can constitute a problem when compared to possible alternative or improved products that can also perform its function. All over the country, people use electricity for heating water, and the electric water heaters they use do exactly what they are supposed to do. But even though they perform up to specifications, they represent special problems to their owners. First, all of these appliances would consume less electricity per volume of water heated in typical use if they were manufactured with additional insulation. Second, they are usually used to the exclusion of devices that can use solar energy to provide hot water. "It costs too much," or "it's not worth the money," are two ways to express a basic consumer complaint. Actually, all users of ordinary electric hot water heaters could make this complaint, if they considered greater insulation and solar energy when they evaluated their expenditures for water heating.

Buyers of life insurance often buy "whole life" rather than "term" policies. If they realized that whole life insurance combines the coverage provided by term insurance with an enforced thrift or savings program, but costs more than term insurance policies and pays lower returns than most savings accounts, they would no doubt consider themselves consumers with grounds for complaints. At the present time, about 20 percent of people who buy whole life policies let them lapse within two years. This is more than twice the rate of such lapses twenty-five years ago, and is a clear response to the difficulties in understanding how insurance policies work and what insurance buyers get for their payments. [12]

A final example of these "there's a better alternative" consumer problems concerns virtually everyone who has ever bought anything. This broad statement can be made because the example is all homogeneous package goods. Package goods are low priced, frequently purchased items, often sold in grocery stores, such as soap, cereal, bread, and paper towels. Homogeneous package goods are rival brands of such items that are virtually identical in all regards except brand names. People who buy famous brands of ordinary white bread spend millions of dollars a year more than they would spend if they bought identical loaves of bread sold under nonadvertised names. Each buyer of the costlier loaves pays for a combination of bread, advertising, and overhead. [13] The problem these buyers have is not that the bread is stale or below minimum government standards: these buyers (and buyers of all kinds of homogeneous package goods) have been overcharged for their purchases. Evaluating the kind of bread purchased in the context of other available branded on nonbranded bread shows that they spend countless extra dollars for no real benefit. Without realizing it, they buy a wide variety of products at prices far higher than they could pay for identical but less well known items.

Deceptive advertising can create problems by confusing consumers about the attributes of particular products. Where the qualities of an item are not accurately known, it is especially difficult to know whether an alternative might be a better choice. Listerine mouthwash was advertised heavily with claims that it could be effective against colds. After lengthy Federal Trade Commission litigation, it was determined that this claim is untrue, and that Listerine would have to state, in future advertisements for a period of time, that it does not prevent colds or lessen their severity.[14] Consumers who might have been buying the product to obtain a benefit it cannot provide may now learn the truth, but that opportunity comes late and may be missed by individuals who do not happen to see advertisements with the federally required correction.

All of the problems this chapter describes represent losses to consumers. The discernible and nondiscernible shortcomings of products and services that are not what they claim to be, and the implicit shortcomings of products and services that are not what they ought to be, add up to a large assignment for society's complaint-handling process.

In the past, the treatment of consumer complaints has received little attention from the consumer movement. Efforts to improve products or services have approached the problem from the top, looking down. Regulation to improve the quality of products, for example, has concentrated on what occurs before the merchandise is offered for sale. The response to Upton Sinclair's *The Jungle* led to federal regulation of some parts of meat-packing and other industries engaged in producing food and drugs.[15] However, the establishment of standards and even reasonable enforcement of those standards cannot offer a complete solution to the problem of sale of impure foods and drugs. A serious weakness of the regulatory framework is that it does not incorporate pressure from the final targets of production and marketing, the buyers. Regulation can produce drastic improvements in the *quality of goods and services*. But real accountability for the *quality of regulation* can exist only if buyers are able to make known their reactions to purchases coherently and forcefully. Throughout the muck-raking era, government regulation and access to accurate information about products were seen as the reforms which would make the marketplace operate fairly. A well-known article by Wesley Mitchell, "The Backward Art of Spending Money," published in 1912, compared housewives with business executives, and concluded that lack of standards and comparative data prevented household consumers from making the kinds of wise buying decisions that make business efficient.[16] Yet Mitchell did not treat the issue of purchasers' ability to obtain corrective action when purchases are unsatisfactory.

In the 1920s and 1930s books such as *Your Money's Worth* and *100,000,000 Guinea Pigs* carried forward the emphasis on consumer protection through government regulation and availability of consumer information.[17]

Up to the present time, recognition that pressure from victims can improve business conduct has been rare. Even a proposal as valuable and beneficial to consumers as federal aid to dispute-resolution mechanisms has been considered almost exclusively in terms of its aid to consumers as individuals, with little attention to its possible role in benefiting all consumers, as a group, through prevention.[18] The same analysis was made concerning consumer complaint handling by proposed federal consumer agencies.[19] Now that unsatisfactory products and services confront consumers with vast economic risks and unprecedented health risks, every means of improving business responsiveness to buyers' needs must be used.

All consumer problems represent breakdowns of the social order, but from the consumer's point of view, law is usually absent or inefficient, and so are complaint-handling institutions. Our economic system is meant to provide values to buyers: it should give consumers a certain quality of life, and even a certain quantity of life. Consumer problems actually represent thefts of the values people work to earn. A fair system of complaint handling could protect the integrity of workers' incomes. The lack of a fair system lets random allocation of redress substitute for a rational and just distribution. Furthermore, where health and safety are at stake, consumer complaints can do even more than provide a vehicle for securing economic justice. As society becomes more complex, microwave ovens[20] or ozone-destroying aerosols[21] may be supplanted by newer, potentially destructive products. In a broad perspective, consumer complaint handling can become a process for managing the violence of our mass distribution, technological society.

At present, consumers absorb most problems without making complaints. Thus, information about problems, which could be a primary benefit of efficient and fair complaint handling, is denied to government, business, and the general public. With regard to compensation for faulty products and services, the unfortunate fact is that only about one-half of voiced complaints are resolved in favor of the consumer complaints. Taking into account the obstacles that hamper consumers in perceiving and speaking up about problems with purchases, data establish that about one out of every six purchases leads to an ultimately unremedied consumer problem (these data are described in chapter 6). Clearly there are many instances in which sellers fail to provide redress to economically injured buyers. If the apparent difficulty of speaking up about the shortcomings of purchases could be reduced, and if the rewards of registering complaints could be made more equitable and predictable, more people would voice complaints and would receive redress.

Fair treatment of consumer complaints should be recognized as a powerful mode of consumer protection, as valuable as both regulation, which seeks to improve the overall quality of goods and services, and consumer education programs, which aim to provide people with better information about products and services and the ability to use that information.

This study describes major flaws in current complaint handling, and suggests improving opportunities for just consideration of complaints. Greater likelihood of fair treatment can encourage buyers to voice complaints they might currently withhold because they believe the effort of complaining is not balanced by adequate opportunities for fair resolutions. The next three chapters deal with three stages of the consumer complaint process—problem perception, complaint voicing, and complaint resolution—by describing difficulties in fair problem resolution. The discussion of the three stages of complaining is followed by a chapter covering special problems with third-party complaint handlers, and a chapter describing the results of our survey and other quantitative research. Finally, the study explores reforms, emphasizing the need for procedures to enable consumers to make businesses accountable for the shortcomings of products and services. At the buyer-seller level, sellers could be required to establish clear procedures for handling complaints, to respond to complaints within specified time periods, and to maintain records that will permit easy monitoring of their complaint handling. For disputes that are not resolved at the buyer-seller level, mediation, arbitration, legal services, and small claims courts must be made more accessible and effective.

PART TWO

Obstacles in the Consumer Complaint Process

Two

Perceiving Problems

THE CONSUMER complaint process can usefully be divided into three stages: perception of problems, voicing of complaints, and resolution of complaints. *Complaint process* is a term, however, that needs a clear definition. It can be thought of as simply the transactions that take place when buyers complain to sellers about shortcomings in purchases. A broader definition would add actions taken by buyers who voice complaints to sellers but are dissatisfied with the reolution offered by sellers; such actions include appeal to third parties. But perhaps the most useful definition is based on the idea that complaints allow sellers to fulfill their obligations to buyers. Sellers owe buyers delivery of whatever is offered and bought; when this delivery is not accomplished, for whatever reason, the buyer has been disserved, and a process, probably involving complaint, ought to operate to inform the seller that it has not yet met its obligations to the buyer.

A seller who wanted to provide a product that would fully meet both the customers' needs and the representations made by salespeople or in advertisements could devise a quality control system that would keep deficient products from reaching customers. Alternatively, sellers could practice less stringent quality control and compensate buyers who detected and complained about defects. This alternative is the choice of virtually all sellers and manufacturers. That business relies on the consumer to perceive deficiencies in products and services and to complain about them demonstrates the importance of knowing actual patterns of problem perception.

This chapter examines the first stage of the complaint process, perception of problems. Based on the case studies, it describes the major impediments to the perception of problems by purchasers; impediments which block the consumer complaint process at its very beginning. The lack of clear perception of problems hampers both the fair distribution of individual corrective measures and the collection of information for general preventive actions.

The case studies show a number of significant obstacles to accurate observation of problems by consumers. For instance, facts may be hard to determine. Rights may be hard to define. Problems may change over time. Individuals may generally be disinclined to acknowledge consumer trouble.

Difficulty of Determining Facts

Understanding the relevant facts is the necessary precondition to making complaints. Many of the case studies collected by our researchers illustrate the difficulty of determining these facts. The case studies involve problems that people have perceived and made complaints about, usually to third-party complaint-handling institutions. Thus, they deal with a special group of consumer problems: experiences that have led to strong and persistent efforts to receive redress. As will be seen in chapter 6, complaints are voiced to third parties only in a minority of the instances in which people perceive problems. Nonetheless, many of those experiences show that identifying problems accurately can be a hard task, and that often even people who want to make complaints may not know enough relevant facts to be able to complain about the actual causes of their problems.

For example, Washington, D.C., resident Alan Krieger* bought and renovated two houses. Months after completing his work, he received a very high electric bill from Potomac Electric Power Company (Pepco). He tried over the course of nearly a year to find out why the bill was so high: Was it a charge associated with turning the power off and then on at the renovated houses? Did he owe money for a long-forgotten bill? Every time he called Pepco, he related the facts he knew to a different employee. Finally the company began to dun him for payment, but still would not provide enough information so that he could decide whether to pay

---

* In references to case studies, the names of consumers have been changed to protect the privacy of individuals. Names of businesses and complaint-handling institutions have not been changed. The case studies were conducted from 1974 to 1976. The sources of the cases are described in the Appendix.

the bill or complain about a billing error. Ultimately, the company threatened to turn off the power. Still unable to find out the facts, Krieger sued Pepco in small claims court. This action succeeded in getting the truth out of the company and led to an out-of-court settlement Krieger found acceptable.

Mrs. John Harrison bought a Bilt-Rite baby carriage from a store in Cheetowaga, New York. One of the wheels kept falling off, and during more than six months of complaining, all that Mrs. Harrison's efforts produced was a number of new wheels, none of which fit properly. At one point, she expressed her complaint, in writing, to a Better Business Bureau:

The wheel of the baby buggy does not stay on the frame. This makes it dangerous to leave the baby in the buggy. Since the company was notified immediately before the birth of the baby, I feel by now the wheel should have been replaced. The baby is five months old now. I have called and stopped in at least once a month. . . . Soon we will have wasted our money because the baby will be too old to use it.

Unbeknown to Mrs. Harrison, the carriage had been manufactured in Spain, and Bilt-Rite's only association with the product was to put its familiar name on it and distribute it. The company did not have adequate replacement parts available. The problem Mrs. Harrison faced was that an unfamiliar and hard-to-service product was sold under a familiar and well-regarded brand name. Since Mrs. Harrison was unable to discover the real source of her trouble, her complaints never mentioned it. Our research uncovered the reason for the poor performance by the store and the manufacturer, but Mrs. Harrison did not have that information as she dealt with the problem, even though she was highly active and creative in complaining.

A case involving possible injury to a child further demonstrates that knowledge of underlying facts can be crucial to successful participation in the complaint process. Special shoes were modified according to a doctor's prescription for Marc Shick, a four-year-old suffering from an illness which impaired his ability to walk. During three days that Marc wore the shoes he cried in pain. His mother then examined the shoes closely and saw that the width was marked B, the proper width for Marc, but saw also that the B had been inked over a partially scraped off C width mark:

the difference in width was critical, was causing Marc pain, and was nearly impossible for Mrs. Shick to discover. At first, two employees at Lord's, a Danielson, Connecticut, store that had sold the shoes, denied that the size was incorrect. But Mrs. Shick's view finally prevailed, based on the factual evidence she was lucky to discern. If the only fact Mrs. Shick had known was that her son was in pain, successful resolution of the complaint would have been highly unlikely.

When the relevant facts are difficult to establish, the consumer is prone to absorb losses without complaining. Yet these facts can involve subjects no more complicated than the ability of a garment to withstand dry cleaning or the amount of satisfaction a consumer can derive from a nearly new automobile which has broken down repeatedly.

Kevin Partyka, of Buffalo, New York, had a corduroy sport jacket with vinyl trim around the pockets. When he picked up the jacket from the dry cleaner, he discovered that the trim was cracked and discolored. Partyka was unable to determine whether the dry cleaner had used improper procedures, or whether the manufacturer of the garment had incorrectly labeled it "Dry clean only." He complained to the dry cleaner, and then to the local Better Business Bureau, but was never compensated for the damage to his jacket. If he had not been in doubt about the real cause of the problem, he might have been able to plan a successful strategy for presenting his complaint.

Facts are particularly hard to ascertain when a swindler contrives to conceal them. Alan Brewster, of Manchester, Pennsylvania, spent his life's savings of $6,000 to buy a so-called distributorship from a seller known as Consolidated International Tool and Oil, Inc. (CITO). The CITO salesman convinced Brewster that the well-known STP company stood behind the business deal, and that Brewster would be provided with twenty customers interested in buying STP products from him. In fact, STP was unrelated to CITO, and CITO did not provide Brewster with the customers as promised. But Brewster went on believing for months that he had dealt with STP, and when he complained about his problem, he complained about STP. Unfortunately, Brewster's real problem was with CITO. CITO and its president are now bound by a Federal Trade Commission consent order to cease misrepresenting their connections with well-known companies, but Brewster has never recovered his money.

Difficulty of Defining Rights

Understanding the rights of buyers and the obligations of sellers in particular situations can be difficult, thus making it hard for people to discover or acknowledge consumer problems. In a number of the case studies, underlying problems were difficult for consumers to ascertain because they had difficulty determining what was legally or morally right.

For six months, Jack Boroni of Brooklyn, New York, had problems with a new Chevrolet. On a vacation trip to Florida the motor knocked so badly that the Boroni family delayed its travel twice to have General Motors dealers repair the car en route. Soon a new engine had to be installed. Then the car was subject to a GM recall notice for brake repairs. In all of these instances, Boroni knew what the symptoms of the problem were, and was willing to complain about them. When he talked about the car to our researcher, he said, "I bought the car because I wanted a new car. Right away it broke down, and the car has been taken apart so many times, so many hands have been on it, that I feel I have a used car . . . I have no faith in it anymore. This one feels like a used car . . . it's no fun." Ultimately, Boroni was unable to articulate the real essence of his problem, the failure of General Motors to furnish him with what he and most other people have in mind when they buy a new car. The right to exchange a lemon for a new car, although a legal possibility, was not a practical alternative for him.

A recent judicial decision describes an experience similar to Boroni's but involving worse performance from an even more costly car. The owner of a new Cadillac sought to return it to the dealer because it burst into flames after having been driven only seventeen miles. General Motors and the dealer both refused to take the car back, but in a lawsuit against GM the buyer was successful. The court stated that an owner's confidence in a new vehicle is brought about by advertising, and held: "Once such confidence is shaken, a repair is not proper tender of the goods purchased."[1] Boroni might have achieved a similar resolution of his problem if legal help had been available and if he had perceived his rights more strongly.

Richard Warren, of Cleveland, Ohio, wanted to get a better job, to earn more money, and increase his self-respect. He wrote for information about a correspondence course in digital industrial electronics, and was then visited by a salesman for Bell and Howell correspondence schools. Warren was concerned that he might not have enough mathematical aptitude to study electronics, but the salesperson convinced him that the normal mathematical ability he must possess as a high-school graduate would see him through to successful completion of the course. The first materials arrived, and Warren made a partial payment of $140. After he had completed the first four of several hundred lessons that comprise the course, the material began to exceed his capacity for mathematics. His fifth lesson was returned to him several times with advice and criticism from the school. Warren asked to drop the course, and was given permission to do so. He considered the $140 he had spent to be a total loss. Several years later, Bell and Howell sought to collect the balance of the payments for the course. At that time, Warren complained about their practices, but maintained only that *additional* payments should not be sought by the school. Had Warren known his rights, he could have sought a refund of his original payment, because a home study course must in fact be reasonably similar to a salesperson's description of it to a prospective customer.

David Knox bought carpeting at a local store, and when the carpet was installed in his home, he thought it was inferior to the sample he had selected at the store. The complaint he made to the seller, however, was rejected quickly. In the store owner's opinion the differences Knox noticed between the sample and the carpeting actually installed were not differences at all; he called them "normal variations" in weaving and pile. Thus, Knox and the store agreed on the facts, but disagreed on what the consequences of those facts should be. This case ended happily for Knox, however, because he sued the store in small claims court and received a satisfactory judgment. But it shows that perceiving grounds for a complaint can depend on a person's conception of his or her rights.

Mrs. Jane Czajkowski, of Cleveland, Ohio, bought a new Ford equipped with a $400 stereo radio system. During the first few months of use the radio developed problems with static and one of the speakers cut out intermittently. Mrs. Czajkowski complained to the dealer, LaRiche Ford, and a replacement radio was installed. The replacement, however, had been designed for the previous year's models and did not fit her car properly. Mrs. Czajkowski did not know who was responsible for this flaw—the dealer, the Ford Motor Company, or the manufacturer of the replacement radio. Mrs. Czajkowski's husband suggested accepting the poorly fitting radio. In part, not knowing exactly who had done something wrong may have made it harder to characterize the situation as one in which a reasonable complaint could be made. Finally, Mrs. Czajkowski presented her grievance to the dealer with the help of a local consumer action group. Only then did the dealer respond with a satisfactory adjustment and accept the burden of identifying who should suffer the loss: LaRiche Ford, Ford Motor Company, or the radio manufacturer.

In an almost infinite variety of circumstances, uncertainty about rights and obligations inhibits people from realizing that particular circumstances constitute valid grounds for complaint. A Buffalo, New York, housewife, Mrs. L. Hanson, called a plumber to repair a leaky faucet. The work covered a span of more than seven hours, partly because the plumber took a three-hour lunch break and partly because he seemed inexperienced and had to telephone his office for instructions. Mrs. Hanson's only complaint was that she was charged for the worker's lunch time. She had no thought that the worker's level of competence was itself grounds for complaint.

J. F. Roderick, of Alexandria, Virginia, signed a contract with M. E. Flow, Inc. to add central air conditioning to the heating system of his two-story home. The company installed the unit, but when hot weather came the upstairs rooms did not get cool. Roderick examined the system as well as he could, and concluded that the company had done the work called for in his contract, but the house was still uncomfortably warm. He complained to Flow and pressured the company with the use of third-party complaint handlers for more than two years. Finally, Flow corrected the problem by adding some ducts to the system. Roderick worked hard to have his problem remedied, but because he believed that the Flow company had obeyed its written contract, he never thought he had been cheated. He believed the problem was partly his fault, "for not knowing the system's capabilities," and only partly the seller's fault for not "educating" him. What Roderick did not realize was that the claim made by Flow's salesman that the new system would cool his house was a legally significant part of his agreement, and that it was the seller's responsibility to fulfill the terms of such an agreement.

For the model years 1969 through 1972, many Ford cars were manufactured with unusually poor resistance to rust. Ford recognized the problem and decided that the proper action would be to pay for expensive repairs to the affected cars. Because Ford notified its dealers but not its customers of this decision, many Ford customers suffered from arbitrary applications of the policy by individual dealers. One of our case studies followed the experiences of Martin Kron, whose new Ford car became so badly rusted that he gladly sold it to a dealer for $600 when it was less than two years old. No one told Kron that Ford itself had decided that many owners of such cars deserved free repairs. Deprived of this knowledge, Kron perceived his problem as an irremediable occurrence whose cost he would have to bear; had he known Ford's probable opinion of his rights, he might have viewed the problem differently, and sought a different solution.

Similar circumstances involving 1974 to 1977 Fords led to formal Federal Trade Commission litigation. The cars were equipped with engines that were subject to a defect known as piston scuffing. Although Ford told dealers that owners of such cars could receive compensation, the owners themselves were never contacted. A settlement in 1980 required Ford to notify car owners in the future if it decides to extend warranty provisions to take care of special problems; in addition to eliminating "secret warranties," the company also agreed to publicize the availability of technical bulletins about possible engine and transmission problems and how they can be repaired.[2]

Problems May Change over Time

In other patterns of purchase shortcomings, individuals have difficulty in perceiving problems because the problems change as time passes. This sometimes makes it seem that consumers do not articulate their complaints clearly. One cause of apparently confused presentation of complaints may be that in the initial stage of noticing problems, consumers must deal with fluid and sometimes confusing sets of circumstances.

Chances for a changing perception of problems as time passes are greatly increased where a service or product is used over an extended period of time. Home improvement services illustrate this point. Mrs. Barbara Wells, of Philadelphia, suffered through more than two years of disappointments and severe economic and emotional stress because of an informal contract she made with James McHannon to renovate portions of an old house in Philadephia she had recently inherited. She paid $900 as a starting fee, and paid $1,000 about a month later, but the contractor failed her in many ways. After demolishing the portions of the interior that were to be replaced, he asked for additional payments. He put an undesirable kind of paneling in one of the rooms. He refused to perform all the work specified in the contract, although the job involved payments totaling $5,000 and work in many rooms of the house. As time passed, Mrs. Wells hired a lawyer and began to negotiate with the contractor. She agreed to terms suggested by McHannon's lawyer, but then McHannon refused to abide by them. Pipes froze and broke in the basement because the house was unheated during the winter. She had to pay to put her furniture in storage, since her move into the house was delayed.

Mrs. Wells's problem occurred over the course of more than two years. They are hard to separate into individual issues, and they are also hard to describe in an organized manner. In this case, Mrs. Wells's response to such heavy burdens was to seek help from a consumer action group. She eventually surrendered her hope of seeing the work completed or receiving reimbursement for the money she had lost, and instead worked for legal changes to prevent others from suffering similar problems in the future. But her case history clearly shows how problems can multiply and thus, at any given stage, become harder and harder to perceive clearly.

A case that involves a far smaller amount of money also illustrates this process. Robert Engel purchased a tape recorder at Korvette's Department Store in Rockville, Maryland. After a few months it broke. Engel's experiences following that breakdown constituted a galaxy of additional problems, but throughout his efforts to receive fair treatment, his perception remained fixed on the initial tape recorder failure. When he took the tape recorder back to the store where he had bought it, it was accepted for repair. Months passed, and Engel received no word about the machine. When he tried on several occasions to ask about it, he was usually put off or misled by uninterested or unknowledgeable salespeople. Finally, a store manager investigated and discovered that Korvette's had sent the unit to an independent repair shop that had not yet begun to work on it. The manager then sent the unit to a second repair shop. Months of delay had already characterized this case, but when the tape recorder was finally returned to Engel, its cover was broken. More delay and some acrimonious negotiations followed. A broken recorder, poor treatment by store employees, no work done by the first repair shop, actual damage to the unit while it was out of Engel's hands, slow work by the second repair shop, harsh treatment when compensation was sought for the broken part of the tape recorder—these are all elements of the problem. But when Engel thought about the incidents he kept only one or two of the events in mind. It was perhaps too complicated and time consuming, or too frustrating, to focus on the whole story of poor business performance.

The ability of consumers to discern problems may also be undermined if, in a series of events, the significance of an initial problem is overshadowed by a subsequent occurrence. For example, Horace Shean was treated by Dr. William Pierce during a weekend when his own doctor was away from the city. The doctor examined him briefly, prescribed an antibiotic, and asked Shean to return in two days. Before Shean returned he telephoned the doctor and felt, in the course of the conversation, that the doctor was confused about who he was and about what was the matter with him. Nonetheless, he went to the doctor's office. There, the doctor referred to a record card for a patient other than Shean. Later, Shean called the doctor to complain about the possibility that mistakes had been made in his diagnosis or treatment, and the amount he had been billed for. The doctor seemed rude to Shean, and when Shean and his wife finally complained to a third party about this pattern of poor service, they concentrated on the rudeness and on the size of the bill, rather than on the overall quality of the treatment.

Another characteristic of continuing problems is that when the underlying difficulty is not corrected, grounds for complaint can multiply. When the management of Arthur Snow's luxury apartment building was unable or unwilling to have the rats that infested it exterminated, Snow, a lawyer, kept a complete diary of events. His problems initially included both the presence of the rats and the management's lack of responsiveness. As months passed, however, the rats damaged some plants and other possessions in the apartment. During the early stages of complaining, he tended to focus on the most recent problems. But because he had kept records, he was able to present the apartment management with a clear and cogent list of grievances, and was prepared to document his losses should the management eventually agree to settle the dispute.

Impact of Low Expectations

Past studies have suggested that at the second stage of the complaint process, voicing complaints, people of low socioeconomic status do not participate as often or as well as other people.[3] Our survey, discussed in detail in chapter 6, is consistent with this finding, although it shows that additional factors are likely to be as important as social status. The present inquiry, however, is concerned with the first stage of the process, perceiving problems. A major difficulty in considering how people perceive problems is developing a proper means of measuring how well a service or product has met the expectations a consumer should reasonably have for it.

One possible treatment of this measurement problem is to assume that all purchases fail with approximately the same rates and magnitudes of failure, regardless of the purchaser's socioeconomic status. That is, there is little reason to assume, if poor people tend to buy items that are avowedly offered as items of medium quality, for example, that those items will meet the fair measure of medium quality any more or less often than rich people's avowedly high quality purchases will meet the fair measure of high quality. This approach will be used in our survey analysis. It is also possible to examine specific cases in which intuitive estimates of the actual deficiencies of purchases can be made. In a number of our case studies, relative youth, low economic status, or the impact of racial discrimination seemed to make it especially difficult for the disadvantaged buyers to perceive problems that might well have seemed clear-cut to other consumers.

One such case involves Jimmy Groves, a twenty-three-year-old resident of St. Louis, Missouri. He had been employed as a factory worker for some time, but had also suffered periods of unemployment. During one layoff, Groves found himself facing many more bills than he could pay. He was attracted by an advertisement that suggested large debts could be handled by single payments to a single company. He answered the ad and signed a contract, but did not realize for several weeks the exact nature of the agreement. He had not made a new loan or new agreements with his various creditors. Instead, he had merely agreed to pay a debt-pooling company a service charge for collecting money from him and sending it out to his creditors in proportions to be determined by the debt-pooling company. Before Groves came to understand the differences between a debt-consolidation company and a personal loan company, he wrote angry and confused letters to many of his creditors, accusing them in effect of dunning him for bills that were already being paid. Groves was chagrined when he realized the nature of his agreement. Although he complained and eventually saw his problem resolved, his experience clearly suggests that being poor and subject to stressful financial circumstances can cloud one's judgment, making one far more receptive to disadvantageous business dealings than he or she ordinarily would be.

Another young St. Louis man, living by himself for the first time, evinced a pattern of changing and sometimes lowered expectations during a dispute with a furniture store. William Devon was earning a modest income working as an X-ray technician. Obtaining attractive furniture for his apartment was important to him, and he decided to buy a blue velvet sofa, sold at a sale price by the Berger Furniture Store. When the couch was delivered, Devon noticed that its cushions were sewn so that the fabric nap faced in the wrong direction on one side of each pillow. When the pillows

were turned over, they appeared not to match the rest of the upholstery. For several months, he complained about the problem.
Yet on several occasions during that period, he decided that there
was *no* problem. Salespeople at the store were often able to
persuade him that he was too critical or, alternatively, that one
side per cushion is all that a person needs or ought to get when he
buys a sofa. Devon persevered, but he had come close to being
dissuaded. As he told our researcher, "When they talked to me
about the cushions, I began to think, maybe I'm wrong. Maybe
that's the way it's supposed to be."

Low expectations can result from a realistic appraisal of the
kind of products or services usually furnished by marginal or unconventional businesses. Peddlers, for example, do not provide
wide selections of good quality merchandise, and someone who
deals with them may be particularly accepting of certain selling
practices. For instance, James Roja had a neighbor who operated
a small car repair business, Jet Auto Rebuilders, which provided
very poor quality service. The neighbor did, however, provide
repairs informally and at low cost. Roja asked him to install a new
windshield and trunk lid in his car and to paint the car. The
neighbor promised to complete the work in "about a week," but in
fact had still not finished it more than a year later. In addition, he
kept the car outdoors where it was jumped on by neighborhood
children and damaged by rain water which collected inside it. Roja
repeatedly asked when the work would be completed, and the
neighbor, described by Roja as having a real gift for gab, kept saying it would be completed soon. Roja accepted this poor service as
a natural concomitant of dealing with a small neighborhood business.

A study of a single ghetto retail store (Walker-Thomas in
Washington, D.C.) provides additional evidence that poor consumers who deal with businesses of questionable integrity are
sometimes unable to perceive problems that other consumers
might readily identify.[4] Most customers of the store buy its merchandise (primarily home furnishings and appliances) from
salesmen who visit their homes. The salesmen are friendly and
helpful, and spare their customers problems sometimes faced at
conventional retail stores: language difficulties, being watched sus-
piciously by guards, and feeling intimidated about asking ques-

tions. The salesmen also offer to cash welfare checks at their customers' homes. This is a significant help to the customers, and it
also enables the store to collect its installment payments promptly,
since the salesmen deduct what is owed from the cash they give the
customers.

In the context of this relationship, two kinds of grounds for
complaint are frequently rendered imperceptible to the customers.
Almost all the customers pay high charges for credit, and the
records of payments made and accounts due are maintained by the
salesmen in notebooks they carry. A customer could keep his or
her own record, but the transactions often become complicated
due to missed payments or charges for repairs or additional merchandise. For this reason, most customers simply pay a sum
specified by the salesman each week; thus they forego an opportunity to understand the details of their credit arrangements.
Many customers are aware that the total cost of their credit is
high, and that haphazard accounting practices go along with its
high cost. However, since these policies are part of the store's way
of doing business, the vast majority of customers accept them as
unalterable and do not consider them grounds for complaint. The
store has repossessed merchandise without judicial authority, and
has harassed customers by asking their friends and relatives to
pressure them into making larger or more frequent payments. Yet
every customer interviewed in an FTC study of such tactics stated
that the store had done nothing wrong. In the customers' frame of
reference, missed payments allow the store to commit acts that the
FTC deems illegal.[5]

Where the actual quality of merchandise is concerned, a second
basis for complaints develops in many of the store's transactions.
With these problems, too, the store takes advantage of the personal nature of relationships between its salesmen and customers.
Much of the furniture the store sells is defective or imperfect.
When the furniture breaks or shows some severe premature wear,
the salesmen use a standard technique for dealing with complaints
from customers: they blame the damage on the way the customers
have used the furniture. They may be successful, for example, in
claiming that the customer's children have treated the furniture
too roughly. In some cases, the salesman will persuade the customer to order repairs, to be paid for by a small addition to the

customer's monthly payment amount. These customers put the blame on themselves rather than on the seller, where it ought to be.

Disinclination to Admit Victimization

We asked our survey respondents how they thought the number of consumer problems (not *complaints*) they have experienced compared with the number of such problems that "other households" have had. The question was: "Do you think you and your household have more, less, or about the same number of problems with products and services as other households have?" It was intended to test a hypothesis that many people have a general disinclination to report consumer victimization.

The survey data tend to support the hypothesis. In the context of lengthy interviews focused on the past year's experiences, the middle-of-the-road evaluation, "about the same," was reported by 62.7 percent of the respondents, and the evaluation "less" was reported by 32.3 percent. Thus 95 percent of households told our interviewers that they had not suffered more than an average number of consumer abuses. Many of those respondents were probably incorrect. Even if purchase shortcomings were distributed among the population with perfect randomness, the 32.3 percent of the sample that replied "less" would likely include many households whose answers are objectively incorrect. Furthermore, since instances of purchase failure may in fact be unequally distributed among households, it is remarkable that so large a majority of respondents considered themselves to be victims of only an average number of consumer problems. Many of their estimates must be wrong; one probable explanation for the error is that people are reluctant to acknowledge that actions as important as spending money have had undesirable consequences.

For some people, a disinclination to characterize themselves as victims may be related to an underlying inability to perceive themselves as possessors of rights that have been abused. *Civil Justice and the Poor* describes "legal competence" as an attribute that affects a person's ability to take advantage of legal rights. It states generally that legal competence "would appear to consist of one part *awareness* and one part *assertiveness*."[6] This analysis can be applied to competence to deal with consumer problems. People of low socioeconomic status have been described as particularly lacking in legal competence. To the extent that poor people do lack a general ability to use the legal system, it is to be expected that they would be similarly disadvantaged in use of the consumer complaint process. However, some factors supporting the theory that people of low socioeconomic status lack legal competence may also apply to consumers on all social levels.

Poor people may be hampered in becoming aware of problems with consumer purchases because of relative inexperience with abstract issues or because of relative difficulty in objectification of events.[7] This is not to say that people do not know, for example, that a toaster is broken; rather, it suggests that for some people a broken toaster may not be perceived as a problem that can be the basis of a complaint. It is an old joke that everyone complains about the weather, but no one does anything about it. In fact, no one really does complain about it, if to complain is defined as to seek redress. No one complains because no one thinks it can be changed. The question is whether there are customers to whom deficient purchases seem more like the weather in that sense than like reasonable grounds for complaint actions. Limited experience in heterogeneous environments may typically put people of low social status at a disadvantage in obtaining information, developing powers of judgment, and discerning relative importance of problems. However, people of any social status may have similarly limited experience with purchases of particular kinds of products or services or with particular kinds of sellers.

It has even been suggested that Americans, as a group, are particularly accepting of low quality and unfair prices. Tibor Scitovsky has written that we "believe we act rationally when we save ourselves the bother of careful shopping in everyday purchases," but that Europeans devote great energy to bargaining, comparing, and seeking the best brand. He suggests "it is as if they did it for sport, or for the principle of asserting the consumer's expertise and ability to fend for himself. . . . "[8] A number of studies have shown that Americans in general are indeed poorly informed about their legal rights in common situations.[9] It has been found, in comparing people's knowledge of criminal law to their knowledge of civil or consumer law, that while knowledge in both fields is usually low, knowledge of consumer law is lower.[10] A study in Michigan found that higher education levels are related to better knowledge of criminal law, but not to better knowledge of consumer law.[11]

For poor people, past encounters with the legal system have been generally negative. And their way of life may make it hard for them to expect that present effort will lead to future reward. To some extent, all people have had consumer experiences which teach that complaint efforts will be unrewarded. If poor people are not inclined to perceive events in their lives as problems about which legal action might be taken because they lack positive past experiences with the legal system, perhaps some consumers are similarly disadvantaged with respect to their consumer complaint behavior. This may help to explain the reluctance of many people to identify themselves as recipients of unfair treatment by businesses.

Implications of the Obstacles to Problem Perception

The factors that make it difficult for people to perceive and acknowledge deficiencies in products and services are not unique to consumer transactions. In many aspects of life, people have difficulty defining facts and rights, problems may change as time passes, and individuals with low socioeconomic status may have relatively reduced expectations. In the context of consumer problems, these factors may have particular force because they operate in conjunction with the widespread disinclination of people to think of themselves as victims of consumer abuse.

Voicing more complaints could show individuals that products and services can be measured against reasonable standards and found inadequate. But this greater number of voiced complaints cannot be expected to come about unless people increase the rate at which they perceive problems. This circularity indicates that the best technique for showing consumers how to overcome the obstacles to problem perception is itself limited by the inefficient problem perception behavior it might be able to remedy. Nonetheless, since people learn from (and imitate) their neighbors and friends, any small increase in complaint voicing will have a general instructive effect: it will provide varied examples showing the legitimacy of perceiving problems (and voicing complaints).

Perceiving problems is the vital first step in obtaining redress for deficiencies in purchases. Thus, businesses are the beneficiaries of the current low levels of problem perception. When buyers fail to notice deficiencies in products or services, they do not complain about those deficiencies, and sellers do not have to provide them redress. The fact that low levels of complaining provide businesses with unearned income suggests that businesses themselves could fairly be looked to for the financing of remedial measures intended to increase people's competence in dealing with consumer problems.

Another economic consequence of the current rates of problem perception is that businesses are relieved of pressure to improve their products and services. When all the costs of operating a business are internalized, a business operates with maximum social efficiency. Quality control will always be less than optimal when the likelihood of having to compensate buyers for business failures is low.

Three

Voicing Complaints

AN EFFECTIVE consumer complaint process would correct the injustices consumers suffer with defective purchases, and would tend to decrease the number of such purchases. We have seen thus far that there are indeed a great many consumer problems, so that there are many instances in which buyers do deserve to have refunds, repairs, or additional performances of services. There is also a clear need for the kind of preventive action that a fair system of complaint solicitation and resolution could provide. Unfortunately, many kinds of problems may be virtually impossible for individual consumers to perceive. And the preceeding chapter has demonstrated that many factors can operate to reduce consumers' recognition of even those problems that are within the range of ordinary knowledge and powers of observation. Notwithstanding these limitations, it would be a great step in the right direction if the problems that people do notice could be treated properly. But there are many obstacles between noticing a problem and obtaining proper redress; this chapter examines them at the voicing stage of the complaint process.

Once aware of a problem, an individual must choose between action and inaction. Many times, consumers choose inaction. And often those who do choose to act are significantly hampered in the actual presentation of their complaints. Many factors contribute to the choice of inaction and to difficulties once action is attempted. In broad terms, complaining is a costly activity. The case studies show that many complaints require large investments of time and energy, as well as money for professional help, travel, telephone calls, or compensation for time lost from work. Businesses may intimidate customers to discourage complaints. Practically speaking, in disputes between businesses and their customers there is at present a vast imbalance of power favoring businesses. With businesses in essential control of the complaint process, consumers are sometimes forced to follow cumbersome complaint procedures or to characterize their problems according to standards or categories set up by businesses. Another common difficulty buyers face in complaining is that describing a problem clearly can sometimes be very hard. Related to this difficulty (as well as to other factors that hamper complaining) is a final universal flaw in the complaint process: advice or other assistance is rarely available. People have only slight knowledge of third-party complaint-handling institutions. Access to the legal system is mysterious and costly. Some institutions themselves mislead consumers about the kinds of assistance they can offer. Books and television programs meant to help consumers are sometimes too general to be worthwhile or too optimistic to be accurate.

The Costs of Complaining

Expenditures of money, time, and energy, and the impact of these expenditures on personal and family life, are the costs of participating in the complaint process. These costs are suffered *in addition* to whatever loss results from the purchase failure that is the basis of the complaint. In our case studies, losses due to purchase failures range from the cost of a magazine subscription or a man's shirt to large losses related to serious flaws in cars or houses. A study that asked consumers to put a dollar value on problems they had recently complained about reported that the average loss (not counting whatever costs were involved in taking complaint action) amounted to $142, with reported possible losses ranging from $1 to $3,000.[1]

The case studies show that consumers are sensitive to the costs of making complaints. Bob Frey, a twenty-seven-year-old welder, lived with his wife and young baby in a mobile home in Gary, Indiana. For more than two years Frey made complaints about the mobile home's insulation; noting that frost formed on the inside of all the walls during very cold weather. He wrote letters to the company that sold the trailer, the company that manufactured the trailer, Ralph Nader, newspapers, and the Indiana attorney general. In spite of his complaints, no satisfactory repair or inspection of the trailer was performed. Frey finally described himself as "tired out." "I don't want to fight them anymore," he said. He stated that complaining should be reserved only for especially serious problems. A toaster he bought recently did not work at all, but he reported that complaining about it would not be worth the effort. For the problems with his $11,000 mobile home, however, Frey made more than a dozen local and long distance phone calls, each of which required significant effort. On several occasions, the Freys waited at their home for inspectors or repairers who never came. They did not put a dollar value on the cost of making their complaint, but clearly they considered it hard work.

In another case, Fred and Elaine Reeves fought eighteen months for a settlement concerning defective flooring installed in their kitchen. The seller of the flooring made a statement to a researcher which reveals even his knowledge that complaining is costly. J. Miller said that it is not worth it "to tear yourself up" over something that only costs $1,000, and the customer who gets that way "doesn't know what life is all about." Miller's customers would agree that complaining takes so much work that it ought to produce rewards of many thousands of dollars, but they learned that even when less money was at stake, colossal effort was needed to secure fair treatment.

The Reeves ordered linoleum from Miller's Home Center West, in North Olmstead, Ohio. For $979, they were to have linoleum installed in the kitchen, entrance area, and on the steps of their home. Soon after the installation, seams began to separate and several corners of the flooring appeared to be loose. The Reeveses then began a complaint action that eventually yielded them a settlement of $331. Their efforts included making at least eleven telephone calls to Miller, writing letters to the Armstrong Cork Company (manufacturer of the flooring), arranging for an inspection by Armstrong, joining Consumer Action Movement (CAM), a consumer self-help organization in Cleveland, attending numerous CAM meetings, visiting the seller with a delegation from CAM, and picketing the store on more than seven days or evenings. When they picketed, the store had its employees photograph them, and on one occasion sent an employee outside, to march with a "Sale" sign. At one point, upset by the difficulties of complaining, Mr. and Mrs. Reeves took a vacation trip partly "to get away from all this garbage."

As the Reeves case suggests, complaining can involve physical and emotional costs in addition to financial burdens. Consumers plagued by the consequences of typically unfair credit transactions have been shown to suffer from increased incidences of illness symptoms generally associated with psychosomatic problems.[2] In many case studies, respondents reported that both the occurrence of a consumer problem and the effort of complaining led to tension and disagreements within the family. Sometimes in our interviews family members reported these phenomena but described them as primarily affecting others in the family. For example, Frank Mullen had metal siding installed on his house, and it immediately loosened. Two of the corner sections fell off and blew a small distance away. The Mullens complained to the seller and then to an arbitration hearing sponsored by the local Better Business Bureau. No resolution satisfactory to the Mullens was reached. Mullen told our researcher that the experience had increased tension in the household, and that he and his wife still argue about the matter at times. "I ain't the type to let something like this drive me to the nut-house," he said, "but it bothers my wife, and then she bothers me."

Nat Ramsey, of Philadelphia, fought a heating company fraud that was aggravated by errors of a gas company's repair personnel. The gas company employees misplaced or threw away a defective part that would have been crucial evidence against the heating company. It took a year of efforts by Ramsey and members of a Philadelphia-based self-help group, Consumers Education and Protective Association (CEPA), to persuade the heating contractor to reimburse Ramsey for fifty-seven dollars he had paid the gas company for emergency service.

Bill Heinz of Waynes Lake, Illinois, suffered the aggravation of returning a brand new Ford to its seller on thirteen occasions. All of this effort left Heinz feeling "tired out," and the problem went unremedied.

When pursuing a complaint requires the help of professionals, the cost obviously is a major reason some consumers drop out of the complaint process. When Jean Day, of Washington, D.C., found hairs in a box of the General Mills product Bisquick, she sent a sample of the product to the company. In response, she received a letter stating that, to the company's regret, the Bisquick had contained some slivers of paper. A private laboratory tested another sample of the product, at the request of the Center for Study of Responsive Law, and found hair in the sample. Without the intervention of our researcher, the General Mills explanation would have left Ms. Day with no choice but to drop her complaint. She could not have afforded to hire an independent laboratory or to take time from her work to transport the sample to a laboratory.

The case studies illuminate the primary reasons some consumers are reluctant to hire lawyers, even though these studies examine complaints that were generally made with more frequent than usual response to third-party assistance. The reasons often relate to cost. Consumers described experiences such as: being told by a lawyer that to sue the Ford Motor Company would cost more than the price of a new car; threatening to hire a lawyer but deciding not to sue when the seller also proposed to hire a lawyer and thus burden the buyer with large legal fees; deciding that a dispute was not large enough to merit paying for a lawyer's help. According to our survey data, individual lawyers, small claims courts, and legal aid services are involved in fewer than one of every one thousand consumer problems that people perceive.

Intimidation and Retaliation

The case studies document a variety of ways in which consumers who complain are faced with aggressive responses by businesses such as intimidation and retaliation. Threats that a buyer's job will be put in jeopardy, that an individual will be prohibited from ever again buying something from a particular seller, and arbitrary withdrawing of settlement offers are all techniques that have been used against consumers. These techniques not only affect the individual against whom they are directed, they also affect future complaint behavior by that consumer and by others who find out about them.

The arbitrary withdrawing of settlement offers was observed in a great many of the case studies. During negotiations, a seller would suggest (or a buyer might infer) that if the buyer would not accept the seller's offer of settlement, the seller would withdraw the offer. This technique of implicit threat discourages the buyer from pressing the seller forcefully, and especially may discourage the buyer from seeking help from third parties.

The Walker-Thomas ghetto enterprise has used a network of neighborhood informants to gather incriminating information about some of its customers. These customers knew that if they protested the store's actions, the store could inform governmental authorities, for example, that they have violated regulations concerning public assistance payments. This well-known and sometimes carried out threat bears no direct relation to a customer's dealings with the store. It is, nonetheless, an effective method for squelching legitimate buyer protests. A more aboveboard technique used by Walker-Thomas is the threat that a complaining individual will no longer be welcome as a customer. While freedom from the Walker-Thomas deceptive practices might seem a blessing rather than a penalty, for many customers such a store can serve a valuable function. They see it as the only practical source of household furnishings. Yet many stores shun complaining customers, and cast the innocent buyers as trouble-makers rightfully excluded from doing business with the company.

In at least one instance, Tiffany & Co., the New York jeweler, used a similar shunning technique. After Tiffany ran advertisements announcing positions of the company on national economic issues and civil responsibilities, Mrs. Hamilton Foley, a customer, wrote to the store expressing her disagreement with its expressed political philosophy. In reply, the store canceled her charge account, asking her to take her business elsewhere.[3] This incident was publicized, and although the loss of a charge account is not likely to be a serious problem to an individual in a financial position to maintain one in the first place, the store's action nevertheless is clearly intended to discourage customers from criticizing the way that the store presents itself to the public.

Retaliation and intimidation are of course most easily practiced in situations involving a continuing relationship between a buyer and a seller. For example, owners of mobile homes are particularly liable to be victims of such business practices, because they usually must lease space on which to install their homes, and because they often lease this space from the same business that has sold the mobile home. In the above-mentioned case of Bob Frey, a service representative of the trailer manufacturing company told Frey that if he caused any more trouble, they would hook up his home and "move it out right then and there." This threat influenced Frey to stop complaining. People who have bought new cars sometimes feel that they are dominated by the car dealers and manufacturers. Unlike Frey, they do not fear eviction, but they are dealing with a single company, and usually a single dealer, concerning cars in which they have a very large financial stake.

Alan Hamilton, of Concord, North Carolina, bought a new Chevrolet from a local dealer. It was delivered with partially bubbling and mismatched paint, a defect that allowed rain to leak in on the driver's seat, and with additional flaws that destroyed Hamilton's confidence in the car. He complained to the dealer and to the Chevrolet zone office for about five weeks, and even advertised his new car for sale in the local newspaper. When no one responded to his advertisement, Hamilton decided he would have to keep the car. He then wrote a detailed letter to Chevrolet's Detroit headquarters, and sent copies of it to the president and board chairman of General Motors, the President of the United States, several members of Congress, and a number of government and private consumer groups. He also sent a copy of this letter to his dealer. The next time Hamilton saw the dealer, he was told that unless he could prove all the claims he had made in his letter, he would be guilty of libel, might lose his job, and might go to jail. All this might happen, the dealer told Hamilton, unless he wrote a letter of retraction and sent copies of it to every person and agency to which he had sent the original letter. Hamilton complied, and wrote retractions of his first letter, saying, "I hope that it has not been injurious to anyone, organization, entity, etc." Subsequently, when the dealer made some repairs on the car, he asked Hamilton to sign a statement that they were satisfactory. Although he did not consider the repairs acceptable, Hamilton signed the statement in order to avoid further trouble.

What a Chevrolet dealer was able to do with Hamilton, who was a young man with a very modest annual income, is similar to Ford's actions against Dr. Thomas James, a surgeon with an annual income more than seven times that of Hamilton. Dr. James bought a used Continental Mark IV, and from the start of his ownership, the car broke down repeatedly. A brake cable ruptured, and locked the wheels, a problem Dr. James believed could have caused a fatal accident had he been driving at high speed when it occurred. A more costly problem led Dr. James to complain. The motor block was severly damaged by a defective rod, and repairs cost more than $1,200. Dr. James asked the dealer who had sold him the car to pay for this repair, claiming that the engine should have been strong enough to withstand the failure of the rod. He also wrote to the president of Ford. A middle level complaint handler at Ford offered Dr. James $260 for "good will," but imposed a condition that he make no further complaints about the problem. Dr. James refused the offer, and Ford withdrew it. Later, he was offered $160; this was apparently the reaction of Ford and the car dealer to Dr. James's earlier hard line stance. In the end, Dr. James accepted the $260 offer because Ford's intransigence convinced him that he really would lose nothing by giving up his right to seek additional compensation. Ford's earlier total withdrawal of the $260 offer had influenced this decision.

A problem with the drainage on the grounds of a newly purchased house led to a number of stressful confrontations between the owners, Mr. and Mrs. Paul Remsen, and the construction corporation. Mrs. Remsen became so convinced that the builder's representatives were willing to lie and distort the truth that she became reluctant herself to discuss the problems concerning the house. She told our interviewer that the corporation might use her recital of the truth as a basis for suing her, to bankrupt her with the cost of a legal defense.

Buyers with small grievances can also feel intimidated. One case study involves a twenty-five-year-old woman who was afraid to ask a store manager to exchange a defective pair of shoes, even though the shoe manufacturer had written to her that an exchange should be made. As a favor, a friend went to the store for her, but the store manager berated the friend, saying that no exchange would be made through an intermediary.

Negative Attitudes about the Legitimacy of Complaining

Just as many consumers seem reluctant to acknowledge that they have been victimized by unusually heavy problems, in a similar fashion many consumers characterize their complaining patterns in ways that underestimate the number of complaints they make. More than 90 percent of our survey respondents stated that compared to "other households," they make less or about the same number of complaints about products and services they buy. Many of these respondents are objectively incorrect; it is significant that the common error is to underestimate complaining. Only a small group of respondents answered that they had made more complaints than other households.

Prejudice against complainers and partial acceptance of sellers' sometimes harsh attitudes toward complaining show up even in our case studies of consumers who took forceful steps in handling their own complaints. Ruth Black bought a Caloric gas range which emitted a nauseating odor when she used its oven. She complained about it to the company, and was told to let the odor "burn itself out." She spent many hours in her backyard avoiding the odor of the stove while she followed this suggestion. She complained to the Consumer Product Safety Commission, but never discussed the problem with friends for fear that they would consider her a chronic complainer. She was also unwilling to discuss possible problems with other purchases when she talked with our interviewer.

Confusing Presentation of Complaints

Many times, the deficiencies of a product or service are complex, or a simple problem becomes complex due to the initial treatment it is given, so that when the buyer returns to the seller to explain the problem, the explanation itself is complicated and confusing. Written complaints can also be presented confusingly, since written expression is particularly difficult for some people, and since by the time a complaint has progressed to the stage of being written, it has often become particularly complicated. Phenomena that lead to confusing or complicated presentation of complaints include: complex fact situations; personal closeness to the problem that makes all issues, large and small, seem equally important; and difficulty in determining the identities of the individuals and businesses involved in the problem.

The case of Mr. and Mrs. Harold Conrad typifies a consumer problem with so many aspects that there is no way the complainant can describe it succinctly. The Conrads bought a house under a Veterans Administration (VA) home loan guarantee program for $20,900. They mistakenly believed that the VA would take care of any problems that turned up. Also, because the VA provided a loan and a Certificate of Reasonable Value, the Conrads thought that the government considered the house a reasonable investment. Unfortunately, dozens of things were wrong with the house. To repair them would cost from $7,000 to $10,000. Each defect could be thought of as a separate problem. The treatment the Conrads received from the Veterans Administration home loan program was an additional problem. During the first sixteen months of living in the house, they discovered major flaws in the electrical wiring and fixtures, major flaws in the plumbing, severely cracked beams, and periodic total flooding of the basement. They complained about these problems to their real estate broker, to the former owner of the house, to the VA, and to a local television station's complaint service. But as they complained, the number of problems they had to mention kept increasing because additional problems occurred.

The repeated experience of seeing major flaws develop in the newly purchased house also affected the Conrads emotionally, so that some of the complaints they presented in person or on the telephone may have seemed particularly troublesome to the businesses and agencies that should have helped them. Because the Conrads seemed extremely upset, real estate agents or workers at the Veterans Administration may have become, consciously or unconsciously, less cooperative than they might otherwise have been. At one point, one real estate agent referred Mrs. Conrad to a second agent, who was supposed to be supervising a repair. Mrs. Conrad told our interviewer, "When I called Plachem and he gave me the runaround, and then Brook-Park jumped all over me, I sat down and cried—this just can't be happening to me—we were struggling just to get in here, just so the kids can have a yard to play in, where they can get out and be free and play, and here's the house ready to fall down around us." As tension built up, each successive complaint involved not only the most recently discovered problem, but also concerned the fact that *previous* complaints had not been treated properly. When the Conrads wrote letters about their problems, even giving only slight detail about each element of their troubles made their letters long and difficult to follow.

In many complaint letters, the writer does not see the forest for the trees. In other cases, the forest may be seen, but the trees are overemphasized. An Oshtemo, Michigan, woman bought a new Chevrolet which was delivered with a serious defect. The inside of the windshield developed a haze so that "all you see when you are driving in direct line of the sun is nothing." This is the concise description of the problem she set forth in a letter to Chevrolet's Area Service Manager. However, the letter also touches on the following points: the dealer is thirty miles away from her home; she was informed once that the haze might be due to the effect of heat on the car's plastic upholstery, but was told another time that it was caused by exhaust from other cars; the car did not have the precise interior she had ordered; once the dealer had kept her car overnight only to return it saying nothing could be done about the problem; and whatever caused the haze may be harmful to her health.

In another case, Louise Hemingway was plagued for several years by receiving unsolicited records (and bills for records) from the Longines Symphonette Society. Each time she received a record she returned it. When she received dunning letters, she replied that the records had been returned. For several years, Ms. Hemingway concentrated in her correspondence with the mail order company on each particular refused record rather than on the bizarre history of the company's mistakes.

Another source of delay and—sometimes—unsatisfactory resolutions in complaint processing is difficulty in properly identifying the particular individuals and businessmen involved in the failed transaction. Henry Gibbs, of Alexandria, Virginia, bought a used car from Wissinger Chevrolet, a local dealer. Mr. Gibbs made an extra payment at the time of purchase to obtain a warranty for the car's engine. A $600 repair on the engine was soon needed, but Wissinger refused to pay for it, claiming that the car had not been maintained properly before Gibbs bought it. Gibbs attempted to sue for the $600 in small claims court, but his suit was initially rebuffed when the lawyer for Wissinger Chevrolet asserted that General Motors Corporation, not the dealer, should have been the defendant.

Gibbs is a self-confident middle-aged man, accustomed to dealing with businesses. But Nat Ramsey, whose home heating problems were discussed in connection with the costs of complaining, is not self-confident, and seems withdrawn (although in his terms he has found "inner peace"). In describing his problems with a heating equipment installation firm and the Philadelphia Gas Company, Ramsey did not know whether particular people he had talked to about the problem worked for the gas company or the heating equipment company, nor did he know their names.

Scant Knowledge about Third Parties

In the 1940s, Earl Loman Koos showed that social service agencies were notably ineffective in making themselves known to people they were supposed to help. Even agencies located only a few blocks from the particular New York City block Koos studied in *Families in Trouble* were unknown to many of the households that might have benefited from their services.[4] In the 1960s, David Caplovitz' *The Poor Pay More* reinforced this finding.[5] Our survey of urban consumers confirms this pattern. The case studies show that consumers have great difficulty distinguishing between various third parties, that consumers often expect more from third parties than they are likely to receive, and that when third parties fail to help consumers those failures do not necessarily educate consumers about the weaknesses of the third parties.

Although the case studies all involve consumers who did voice complaints to third parties, they reveal numerous instances of misimpressions about the work those institutions perform. About Better Business Bureaus (BBBs), for example, the following inaccurate comments were made to our researchers: "They check into things consumers complain about and let you know if you're right or wrong," "[when] you have trouble, you're supposed to notify them," "You can't use a Better Business Bureau when a case involves credit instead of merchandise." These statements are not correct, as will be shown in chapter 5. Better Business Bureaus do not often tell buyers whether they are "right or wrong;" notifying the BBB about a problem is voluntary; and all kinds of buyer-seller problems, including problems about credit, are within what BBBs define as their scope of interest. It should be noted that many of the case study subjects did have accurate impressions of the work of Better Business Bureaus. Yet the fact that even among our sample of third-party users a good many had incorrect or distorted impressions suggests that the number of misimpressions is far greater among the general population, where imprecise notions about third parties are more likely to be found.

We asked consumers what they knew about their state's attorney general's offices. Many said they knew nothing, and one person replied that the attorney general is the president's lawyer. Asked about media-related complaint handlers, such as newspaper and radio or television "action lines," many respondents again gave partly incorrect answers, such as, "You send them your problems and they look into it." (Actually many such third parties act only in a minority of the problems people present to them.) With regard to small claims courts, there were similar misconceptions among the complainants, such as, "You have to have a lawyer there," and "It settles small cases, three- and four-dollar items."

Additionally, we asked the complainants if they knew of the federal Office of Consumer Affairs, the Federal Trade Commission, the Food and Drug Administration and, where appropriate, local consumer protection agencies. Relatively few of the answers recorded were good descriptions of the duties or accomplishments of these agencies.

General lack of knowledge about complaint-handling third parties leads some people to expect more from them than they provide. Many local consumer agencies are much less powerful than some customers believe. In New York City, for example, Sidney Berger complained to the Department of Consumer Affairs that a local automobile repairer, with a Great Bear Company franchise, had performed unneeded and unapproved repair work on his car. The department held a brief hearing, attended by Berger and a representative from the repair establishment. The result of the hearing was an agreement by the repair shop to pay $50 to the City of New York. Berger got nothing more from the department than advice to sue in small claims court, because the department has no authority to order a payment by a seller to a buyer. After his experience, Berger stopped pursuing his complaint. Explaining to our researcher why he did not go to court, he said, "I was afraid I'd make a fool of myself." Part of the source of that fear may have been the frustration of the fruitless (for him) efforts of the Consumer Affairs Department.

The same pattern is seen, too, in the typical workings of state consumer affairs offices. For instance, in Illinois, the Attorney

General's Division of Consumer Frauds conducts hearings which do not even have the potential of requiring a payment to the state by the accused business, and which, as in New York City, cannot impose a decision on a seller, but can only hope to encourage a compromise settlement.[6]

Consumers develop false expectations about third parties in many ways. The general cause is lack of knowledge. Some complaint handlers disseminate misleading information about what they can or will do for consumers. The Illinois Attorney General's Division of Consumer Frauds, for example, solicits complaints from consumers with claims such as: "Any Illinois consumer who believes he has been treated unfairly in any transaction can receive assistance from my office."[7] Better Business Bureaus use a form for receiving complaints which instructs the consumer to check an appropriate box to classify his or her problem, and says that if the problem fits a BBB category, it will be worked on. Nine categories comprise the check list, including as category number nine, "Other." Although the categories admit all possible problems, BBB policies exclude some kinds of disputes.[8] This discrepancy between the intake form and actual practices can give consumers unrealistic ideas about the kind of help they can expect from Better Business Bureaus.

A natural impulse to help people in need has sometimes made workers at third-party institutions hold out prospects of greater assistance than they can actually provide. It is possible that when the third parties are trade associations, such false offers may have less innocent motivations. All such inaccurate representations give consumers false expectations. In the case involving drainage problems with his new house, Paul Remsen tried to secure help from a number of third parties. He was pleased that a local builders' association, Niagara Frontier Builders Association, Inc., offered to help him. Events proved, however, that the association was unwilling to back up its promise of help with significant actions. Our interviewer asked the executive secretary of the organization, Ms. Jan Juhl, whether she thought the association had raised Mr. Remsen's expectations falsely. She replied, "You go into these things with a positive attitude. . . . It would be terrible if I said, "Sorry kid, can't help you.' People would be even more bewildered then."

Lack of Access to Law

The problems consumers have with using law are threefold: determining whether or not legal help can be useful in a given set of
circumstances; locating competent legal help; and paying for legal
help. These problems have interrelationships that add to the difficulties of using law. For example, legal help is usually expensive,
and its cost is rarely fixed in advance or easy to predict. This
makes people reluctant to employ lawyers, and thus reduces opportunities for people to learn about the relevance of law to different kinds of disputes.

The basic question, whether many people who could benefit
from legal assistance are currently unable to obtain it, cannot be
addressed with very much quantitative information. Although a
massive national survey was sponsored by the American Bar
Association (ABA) in 1974, a problem about quantitative data is
that there can be a distinction between need and demand. There
may be much more *need* for legal help than there is *demand* for
legal help. A lack of demand could itself be evidence that the consciousness people have of the role of law is lower than it ought
to be.

Even without much numerical data, all writers on the subject
agree that there is drastic underdelivery of legal services to all but
the very rich. Roughly a third of the population has never used a
lawyer. Roughly another third of the population has used a lawyer
on only one occasion.[9] When the federal legal services program
began in the mid-1960s it worked on half a million cases a year.
With more resources, it could have given service on 5 million
cases.[10] A study of legal services and people of moderate means,
conducted for the ABA-supported American Bar Foundation, estimated that middle income people have about 2 million cases each
year that could benefit from legal help, but that all of these cases
are currently handled by individuals with no help from lawyers.[11]
And the Center for the Study of Responsive Law survey shows
that about one in every six purchases leads to recognized grounds
for complaint that are never resolved to the satisfaction of the
household. Not all of these problems are complained about to
business, nor are they all appropriate problems for treatment in
the legal system, but the existence of so many problems reinforces

the conclusion that there is substantial need for application of law to consumer transactions. Yet use of law, either with or without the involvement of lawyers, takes place in only a tiny fraction of the instances in which people perceive consumer problems.

Many consumers interviewed stated that the next time they suffered serious problems, they would seek help of a lawyer. On the other hand, fear of high costs and of appearing to have been victimized kept some people away from legal help. Some struck a middle ground: although they told businesses they might sue, or indicated in complaint letters that a copy would be sent to a lawyer, in fact they did not really plan to take such actions.

The case studies do show that some lawyers are willing to work for low fees for consumers who are linked to them through friends or family. In addition, prepaid legal services plans provide legal aid for their relatively small memberships, and for some of the country's poorest citizens, government-funded lawyers may be available for consumer problems. However, the government Legal Services programs often give individual buyer-seller problems low priority, because they can be relatively time consuming and are not likely to produce broadly applicable legal reforms.[12]

The case histories track this assessment. A Memphis businessman, William Maxwell, argued in Rio de Janeiro with the director of a university alumni association tour, and was left behind in South America, barred from flying home on schedule with the alumini group. He found a lawyer willing to sue the travel agency on a contingent fee basis, and collected a settlement of $1,750. (The contingent fee is a share of whatever money is received if the case is won or settled; in this instance the fee was $600.)

During one Milwaukee winter, the refrigerator in Ethel Koenig's apartment broke down. She complained about it to the manager of the apartment building, but he brushed aside her problem, telling her, "You know, we're really busy with heating problems this time of year. We'll get around to your problem when we get there." "That's when I decided to fight," Koenig told our interviewer. She withheld some rent in protest. The owner then began a legal action to evict her and force her to pay the withheld rent money. This prompted Koenig to seek legal help, although it might easily have led to her giving in without protest. Through a friend, she located a lawyer who charged her $35 and produced a settlement which gave her a net recovery of $50. Koenig chose to move out of the apartment, but the building owner never received more than the rent Koenig thought was fair considering the poor service that was provided.

Dick Meagher took a truck-driving course in Cleveland, Ohio. Although he completed the course, he never received a diploma. He complained about this without success to the local Better Business Bureau, a television station complaint service, and the Veterans Administration (which gave financial support to the driving school). When asked by a researcher what would he do differently in a future problem, he replied simply that he would hire a lawyer, if he could afford it.

The Imbalance of Power

Almost all of the difficulties people face in identifying their consumer problems and voicing complaints about them reflect a basic fact: Sellers are generally much more powerful than buyers. Sometimes this is true because a business that has received money from a buyer can hold on to it in the spirit of the adage "Possession is nine-tenths of the law." Many other situations arise in which businesses have far greater power than their customers. A single angry customer cannot affect the profits of a giant corporation. And without organization or careful use of certain highly restricted legal procedures, even thousands of angry customers can have little hope of affecting the profits of a large automobile company. Almost every customer who pledges never to buy another Ford car is balanced by someone else making the same vow about General Motors cars.[13] Sellers thus deal with consumers from a position of strength. Some of the manifestations of this strength include monopolizing vital information, making credible threats, delaying the resolution of complaints for long periods of time, controlling the definition of issues in dispute, and having the ability to withstand most complainant pressures in the context of large ongoing businesses.

The power of information is illustrated in two disputes that involved small amounts of money. Each case concerned a dunning letter sent by the Magazine Collection Bureau to a *Ladies' Home Journal* subscriber. The subscribers had paid for their subscriptions by check and had records of payment. Yet the dunning let-

ters upset them, and prompted them to write serious and length
letters to the magazine, the collection agency, and numerou
public bodies. The subscribers were upset because the letters state
that credit bureaus might be notified of the subscribers' failure t
pay their bills. To everyone, this could seem to be a serious threat
to the complainant in one of the case studies, it was particularl
serious because she and her family were about to purchase a hous
and were especially concerned about their credit rating. Both prob
lems were resolved quickly and to the satisfaction of the con
sumers, but neither the consumers, law enforcement agencies tha
became involved, nor our researchers were able to discover ho
common such slip-ups are, or what precautions are taken t
prevent them. That information, if it exists at all, is currently ir
the possession solely of the collection bureau and the variou
magazines for which it performs its services. Thus, a more far
reaching complaint cannot really be made by a consumer o
agencies that operate on the behalf of consumers, because of the
difficulty of amassing a truthful description of the seriousness o
the problem. On the other hand, the seller's agent, the collection
bureau, is willing to use some of its information, selectively, to affect the credit ratings of consumers.

When a business operates unfairly, and overtly refuses to be
bound by normal standards, the imbalance of power is clear. The
dynamics of a dispute with a swindler are the same as those of a
dispute with a legitimate seller, but the potential for a satisfactory
resolution is virtually nonexistent with a swindler. For example,
there is a kind of anarchic power in a travel agent who accepts deposits for a charter flight from a group of people, uses the money
himself, and never arranges a flight, and who then becomes
bankrupt or in some other way avoids a legal judgment. In the
case of Travel Way Travel Service, Inc., apparently a fly-by-night
business formerly operated in the District of Columbia, dozens of
individuals who planned to fly to an annual meeting of a college
fraternity lost deposits of about $200 each. The assets of the com-
pany could not be reached even by a customer who obtained a
small claims court judgment against the company.

The developers of a resort and community in Illinois rebuffed
many efforts by dissatisfied buyers to obtain refunds or partial
refunds of money they paid for building lots. Candlewick Lake

Associates used high-pressure sales tactics, and promised its customers that it would construct a lake, that there would be a
community association with low annual fees, that roads would be
built, that there would be four beaches, and that there would be a
properly functioning sewage treatment plant. Most of the promises
were broken, in varying degrees. In addition, the company violated
federal land development regulations. In one instance of a clear
violation, the company had to rescind its contracts with certain
buyers and refund their money. When those buyers contacted the
company, according to their attorney, they encountered long
delays and the company's refusal to accept registered mail (which
contained requests for such rescission and refund). Through this
pattern of operating, the company virtually exempted itself from
the normal constraints of law. Its success in avoiding obligations is
restricted only to the extent that individual consumers can obtain
skillful legal aid or can influence the government to assist them.
Unfortunately, seeking government assistance in a case like this is
not likely to lead to compensation to individual consumers. Here
again, inertia is on the side of the probable lawbreaker.

In numerous other situations, businesses show great strength
and staying power, as compared to consumers' resources. The
pressures that some businesses are able to withstand and the
burdens they are able to put on the shoulders of complainants
contribute to the difficulty of voicing complaints.

The resistance faced by the persistent and energetic consumers
who are described in our case studies suggest that in other
instances lesser pressures or weaker efforts to achieve just results
would probably be unsuccessful. For example, Mrs. H. A. Cosey
bought a new Dodge automobile from Holman Motors of Jericho,
New York. When she picked up the car, a number of defects were
noticeable, the most important of which were a jammed seat belt
on the driver's seat, a driver's door which would not stay closed, a
dead battery, a loose brake pedal, and fluid leaking from the
power steering mechanism. The dealership asked for some time to
repair the car, and refused to return to Mrs. Cosey the car she had
traded in. A long series of failed repair attempts and possible de-
ceptions took place. Mrs. Cosey then contacted the New York
State Motor Vehicle Department, and had the car inspected by a
state trooper. This led to the discovery that Holman Motors had

improperly certified the car as meeting the standards of the New York State motor vehicle inspection regulations.

Mrs. Cosey consistently asked for repairs, for the loan of a car while hers was being repaired, and for replacement of the car she had bought. Almost all of her requests were denied, even after she participated in a hearing which led New York State to revoke temporarily the dealer's licenses for registering and inspecting new cars. Even this strong action caused no noticeable change in the dealer's treatment of Mrs. Cosey. "Go home and write some more letters," she was told on one occasion when she presented the car to the service department for additional repair work. Finally, Mrs. Cosey sued the dealer in small claims court, seeking $240 for expenses she had incurred due to the loss of use of the car. The dealer settled the suit out of court, but never was able to repair the car to the satisfaction of Mrs. Cosey. All of her persistent and decisive actions seeking resolution of her complaint had very little effect; clearly the dealer preferred suffering the minor irritations of her actions to replacing or adequately repairing the car. A possible reason the dealer tolerated the effects of its refusal to satisfy Mrs. Cosey may be found in the relationship between automobile dealers and automobile manufacturers: each party claims the other is responsible for consumer complaints. Nonetheless, if Holman Motors was unwilling to grant Mrs. Cosey's requests because it believed that the cost of meeting them was the responsibility of Chrysler Corporation, the result from Mrs. Cosey's perspective remains unsatisfactory.

A Madison, Wisconsin, dentist who specialized in the treatment of children accrued a record over a period of eight years of reports that he slapped and hit his young patients, that he was abusive of them, and that he performed expensive procedures such as capping teeth without asking prior permission of his patients' parents. After persistent complaints by a number of parents who believed their children had been mistreated, a hearing by the State Dental Examining Board led to a decision that could involve temporary suspension of the dentist's license. But the significant lesson of this case is that for at least eight years prior to the time of the hearing, complaints had been made against the dentist. His ability to continue in practice for so long indicates that changing a doctor's method of practice by complaining requires a huge investment of time, dedication, and energy.

Calculated intractability by a business can be a serious problem. Two cases involving low cost, frequently purchased services (car parking and shirt laundering) depict this pattern. In both cases, involving Washington, D.C., businesses—Parking Management Corporation and Manhattan Laundry, Inc.—employees carried out their tasks imperfectly, allowing hubcaps to be stolen and losing several shirts. Both businesses responded to complaints by admitting that they had certain liability, and both companies offered payments to the customers. The customers then asked for more money than the companies had offered, and in both instances, the companies simply did not reply to the customers' counteroffers. Representatives of both companies admitted in interviews that when consumers reject settlement offers, the companies usually stop communicating with them. This silent treatment often ends the dispute, with the consumer receiving no money at all. In both of our case studies however, the buyers commenced lawsuits in small claims courts and the companies settled quickly for amounts that the buyers considered acceptable.

Sometimes possession can work to the disadvantage of the possessor. In the case of Phyllis Lupo, of Cleveland, Ohio, a dishwasher purchased from the Kennedy & Cohen appliance store did not work properly. She tried a number of times to have it repaired by the store, but her efforts produced only some ineffective repair attempts. She then asked that the futile repairs be stopped, and that the store replace the defective machine. When the store refused, Ms. Lupo contacted a lawyer who asked the store to accede to the demand. The store then agreed to replace the dishwasher. However, the lawyer did not work out a precise plan for the store to pick up the dishwasher, and this led to a final vexation for Ms. Lupo. The store refused to make an appointment to honor its promise. Finally, Ms. Lupo and some friends loaded the machine themselves into a friend's truck and delivered it to the store. Possession worked as a burden, in this case, where the object possessed was of no value.

Trial lawyers know that a person who is a frequent participant in trials gains a number of advantages over people who are occasional or one-time participants.[14] Businesses, for example, have fixed costs for complaint-processing personnel, while a consumer who considers complaining faces unanticipated expenditures of time and money. Nearly always, whoever defines the ground rules for a competition secures a significant advantage. In buyer-seller disputes, this advantage usually goes to the sellers. They achieve it defining the issues presented by buyers in ways that are susceptible to quick but possibly inappropriate resolutions, and by monopolizing knowledge of their internal procedures for processing consumer disputes.

In automobile problems, for example, dealers and manufacturers treat complaints by asking whether the car in question measures up to the ranges of tolerance set out in their own specifications. In one case study, Jimmy Raven of Gulfport, Mississippi, bought a new Ford. He noticed a suspicious sounding rattle, and took the car back to the dealer, Bubba Oustalet, Inc. Many attempts were made to correct the problem, but each effort was unsuccessful. Finally, Raven asked that his car be exchanged for a new one at Ford's expense, a resolution which Ford rejected. The noise Raven found objectionable was determined by Ford to be within the range that the company deems acceptable. Furthermore, the idea of exchanging what Raven considered to be a "lemon" was virtually unthinkable to Ford; whether the car should be replaced was not even given serious consideration. That issue was transformed into one more amenable to Ford's own complaint-handling procedure: whether the long series of repairs had accomplished the job of making the car meet Ford specifications.

Bernice Simpson, of Philadelphia, noticed that the Mattel Toy Company, which manufactures dolls with either black or white skin color, was featuring only its white dolls in pre-Christmas television advertising. Ms. Simpson is black and had bought a black version of a Mattel doll for her daughter, but she anticipated that the child would be disappointed by receiving a doll not exactly the same as the one shown in television advertisements. She explained this concern in a letter to the toy company, but the company replied by telling Ms. Simpson that the ads were truthful. The company refused to consider a complaint about its advertising in the context of any issues other than truthfulness and adherence to government and trade association rules.

Businesses clearly have the power to establish their own procedures for complaint handling. But when these procedures are not disclosed to the public, sometimes people with complaints take unnecessary or inappropriate actions. For example, Betty Griffin is a medical school professor with a Ph.D. in anatomy. She applied to a Washington, D.C., supermarket corporation, Giant Food, for a check cashing identification card. Giant Food interpreted the information Ms. Griffin furnished and printed a card for her naming her as "Mrs. Dr. William Griffin." Ms. Griffin wrote an angry letter to the company asking for a card issued in the name Betty Griffin. One night several weeks later, an anonymous individual called Ms. Griffin, saying that her letter to Giant Food was not being handled properly by the company, and that she should write a second letter directly to the company's president. Ms. Griffin followed the stranger's advice, and received an apologetic letter and a satisfactory check cashing card within about a week.

On the other hand, large numbers of consumers write letters to the presidents of the automobile companies in the belief that going to the top will help them obtain just treatment of their problems. They would be better advised to write to the middle-level regional officials of the companies who are higher ranked than the dealers but are closer to local experience than the executives in a home office.

The mystery of how to go about complaining and—more fundamentally—of what kinds of service are grounds for complaints is especially prevalent in the field of health care. Perhaps because doctors and dentists have high status in our society, patients who perceive problems with their services are relatively hesitant to voice complaints.

Pennsylvania has sponsored an experimental medical complaint-handling agency. Its director reports that the problem most often brought to the agency in its first year of work was that doctors were not accessible to their own patients. Her report suggests that many malpractice suits may be undertaken by patients who have realized that there is no other way to obtain the attention of their doctors: that "If they are dissatisfied or have questions or are in pain, they are not allowed to speak to the physician. Loyal nurses and secretaries are diligent guardians and unfortunately may become rather unpleasant." [15]

Our case studies of medical complaints show this inaccessibility. Although they involve consumers who did voice complaints, they indicate that the deference medical practitioners usually receive makes it hard for individuals to present complaints about their services. In the case involving the alleged brutal acts by a children's dentist, several families had to persevere for years to bring about the administrative hearing which was itself a difficult event in which to participate.

Robert Howell believed that he had been treated unfairly by an optometrist who fitted him with a set of soft contact lenses. He presented his complaints to a state licensing board, stressing criticisms of both the doctor's fee schedule and his general methods of practice. In disposing of the case, the board considered the fees issue but essentially ignored the more fundamental questions Howell had raised. In the end, Howell was convinced that there was simply no way he could force a fair hearing on the issues of ethics and ways of practice.

Researchers at the New York University Law School Consumer Help Center have shown that in New York City, people with complaints about doctors rarely know how to handle them. Aggrieved patients can present complaints to county medical societies, whose strongest sanction is expulsion of a member (although many doctors are not members of the county societies), or they can seek help from the State Board of Professional Medical Conduct, which can take actions that lead to revocation of a doctor's license. The NYU Help Center found that most medical problems are absorbed by the individuals without taking any action involving a third party. [16]

An innovative procedure currently used at two hospitals reflects an understanding of patients' ordinary reluctance to complain. These hospitals inform patients that their services are provided with a money-back guarantee. Although the policy is formally limited to services such as food and lodging, it is sometimes extended to medical care itself, in complaints about emergency-room treatment. This policy attracts attention to the hospitals' interest in resolving problems, and is thought to have led to better performance by hospital employees.[17]

Inadequacies of Consumer-Help Books and Broadcasts

Consumers who look to books and the mass media for advice on making complaints will discover that the same few basic ideas are presented in almost every book, magazine article, or broadcast and, further, that books written to help consumers deal with the consequences of unfair sales transactions are themselves sometimes promoted in misleading ways. A book produced by the Council of Better Business Bureaus claims to provide "all the facts you need before you buy, invest, or sign on the dotted line," but includes the statement that consumers "have only themselves to blame" if they are enticed into buying fantastic bargains that turn out to be frauds.[18] Ralph Charell wrote *How I Turn Ordinary Complaints Into Thousands of Dollars*, but nowhere in his book did he reveal that one of the techniques he used for voicing complaints was to write them on the stationery of a television station.[19] *Consumer Complaint Guide*, by Joseph Rosenbloom, was promoted with the theme that presenting complaints to company presidents will cure consumer frustration, anger, and disappointment. This proposition is doubtful, but is is the basis for a number of similar books listing names and addresses of corporation presidents and executives.[20]

Guides for consumers typically provide two types of information: advice on careful buying, and advice on how to complain. The long lists of officers and addresses of corporations contained in a number of these books are not as useful to consumers as the periodically revised standard corporate directories available at libraries. Furthermore, the complaint techniques the books suggest are elementary. It may be true that there are not any innovative techniques readily available for use by consumers, but all that consumers ordinarily receive for the cost of buying a book is advice that they should complain to the seller, write letters to the manufacturers, contact trade associations, and go to small claims court.

Sometimes this advice can be presented in a particularly clear fashion. John Dorfman sets out an escalation ladder of ten steps in

A Consumer's Arsenal that is theoretically all inclusive. He suggests that consumers take the following steps, in this order: complain by telephone, write to the retailer, write to the manufacturer write to trade associations or Better Business Bureau and Chambers of Commerce, write to local or state agencies, write to federal agencies, take legal action including suing in small claims court seek help from private (often voluntary) complaint-handling groups, appeal to print and broadcast media for help, and use unconventional tactics.[21] The very completeness of this list however, may be a flaw. For many problems, following all its steps will waste time and effort, while following one or two of them might produce a satisfactory resolution. For example federal agencies have jurisdiction over relatively few consumer problems, and writing to them may be useless.

One recent book suggests turning business intimidation techniques around and using them to pursue consumer redress. *Super Threats*, by John M. Striker and Andrew O. Shapiro, recommends that buyers write letters with phrases such as "in the matter of," or "reference is made to," and that the letters make actual use of phrases from judicial opinions and statutes. Their book includes suggested language for what they call "super threat" letters.[22] Whether their techniques will be effective in particular cases is difficult to say. But their point of view cannot be disputed: consumers ought to express themselves forcefully, and ought to cite the same sources of authority that businesses themselves frequently use.

Overly broad recommendation of small claims courts is a kind of generalized advice that may not be helpful. One popular book, *Sue the Bastards*, by Douglas Matthews, ignores the fact that in many states the small claims courts are slow and that judgments are difficult to collect. It urges everyone to sue, even though full-fledged small claims courts are practically inaccessible to a large proportion of the country's citizens.[23]

A model for consumer help books that focus on giving specific advice is *The Compleat California Consumer Catalogue*, published by the California Department of Consumer Affairs. The book is printed cheaply and has been planned to allow for frequent revisions. In about two hundred well illustrated pages, it alerts consumers to possible difficulties in a wide variety of commonly purchased products and services. It also summarizes the possible methods of complaining when something goes wrong, stressing that "if more individuals express their dissatisfaction, businesses will become more responsive to consumer concerns."[24]

The television series *Consumer Survival Kit* devoted a program to complaint handling; once again, the use of small claims court as an ultimate resource was stressed. Where such courts are available, they can indeed be highly useful. But their current role is very small in the overall resolution of buyer-seller disputes.

Interrelationship of Difficulties in Complaint Voicing

The impediments to complaint voicing reinforce one another. Because consumers lack access to law or adequate knowledge concerning third parties, businesses exercise control of the procedures for dealing with complaints. This control sometimes leads to delaying tactics, which increase the cost of complaining. Delays also increase the likelihood that a buyer's presentation of a complaint may be poorly organized or confusing in other ways. The conditions that create the high cost of complaining might change to the advantage of consumers if greater numbers of complaints were voiced, but the potential of greater voicing is made unlikely by the cost factors. For example, fear of retaliation contributes to the psychological cost of complaining. If complaint voicing were to become more common, sellers would be less able to engage in retaliatory conduct; that is, while they now feel free to penalize an occasional rare complainer, if vast numbers of aggrieved customers presented complaints, sellers would be unable to penalize them, for fear of losing too many customers. Unfortunately, this more frequent voicing is itself inhibited by the very practice it might help remove—retaliation.

In a more practical view, probably any actions that do stimulate voicing, even if they accomplish that stimulus by counteracting only minor obstacles, will indirectly help consumers to voice complaints.

Increasing and clarifying the accountability of sellers to buyers for the quality of goods and services and for the fairness of all aspects of sales transactions would allow consumers a greater chance for victories in small claims courts. If such courts were available, or if increased business accountability were applied in individual cases through other processes such as arbitration or mediation, the number of successfully pursued complaint cases would increase. As is true in the example of retaliatory tactics, such an increase in successfully presented complaints could be expected to counteract many of the obstacles to complaint voicing. For example, individuals who become aware that more complaints are being voiced will likely be helped to overcome the obstacle of lack of knowledge about complaining. In this manner, the interrelationships of the hindrances to complaint voicing may work to the benefit of consumers. As progress is made to overcome any single obstacle, the increments in total complaint voicing that come about can help to eliminate others.

Four

How Business Says No

WHEN A CONSUMER seeks redress for a deficient purchase, he or she may encounter some of the obstacles that make voicing complaints difficult and costly. Once a complaint is actually made, a common result is that businesses refuse to offer satisfactory refunds, repairs, replacement of products, or correction of improperly performed services. As will be seen in the detailed description of our survey data, in about 56 percent of complaint cases, businesses offer satisfactory responses. Nonetheless, examining cases in which businesses rebuff complaints can alert us to particular techniques and practices that must be overcome to achieve fair treatment of all complaints. Naturally, buyers make some unjust requests. But the modes of treatment used by various businesses in rejecting requests may well be applied to *justifiable* as well as unjustifiable consumer complaints. This is why the techniques themselves must be examined.

Sellers reject requests for redress in many ways. Many of their techniques are made possible because businesses are far more powerful than consumers, in terms of ability to persevere through long conflicts, strength of financial backing, and access to relevant information. For example, businesses can reject complaints by tactics of delay and confusion—the runaround. Silence is another kind of reaction that powerful sellers can use with virtual impunity; it can terminate the efforts of even strongly motivated complainants.

Businesses also rely on an arsenal of techniques based on the legal system. These strategems include using lawyers or referring to legal rules and decisions to confuse issues, to make problems seem complicated, to intimidate buyers, or to support claims that resolutions favorable to customers are impossible or illegal.

Further, relying on their position of strength, businesses sometimes reject buyers' complaints with the claim that victims of consumer troubles are themselves to blame. In some instances, strong businesses offer only partial redress, justifying this means of simultaneously saying yes and no by implicit or explicit claims that a buyer has acted improperly, or that offering any redress at all is an act not of obligation but of generosity. Refusing to interpret requests for change in terms as broad as those intended by complainants is yet another way businesses prevent satisfactory resolution of some consumer complaints.

This chapter reports the advice that many business people themselves would offer buyers who have perceived problems and want to complain about them. In part, their comments reflect an understanding of the power advantage businesses ordinarily have over their customers. The narratives and analysis throughout this chapter highlight this decrepancy in strength.

While examining some of the principal methods businesses use to reject requests, it is important to remember that the consumer complaint process involves mutual influences among the various stages of problem resolution. For example, unfairness by businesses at the stage of finally denying redress will affect the way people feel about initiating the process of voicing complaints, and may even affect the likelihood that they will perceive and acknowledge basic defects in purchases. Thus it would make sense to consider the abuses this chapter describes as relevant to understanding not only how businesses sometimes act when their decisions about complaints are negative, but as relevant additionally to understanding the overall consumer complaint process. That is, although the techniques are described here in the context of denying redress, they also have an impact on the perception of problems and the decision to voice complaints.

The Runaround

Businesses sometimes fend off a complaint with the runaround, by passing the complaint from person to person without resolving it. Depending on the size of the organization and its structure, this method of refusing to acknowledge complaints can take many forms. A simple type of runaround is evident in a Las Vegas hotel desk clerk's treatment of an angry would-be guest who was told that the hotel had no record of his reservation. The clerk assured the consumer that he would be able to solve the problem in about an hour, and that the consumer should wait, or perhaps gamble, in the hotel's large lobby. The would-be guest did spend an hour waiting, and when he returned to the hotel desk, he learned that the person who had promised to solve the problem had finished his day's work about half an hour earlier and had gone home.[1]

When a company is organized with a hierarchy of complaint handlers, there is a greater likelihood that complaints will be passed from one person to another without being resolved. The case history of Sylvia Klein illustrates this process. She bought a Frigidaire washing machine from Kovatch Appliances, in Cleveland, Ohio. Within two weeks, she discovered that the washer did not clean her laundry adequately. She complained to the store by telephone and was told an exchange would be made. But when she went to the store to work out the details, she was told that someone would visit her home to inspect the machine. Over the course of six months, there were many visits by repairers, without satisfactory resolution of the problem. Furthermore, the washer began to rip and puncture sheets and clothing. Ms. Klein then called the Dayton office of Frigidaire to register her complaint and talked to Mr. Marks, who listened but was not helpful. More repairers examined the machine, and Ms. Klein was told to switch brands of detergent. She followed this instruction, but the problems persisted. She called the Dayton office again but her call was taken by a Mr. Jacobs who knew none of the facts of her problem.

Three months later, Ms. Klein wrote to Frigidaire's vice president in charge of appliances. After a few weeks went by with no reply she called him and was told that the Dayton office would take care of her complaint. Next, a Frigidaire field representative visited her home and examined but did not repair the washer. After about six more weeks of waiting for satisfactory action from Frigidaire or the Kovatch store, Ms. Klein filed a suit in small claims court. This led to a refund for the machine and partial compensation for the damage to her laundry. More than thirteen months had elapsed between the first complaint and the settlement, and Ms. Klein had dealt with more than seven different representatives of Frigidaire and the Kovatch store during that period.

Another case history illustrates the runaround involved in a four-month dispute over the quality of carpet installation. The consumer was directed to four different salespeople or complaint handlers at the carpet store, two different two-man repair teams, then two more store sales employees and a representative of an independent testing company. The consumer in this case believed that the seller was stalling to avoid replacing the carpet. Appointments for visits by the repair teams were not made in advance, nor did the store inform the buyer of the findings of the repair teams. The buyers had to make repeated telephone calls to spur each action by the seller. In the end, the problem was resolved (the store agreed to replace the carpet) after the buyer enlisted the help of a local consumer affairs department.

Any seller can benefit by delaying the resolution of disputes. A postponed expenditure allows the enterprise to continue earning interest on money it would otherwise have paid out. Furthermore, delay keeps alive the possibility that the consumer will give up seeking redress. For some kinds of complaints, notably those involving cars, chances are especially high that people who complain will be given the runaround. Because of the way car sales are organized, a number of potential complaint handlers exist and each has slightly different institutional interests. The same reasoning applies to other products and services marketed by large companies through independent dealers. In one of our case studies, Alvin Hand had a dispute with Waller Motors, in Jenkintown, Pennsylvania, over warranty coverage on a new Mercury. One morning when Hand opened the left door of the car, the window on the right door broke. Replacing the window cost $79. At first the dealer claimed this repair was not covered under the warranty, but Hand persisted, and after about ten weeks of pressing his complaint, received reimbursement from the dealer.

At one point, when Hand was unable to reach the dealer's complaint handler by telephone (he had called several times and left messages that were not returned) he contacted the Ford Motor Company in Detroit, whose representatives told him to continue trying to settle the problem with the dealer. Then he wrote to Ford in Detroit and received a post card saying his problem had been referred to a district office. Reacting to the dealer's tardy treatment of the problem, Hand came into contact with representatives of both Ford's headquarters and a local Ford district office. After his problem had been resolved, Hand received a letter which revealed the tensions between the headquarters and the district office, and which could have delayed and further confused Ford's complaint handling. The letter, from the *district office*, said that the *headquarters office* would soon be sending Hand a survey post card asking if his problem had been resolved. The district office letter asked Hand to return the card to the headquarters office only if he was satisfied and would answer yes, as indicated on a sample form enclosed with the district office letter. The letter said, "If you cannot indicate a 'yes' . . . please hold the original form when it is received and, meanwhile, telephone me . . . in order that I might further pursue the solution to the problem." This put the consumer in the middle between Ford's main office and district office, and it invited the customer to delay and confuse the procedures that one part of the Ford company has established to monitor consumer complaint handling. On the other hand, at the expense to Ford's headquarters of the loss of some accurate information about local complaint handling, the district office letter in this case may have helped resolve the complaint.

This case also exemplifies the business technique of explicit avoidance of responsibility. The manager of Waller Motors wrote to Hand that "the service manager is to be commended for skillfully presenting your case to Ford and obtaining payment under the warranty." From Hand's point of view, no commendation was merited. A flaw in the purchased product had caused him considerable inconvenience, and the seller, Waller Motors, had tried to avoid financial responsibility for repairing it. If there was some doubt whether Ford Motor Company would reimburse Waller Motors for repairing the window, that doubt was not a matter of concern to Hand; for the dealer to write that the service manager had presented the buyer's case suggests that the dealer conceived of itself as a middleman, not a responsible participant in the overall marketing process.

The Silent Treatment

Businesses sometimes respond to a customer's request with a silent treatment. For example, Cyril Morrison hired a small owner-operated appliance repair business in the Washington,

D.C., area to fix a refrigerator. When the work turned out to be ineffective, Morrison called the company to complain. The company is so small, however, that when the owner is out (and even sometimes when he is at his office) an answering service handles telephone calls. Morrison called many times and never got to speak to the owner; furthermore, the owner never returned Morrison's calls. In the end, Morrison sued in small claims court and won a judgment. The owner of the repair business did not appear in court, however; his pattern of dealing with consumer complaints seemed to be to ignore them at every stage. When interviewed, he said that he had not had time to respond.

The earlier examples of this type of claims handling by a laundry and a parking company could also be viewed simply as business techniques for rejecting justified consumer complaints. At hearings before the National Commission on Product Safety, Thomas O'Toole, then Dean of Northeastern Law School, testified that this kind of complaint handling is not restricted to small local sellers. Referring to "a major manufacturer," he stated that the company's procedure for dealing with product liability claims "was to have the claims thoroughly investigated, a file on the case carefully preserved, and then do nothing by way of responding to the consumer's complaints unless and until a suit was filed. In this manner, seven out of every ten claims were buried."[2] Dean O'Toole made the further point that this procedure must have resulted in the denial of justified relief to large numbers of consumers.

Legal Gimmicks

Businesses sometimes use legal concepts or lawyers themselves as bargaining tools or as a means of intimidation. Refusing to honor a buyer's request because of a purported legal principle allows complaint handlers to evade responsibility and can discourage buyers from continuing to seek redress. When a business uses a lawyer to contact a complaining customer, it may in some instances be done with the reasonable anticipation that the fear many people have of lawyers will work to its advantage.

One of our case studies illustrates a business use of a lawyer as a negotiator. Blue Cross of Washington, D.C., (Medical Service of

District of Columbia) informed Elaine Rupert that her health insurance policy would cover a lengthy series of treatments to remove warts. After she had undergone treatment for several months and Blue Cross had paid for the treatments, Blue Cross informed her that she was ineligible for such payments after all. According to Blue Cross, bills she had submitted for payment that had not yet been processed would not be paid. Representatives of Blue Cross told Rupert that if she was not satisfied with this decision she could sue the company in small claims court. This advice really constituted an effort by Blue Cross to change the setting of the dispute to one in which it would be appropriate for a lawyer to represent the company.

Rupert filed suit in small claims court. A Blue Cross lawyer then telephoned her, asking if she was a lawyer, if she had had any legal training, and if she had read a particular judicial decision with facts he said were similar to those of her dispute. He offered a compromise payment which Rupert, discouraged and somewhat frightened, accepted. If Blue Cross considered a compromise appropriate in this case, it should have offered one in its ordinary complaint-handling process. If Blue Cross considered its recommending of small claims court and its subsequent negotiation with a customer to be part of its ordinary complaint-handling process, then it would seem fair that Blue Cross conduct that negotiation through a nonlawyer representative, rather than through a lawyer. Thus, once again a seller used its power (here, its ability to hire an attorney) to force the consumer into a compromise settlement.

The legal system is often used by sellers to delay or discourage consumer disputes. Referring to legal technicalities is one favored tactic to thwart a consumer's legitimate quest for fair treatment. The use of a lawyer to press a consumer to compromise is a counterpoint to another case study, in which a business *avoided* use of a lawyer to achieve a similar compromise. In this case, a small District of Columbia repair business was sued by a consumer in small claims court. At the time of the trial, the owner appeared, as did Harvey James, the consumer, who had commenced the suit. To James's amazement, the trial was postponed. The judge ruled that a corporation must be represented by a lawyer, and that he would allow the business to return to court at a later date, after retaining a lawyer. The business owner was not surprised by this ruling; he had anticipated it and used it intentionally to introduce delay and difficulty. A few days after the hearing the buyer and seller agreed on a settlement.

Beyond the strategic use or nonuse of lawyers, several particular kinds of reliance on legal principles are seen in the case studies. One technique of complaint handling is the process of arbitrarily defining the topic of a complaint as completely controlled by an inflexible legal rule that prevents a finding in favor of the consumer. Thus, parking lot companies print disclaimers of liability for negligence on the receipts they give their customers. Such disclaimers are not valid in the circumstances of many of the lots and garages where they are used, but the businesses that continue to use them must believe that they discourage some people from making complaints.

A case involving a liability disclaimer was that of Lucile Wald, who underwent an operation at the University of Pennsylvania Hospital in Philadelphia in May 1975. Upon being admitted to the hospital, she was required to sign a form releasing the hospital from liability for loss of eyeglasses and prosthetic appliances. At the time of her operation, a somewhat common incident occurred: Mrs. Wald had removed her dentures prior to being sedated and moved to the operating room; when she regained consciousness in her room, she discovered that her dentures were missing. She complained to nurses and, later, to hospital executives, but was told that she had probably left the dentures wrapped in paper tissues, that a cleaning person had probably thrown them away, and that she, not the hospital, would have to bear the $310 loss. "I started to sizzle," Mrs. Wald told an interviewer, when the hospital employees used the "stall tactic" of saying they would look for the dentures in the hospital's laundry. After she repeated her complaint several times, Mrs. Wald sought further help from the Pennsylvania Health Department's Demonstration Complaint Service, and the hospital finally paid for the lost dentures. The instructive postscript to this story, however, is that the hospital revised its release form to include dentures among the items whose safekeeping is explicitly stated to be outside its responsibility. Future complaints about lost dentures will most likely be turned away by hospital staff members relying on the wording of the new forms.

Another technique for fending off complaints is to assert that it is impossible to give the buyer what he or she has requested. This allows the business to disassociate itself in some degree from responsibility for a negative response. An example of this was the treatment by Eastern Airlines of a complaint about overbooking. Richard Persky of New York City planned to send his two young children (accompanied by an adult cousin) to Fort Lauderdale, Florida, to spend a Christmas vacation with their grandparents. Eastern overbooked the flight for which they had reservations; after a great deal of confusion and faulty communication by Eastern, the children arrived in Fort Lauderdale on a subsequent flight about six hours later than they were expected. No one had gotten word of the change in flight to the elderly grandparents, whose grandchildren finally arrived at four o'clock in the morning. Persky complained by telephone to Eastern about the poor service, and was promised a written reply. After six weeks went by without such a reply, he wrote to the company president asking for a refund of the money paid for the tickets and for a payment to compensate him for his inconveniences. The reply he received referred to instances of overbooking as "seating problems," and added, "While I can understand your reaction to this situation and the subsequent handling by our people, an airline is unable to provide compensation for such things as the anxiety you mentioned." This is not a truthful statement. An airline is not *unable* to make a payment in compensation for poor service and anxiety it causes, but Eastern in this case was *unwilling* to make such a payment.

Another stratagem for rejecting consumer requests is the one-sided interpretation of legal concepts. Automobile dealers conventionally take the position that no matter how many flaws a car may have, it belongs to its buyer and cannot be returned to the seller. This philosophy leaves the financial burden represented by defective cars randomly distributed among particular individual car buyers instead of rationally directed back to the manufacturers, who can best bear the losses and who might improve quality control if they did have to take back their most defective products. One case study illustrates this routine method of responding to complaints, but provides an example of an atypical resolution. Jim Denton, a real estate broker in Springfield, Vir-

ginia, bought a new Volkswagen from a local dealer, Lee Volkswagen. During the first two weeks of use, the car performed very
poorly; the worst of many problems was intermittent stalling. In
separate attempts to repair the car, Lee Volkswagen replaced
several portions of the carburetor, but the car continued to
perform poorly.

The last straw to Denton was a drive (to the dealer's service department, ironically) during which the car stalled in an intersection
and was nearly hit by a cement mixer truck, and stalled again almost causing a rear-end collision. When Denton got the car to the
dealer's lot, he left it there, gave the keys to an employee, and announced that he was returning the car. He demanded return of his
down payment and cancellation of a loan he had obtained, at the
suggestion of the dealer, from a local bank. The dealer rejected the
demands, based on a strongly stated position: "If a customer
decides next week that he doesn't like the car, he can't come back
here and demand his money back." Denton then took a carefully
maintained set of records about the car's poor performance to the
bank, United Bank of Virginia, and persuaded a loan officer there
to put pressure on Lee Volkswagen to rescind the transaction. His
persistence in obtaining help from the bank, and his decisiveness in
abandoning the car on the dealer's property broke through the
dealer's distorted legalistic position. Contrary to the dealer's
conventional stance, if a car grossly differs in significant attributes
from the way it is described at the time of sale, a customer can
return it, and a dealer can be obligated to refund the buyer's
money.

When warranties or other kinds of contracts are the subject of a
complaint, sellers sometimes maintain that due to the particular
facts of the buyer's problem, legal rules prevent them from fulfilling the buyer's request. While Eastern Airlines flatly stated it was
unable to honor a request for compensation for anxiety, other case
studies show sellers claiming that payments which would otherwise
be proper are barred because buyers have failed to satisfy certain
legal prerequisites. This kind of legalistic response is seen in the
Gibbs case, already discussed. When Gibbs bought his used car, he
made a specific additional payment which he was told would
entitle him to the benefits of the warranty which had been part of
the sale of the car to its original buyer. The car broke down, and

Gibbs sought reimbursement for the repairs it required. At this point, the dealer resorted to a false legalism. Although engine repairs are within the scope of the warranty, he told Gibbs, warranties apply only if a car is maintained properly. And Gibbs's car, he said, had been poorly maintained by its original owner. Requiring Gibbs to suffer because of past acts by the original owner did not make sense, since Gibbs was offered and he accepted an opportunity to pay for a transfer of the car's warranty. But nonetheless, both the dealer and General Motors Corporation complaint handlers held to the line that Gibbs had failed to carry out the obligation of a warranty owner to maintain his car adequately; they were unwilling to recognize the special circumstances of Gibbs's case until he sued them in small claims court.

Another pattern of facts illustrates a similar business use of legal concepts to reject a legitimate consumer claim. Three college-age sisters and a fourth young woman shared an apartment in Madison, Wisconsin. One of the women arranged for fire and theft insurance for the possessions of all four individuals who lived together; however, the policy she received listed only her name. She called the insurance broker and was told to add the other three names to her copy of the policy. A robbery took place soon thereafter, and all four roommates lost valuable possessions. When they sought payment from the insurance company, they were told that only one of them was entitled to payment, because the other three roommates were not covered by the policy. This dispute eventually involved the insurance company, the insurance salesman, and the brokerage firm he worked for. At various times each of them invoked the legal principle that their obligations were limited by the terms of the written insurance document. It was not until the young women obtained legal advice that they learned there was a legal basis for their position that the telephone conversation with the salesman established their right to be compensated for the losses. The businesses readily gave their own interpretations of how the law limited the applicability of the incorrectly issued insurance policy, but they all ignored the significance of the agreements and assurances that were made in telephone conversations. This case ended with a compromise that called for the salesman to pay for most of the loss suffered by the women whose names had been omitted from the policy.

Blaming the Victim

Another common business technique for rejecting consumer requests is blaming the victim. This response not only directs responsibility away from the seller, but it may also discourage the consumer from voicing complaints about subsequent purchases of poor quality goods and services.

When a laundry lost several expensive shirts, its spokesman told the customer he should not have sent such expensive shirts to an ordinary commercial laundry. A tourist in Houston bought an expensive needlepoint pattern along with a supply of specially colored wool, and was promised that additional wool would be available if she needed it. As the buyer approached the completion of the project, she did run out of some colors of yarn. She asked for additional yarn and was told that none was available. The store owner told her that if she had been more skillful in her needlework the original supply of wool would have been adequate. A suburban homeowner ordered a dining room table and matching chairs from a large furniture store in a nearby city. There was a long wait for delivery, because the items had to be specially ordered from their manufacturer. When they arrived, there were a number of imperfections and slight injuries to the finish of the table and chairs. The customer complained to the store, and was told that an expert refinisher would go to his house and make whatever repairs were needed. But no refinisher was ever sent. For several months the buyer and seller communicated in phone calls and letters. Eventually, the store offered to replace the merchandise. When the buyer refused this offer (since he did not want to do without furniture during another long wait for delivery), the store refused to make any other offer. From then on, the store took the position that the buyer was the cause of the problem for unreasonably seeking a repair instead of a replacement.

A dispute with an automobile dealer over payment for repairs to a used car led a customer to join a citizens' action group. The group told the dealer that it would picket the showroom if a meeting failed to produce a compromise agreement. The dealer then agreed to pay for part of the cost of the repairs. But he did not turn over a check at the meeting or at any time during several weeks after the meeting. He finally paid the buyer the agreed amount when the buyer visited him in person one more time. According to the dealer, when the buyer "came in like a gentleman without all his friends, he got his money." This suggests that the delay in resolving the problem was caused by the customer's bringing the consumer group members with him to negotiate with the dealer. In fact, at the beginning of the dispute, the buyer did deal by himself with the dealer and the dealer totally rejected his refund request.

In a number of the case studies, business complaint handlers expressed generalized hostility to all complainants. The manager of the Korvette's store which mishandled the repair of Robert Engel's tape recorder told our interviewer, "What'll happen if everyone finds out you can get what you ask for?" In fact, Engel did not even get what he really wanted: speedy and skillful repair of the tape recorder. A furniture manufacturer, explaining his general belief that there is too much interference by government in buyer-seller relations said, "We don't need flammable fabrics laws, we need people who don't smoke in sofas." And a Lincoln-Mercury automobile dealer summarized his impression of customers who make complaints, saying, "Consumerism is the people who make things rising up against themselves."

Negative perception of complainants is reinforced by buyers who have legitimate grievances but who also display physical or social attributes that are disfavored by complaint handlers. The possible mistreatment of consumers with conventionally disapproved traits is seen in remarks made by a Frigidaire appliance company complaint handler. He told our interviewer that he hears from three different kinds of complainants: hysterical women, drunks, and people who are unwilling to pay for a product or service. How does he respond to complainants? He says he tries to pacify the hysterical women, he hangs up on the drunks, and explains to the others why their complaints are not justified.

In some cases business representatives condemn all or almost all complainers as unreasonable. The owner of a small floor-installation firm stated that 99 percent of his customers bring no trouble. Those who do complain are themselves the cause of the problem: they are women who "worship the kitchen," who excel at housework, and who therefore notice every tiny imperfection in their kitchen floors and may aggravate any problem with the seams by washing the floor too many times. The manager of a baby furniture store suggested that most complaints are unjustified because

customers often ruin merchandise themselves and then try to
return it.

Some businesses maintain lists of complaining consumers.[3] A
canning company complaint handler who is also head of its claims
department says his only consumer complaint records are copies
of correspondence and a list of names of complainants. When the
company apologizes for having manufactured one of its products
poorly and accompanies the apology with a replacement of the
flawed merchandise, it records the name of the consumer. The
purpose of the list is to save the company from making subsequent
replacements to the same consumer. The company's theory must
be that any consumer who complains more than once or twice is
lying in order to defraud the company. The company does not
assume that a three-time complainer might be a statistically rare
but realistically very unlucky three-time purchaser of defective
products—precisely the customer who is especially deserving of replacements and an apology.

In blaming complaints on consumer ignorance, business representatives often claim to be experts, or use jargon to intimidate
and belittle complainants. According to a Ford Motor Company
district representative who was involved in the case of Jimmy
Raven's car, complaints about items that meet normal specifications as set by Ford are "subjective" and therefore unjustified
"from a purely analytical and logical" point of view. This remark
confines any ensuing debate, for the manufacturer claims a monopoly on rationality. When asked about the "problem" of serious
vibration in a customer's car, the service manager of a Ford
dealership replied that this is "not a problem," it is a "manufacturing characteristic." His choice of words shows that he has
defined a negative attribute as something that is a positive, intentionally included feature of Ford cars. When consumers call
General Mills after having found worms or insects in cereal or
cake mix, a representative from the quality control department
assures them, without actually investigating, that the insects are
merely harmless "pantry-pests."

Yes and No

Partial refunds, repairs instead of replacements, and expressions
of concern but of unwillingness to take corrective action are all

examples of ways in which sellers simultaneously say yes and no:
they reject the requests but try at the same time to make the rejections acceptable to their customers. Compromises may sometimes
be fair resolutions; some of the ways, though, in which businesses
give half a loaf really amount to no more than attempts to buy off
justified complainants at low cost. Once some response is made by
a seller, no matter how insignificant, the buyer wil not be able to
complain to a third-party complaint handler that the seller had
ignored his or her request completely; for a small cost the seller
may thus achieve the appearance of fairness.

The Persky case, in which Eastern Airlines delayed the trips of
three members of a family due to overbooking their flight, was
covered by federal regulations which require financial compensation by the airline, but there was a dispute about whether the
travelers had arrived at the airport as far in advance of departure
time as the regulation requires. Initially, the airline refused to
make any payment. But after a member of the family filed a suit
in small claims court, the airline offered a compromise. It paid the
denied boarding compensation required in the regulations to one
of the three affected individuals. By accepting this compromise,
the family gave up its effort to receive payment for the full amount
to which it believed it was entitled.

In another case, Ann Hammond of Lynchburg, Virginia, paid
$1,400 to the Vulcan Basement Waterproofing Co., for water-
proofing the basement of her house. Her basement was flooded
during the first heavy rainstorm after Vulcan did its work. Mrs.
Hammond complained to Vulcan, got no response, and then complained further to a number of third parties. In response to these
further complaints, the company sent two poorly trained part-time
workers to Mrs. Hammond's home. They worked in the basement
for a short while, but the results of the next rainstorm showed that
their work was not effective. The nearly worthless repair attempt
by Vulcan did, however, complicate the dispute and make it more
difficult for Mrs. Hammond to press for further action.

Another style of reacting to complaints by taking actions which
do not attack the fundamental problems is illustrated in the case
studies. Asked whether most consumer complaints are justified,
one automobile dealer responded. "Anyone who pays money and
who thinks he has a complaint is justified in expecting an explana-

tion of his problem." In a number of cases, sellers told our interviewers that since most complaints are due to consumer exaggeration or misunderstanding, problems can be resolved by clearer explanations of the attributes of the purchased products and services. Richard Eilan, vice president in charge of consumer affairs of Eastern Airlines, said that consumer complaints are of "terrific" utility to the company: if there is an abnormal growth in a category of complaints the "policies and procedures" are reviewed and may be changed. Asked for an example of such a use of consumer complaints, he provided an illustration of a change in the explanations customers receive, not of a substantive change in policy. He said that customers believe that children traveling alone pay full fare instead of a discount fare because Eastern will coddle them, but actually the reason for the full fare payment is that discounts are offered only in combination with the sale of additional tickets. Because of a number of customer complaints reflecting this misunderstanding, Eastern changed a procedure. Now when a reservation is made for an unaccompanied child the reservations clerk is supposed to inform the customer that he is paying full fare because the child is unaccompanied, not because any special care will be provided.

Rejecting Requests for Changes in Policy

When complaints ask not only for refunds, repairs, or replacements, but also that a business change the design of a product or alter its procedures or techniques for providing a service, businesses often ignore or reject the requests. In our case studies, business spokespersons were asked whether past complaints had provided any constructive information to help them serve their customers better. The responses to this inquiry, along with other data from the case studies, show that businesses are often reluctant to learn from the proof buyers present to them of their past mistakes.

In one case study, the manager of a home improvement company stated that the firm had received only one complaint in seventeen years. This seems incredible, given the fact that home improvement businesses are generally one of the most common sources of complaints received by third parties, but it may reflect an idiosyncratic definition of the term complaint. The president of a door-to-door bulk meat and home freezer sales company gave our interviewer a similar report that complaints are rare; comments from customers, he went on to say, are not uncommon. For a business to perceive complaints as neutral comments may lead to a serious consequence: the business may ignore requests for action.

Any single complainant usually does not know if other consumers have also complained about a given subject. Businesses, however, should know, so that the generally applicable lessons of individual complaints can be identified and acted upon. Yet analysis of a number of case studies shows that in many businesses, patterns of consumer complaints can probably not be detected except by personal memory of particular employees. Filing and recording systems are not set up to monitor trends or topics in complaints. A service manager for a Volkswagen dealer, for example, stated that he and his assistant try to resolve complaints when they are made, but that no records are kept. Where records *are* kept, some businesses may not be interested in checking for patterns, and some filing systems may not permit the discovery of patterns. Complaints that are filed only by the names of complainants, for example, cannot yield information about complaint patterns.

Inefficient Management

Failures to make use of constructive components of complaints may be due simply to bad management rather than bad intentions. In some companies, complaints may be distributed inefficiently among organizational divisions. For example, the customer relations manager of Smyth Greyhound Van Lines reports that billing complaints go to one office, damage complaints go to another office, certain other complaints go to a customer relations manager, and still other complaints received by local offices are never communicated to the headquarters office unless they cannot be resolved at the local level. In other instances, company divisions that could correct problems which have been complained about may be unaware of the volume of complaints. A district service manager for a manufacturer of air conditioning systems stated that he has learned of patterns of poor service by particular dealers through consumer complaints. But, because he is not in the marketing division, he has no role in deciding which dealers should be discouraged from selling his company's systems.

The victim-blaming stance which may accompany business rejections of consumer requests also bars businesses in some instances from perceiving and acting on groups of complaints which collectively bear important information about their operations. For example, interviews with plumbers in two separate case studies reveal that complaints about billing practices are prevalent in their businesses because consumers are unaware of the basis for charges. These two plumbers, Jack Harmon and Alan Zoltak, recognize that this lack of awareness is a problem, yet neither suggested that plumbing companies should take the initiative either to change charge practices or to explain them to consumers. They indicated to our interviewers that it is up to the consumer to discover how charges are calculated. According to Zoltak, plumbers often do not have the time to explain the billing practices to consumers. Harmon stated that most consumers are unreasonable and should learn more about the billing practices for plumbing repairs, but, "I'm worried about making a living; I don't have the time to educate my fellow man."

Here is another instance of "consumer ignorance." Both the manager of a Mazda automobile dealership and the customer relations manager of Mazda Motors of America, blamed consumer complaints about poor gas mileage on consumers' driving habits, saying if a consumer does not get the same gas mileage as Mazda's tests predict, then the consumer is not driving properly.

Advice from Business People on How to Complain

Our interviewers asked business people what general advice they might have for consumers with complaints. Some avoided the question by suggesting that consumers shop more carefully. But the replies from business people who did consider the question—What should be done once a failure *has* become evident?—fall into three categories. One type of reply seems to blame consumers for having problems or for speaking up about them; a second type does not blame victims explicitly but nonetheless recommends very conservative complaint techniques; a third type suggests prompt use of third parties or other prompt strong actions. Some of the actual statements are both sources of advice and indicators of the attitudes sellers may have toward buyers who present complaints.

A Ford Motor Company regional service manager gave an answer typical of those which purport to be advice but are really criticisms of people who complain. Referring to customers with complaints, he said, "They should not try to dictate to me or be emotional. Then consideration will be given. I spend 99 percent of my time trying to help customers. They spend 1 percent of their time trying to cooperate." Similarly, a Sears, Roebuck executive said consumers should not argue emotionally: "A lot of them curse at you or scream at you. If they meet us halfway, we're more than willing to meet them halfway." A J. C. Penney executive said that bringing defective merchandise back to the store quickly is important because the more time a customer delays and thinks about the problem, the more distorted it becomes. Distortion, emotionalism, and screaming are referred to in these three comments, indicating that the complaint handlers saw them as frequent impediments to consumers' obtaining justice. This criticism, however, is somewhat circular, since it is natural for a person whose reasonable demand is rejected by a seller to be angry. It is also likely that the failure of a costly purchase will affect a customer's emotions; a store executive deals with problems as part of his job, but a buyer has a financial (and possibly psychological) investment in a particular product or service, and is thus appropriately concerned with all its deficiencies. These sellers are in effect advising consumers to be calm and accept whatever sellers offer them. They maintain this attitude about consumer complaints at the same time that they perceive buyers as emotional and unfair.

A Frigidaire complaint handler's advice to consumers was that they should understand the problems businesses face. Chief among these, he said, is that no one wants to pay for a product anymore, and that people expect good performance from appliances without wanting to pay higher prices for them. A furniture store executive said: "Sometimes it takes technical knowledge to explain the problem rather than get emotional." And a home builder presented perhaps the ultimate in victim blaming or shirking of responsibility, saying: "Sometimes it's best to fix things yourself," rather than to complain. These comments—empathize with business, use technical knowledge, fix it yourself—amount to a stand rejecting the right of consumers to complain in most instances.

Some complaint handlers did avoid blaming consumers for their troubles, but did not offer any significant advice. For example, a car dealer proposed that buyers complain within the company's carefully constructed hierarchy one level at a time until satisfied. A spokesperson for a manufacturer of house trailers suggested that consumers put everything in writing and "be patient."

Against the already demonstrated background of obstacles to perceiving problems and to voicing and receiving satisfactory resolution of complaints, it seems disingenuous if not actually deceptive for business people to advise consumers to be patient or to suggest that those with problems are themselves to blame. Some business respondents did speak to the issue of what an aggrieved customer can do to obtain a fair solution of his or her problem. Our sample of businesses asked to give advice is small and unscientifically selected with respect to this inquiry. But it is noteworthy that a large number of the business responses recommend the use of third parties. This contrasts with the actual practices of consumers, which are marked by generally infrequent use of third parties. A brief restatement of some of the comments illustrates this point. From a retailer of food and appliances: "Go directly to the dealer, and if he won't satisfy you, sue." From a home improvement contractor: "Go to the seller, and then to a Better Business Bureau or Chamber of Commerce; then, take it to court." From an electric utility employee: "For speedy action, contact the public service commission or sue in small claims court." From a complaint handler at Armstrong Cork Company: "The squeaky wheel gets the oil." From an automobile dealer: "Contact consumer protection agencies or call Detroit."

These sellers, and others, obviously do not make these suggestions often in the ordinary course of their dealings with complainants. If they did, and accompanied the suggestions with unbiased information on how to use the third parties, it is likely the overall usage of third parties would be considerably higher. What these comments really may amount to is a kind of joinder of two conflicting themes. The business people recognize that third parties with powers of coercion can really motivate them to reconsider their positions on disputed complaints, so they recommend that consumers with complaints use third parties. On the other hand, business people who are aware that recourse to third parties is typically infrequent can feel free to recommend their use.

They know that few consumers will actually take those difficult and time-consuming actions, and they also may know that even if third parties are brought into disputes, very often businesses can still resolve the problems on their own terms to their own satisfaction.

The Variety of Business Responses

The diversity of the techniques businesses use to reject consumer requests demonstrates that sellers virtually control the consumer complaint process. Nearly all the negative responses—the runaround, silent treatment, blaming the victim, disguising negative decisions, ignoring policy aspects of complaints—succeed only because consumers have little ability to force the application of impartial standards to their cases. Sellers deserve credit for the fair treatment they give to many complaints. But the examples and analysis in this chapter show that sellers can refuse all kinds of requests by buyers. Their arbitrary choice of techniques for rejecting requests is akin to sellers' equally arbitrary decisions on the initial question of which requests shall be granted and which shall be rejected. Businesses' lack of objective standards for the treatment of complaints directly reflects their general freedom from supervision or accountability in complaint handling. Where negative responses are not the product of reasoned calculation, but rather are due to accidental lapses in management or general prejudice against complainants, those responses further indicate the nearly total control businesses exercise over the handling of complaints.

Scrutiny of both willful and random business techniques of refusing reasonable consumer requests shows the need for exposing the techniques to further criticism; their application in many cases is unsupported by logic or fairness. Unfortunately, however, the power of individuals to force such scrutiny is slight. The customer has implicit power to direct his or her future patronage away from a particular seller, but this does not require a seller to explain or justify its decision in any given complaint dispute. It is only through the intervention of third parties that consumers can secure independent evaluations of business responses. Without such independent evaluations, it is difficult to achieve either corrections of individual decisions or systemic improvements in business procedures for responding to complaints.

Five

Shortcomings of Third-Party Complaint Handlers

THIRD PARTIES such as courts, government agencies, Better Business Bureaus, and voluntary complaint-handling organizations occupy a strategic position in the complaint process. Although our survey shows that they deal with only a tiny fraction of consumers' perceived problems, some third parties have legal power to enforce remedies. Others draw power from the fear that most businesses have of bad publicity. Thus, these institutions have the potential to influence businesses to improve their complaint handling. All third parties serve the purpose of offering assistance to disappointed purchasers. Sometimes people seek aid from a third party directly when a purchase has failed; in other instances, they seek aid because they have complained to a seller about the failure of a purchase and have been dissatisfied with the seller's treatment of their complaint.

Institutions that process disputes can be ranked in terms of their power, the formality of their procedures, and the degree to which their resolutions of problems affect society as a whole. Relatively formal institutions are legislatures, law enforcement agencies, appellate courts, and trial courts. Consideration of a dispute (or more likely, a pattern of disputes) may prompt a legislature to promulgate statutes, which are abstract general rules of conduct. Law enforcers act in individual cases to dramatize the statutory rules by citing individuals or businesses as criminals or rule-breakers. Appellate courts treat individual cases and add to the general understanding and elaboration of rules, and trial courts deal with individual cases. The bulk of institutional complaint handling is carried out by less formal entities, however, such as regulatory agencies acting as mediators in particular cases, consumer affairs departments, media-related complaint handlers ("action lines"), Better Business Bureaus, and a variety of voluntary organizations. They can settle disputes, but do not contribute to the prevention of disputes by establishing rules or spreading knowledge about rules. They lack the coercive power possessed directly by courts and law enforcers and indirectly by the legislature.[1]

Our case studies and other data identify certain characteristic shortcomings in the ways that most third parties handle consumer complaints. One significant problem with third-party institutions is that consumers are often confused about the amount and type of help they can offer. In many instances, third parties are responsible for the confusion or are to blame for failing to remedy it. Conflicts of interest between the consumer's goal of obtaining redress and the institutional goals of third parties can operate to penalize particular consumers. Third parties often use case selection methods that are either arbitrary or more closely related to their own goals than to obtaining benefits for the public. In individual cases, third parties sometimes misperceive the topic of a consumer's complaint; aspects of a problem are overlooked or ignored. Sometimes in lieu of facilitating a just solution, a third party becomes a vehicle for or a provider of symbolic rewards to the consumer. Another undesirable aspect of third-party intervention is the legitimizing of business responses in instances where the third party has not obtained enough information to render any judgment.

Confusion about the Extent of Third-Party Help

Almost all third parties handle complaints the same way. They attempt to mediate between the buyer and seller by reporting the buyer's complaint to the seller and the seller's answer, if any, to the buyer. This is the extent of the work that will be performed and the power that will be brought to bear on any single case. In many instances, however, third parties create or acquiesce in consumers' unrealistic expectations of their role.

A nongovernmental complaint-handling institution provides an example of this common discrepancy between apparent power and actual ability to act. Sally Hoover presented a plumbing dispute to the Consumer Protection Association, a well-publicized organization in Cleveland, supported in part by the city's United Torch Drive, an annual charity campaign. Her complaint was that Osborn and Son, Inc., had overcharged for plumbing work, and had violated state regulations forbidding repairers to charge more than 10 percent above an estimate they provide the buyer, unless the buyer approves a greater payment before the work is performed. Mrs. Hoover visited the Consumer Protection Association in person to file her complaint and received an enthusiastic reception. She was told, "If more people like you told us about such businesses our office could do a lot more." However, all the office did for her was to mediate, obtain an offer of compromise, and—when she rejected the compromise offer as too small—refer her to several other third parties which function in almost the same way. This left Mrs. Hoover in what she perceived as a helpless position. Referring to the plumbing company's response to her complaint, she told an interviewer, "By saying that we should sue him, he knew he had the upper hand and that we would never win because he has an attorney who is probably more knowledgeable and knows the ins and outs better than anyone I could get."

In a dispute with the manufacturer and seller of a mobile home, Mr. and Mrs. Jed Wilkins sought help from the Federal Trade Commission (FTC), the California Department of Consumer Affairs, and the Arizona Division of Building Codes. The mobile home had been illustrated in a catalog as having a "Stonehedge" exterior. As delivered, it had the desired exterior on only one end, and there were some problems with its installation. Each of the third parties tried to mediate the problems but no resolution was reached. Mrs. Wilkins herself summarized what all three agencies wound up advising her and her husband to do, and provided an ironic suggestion, in a letter she wrote to the FTC: "Any government agency that is supposed to protect the consumer from this sort of thing is only telling the consumer to hire an attorney. If that is all the information any of them give the consumer—why not just one office to mail out a form letter? 'Hire an attorney.'"

Frequently a consumer with a problem must describe the facts several times to different third parties. This occurs because once mediation fails, complaint handlers typically refer complainants to other complaint handlers. Needless to say, such advice can sometimes be useful. But what sometimes happens is that when a third party's mediation effort fails it refers a consumer to another third-party complaint-handling institution, which *also* attempts only to mediate. This can waste a consumer's time, money, and energy and also waste the resources of the complaint-handling institutions.

The case of Mrs. Gus Shapiro, who was a victim of an unscrupulous collection agency, illustrates this process. In violation of Maryland law, the agency conducted a campaign of harrassment against her. She complained first to the District of Columbia Office of Consumer Affairs. After several months of working on the case, that office referred Mrs. Shapiro to the consumer affairs office of a nearby Maryland county. That office did not begin investigating the complaint until two more months had passed. Mrs. Shapiro wrote to her congressman, who referred her case to the federal Office of Consumer Affairs. That office referred the case to the FTC, and the FTC wrote that it "cannot adjudicate private controversies." Effort and time had been invested to produce no worthwhile result.

Worse than a referral which does no good is a referral which hampers the consumer's efforts to gain redress. Evelyn Huck believed that a home improvement contractor had repaired the roof of her house improperly. She reported her dispute to the Wisconsin attorney general's office, but that office was unable to effect a compromise solution. And in a conversation with one of the staff members of the attorney general's office, Mrs. Huck suggested that she might send her complaint to a local broadcast station's consumer help service, *Contact 6*. The staffer said that *Contact 6* could only get the contractor to do the work again, which Mrs. Huck did not want. But a researcher's interview with an employee of the broadcast station indicated that this was precisely the type of case where *Contact 6* believes its intervention can be useful.

Many kinds of false impressions can be given to a consumer by a third party that has failed to resolve a case successfully. Often, useless referrals are given. As in the Huck case, misinformation is sometimes provided. But especially undesirable, in view of the need for third parties to act as instruments of accountability, is the phenomenon of a third party failing to achieve a resolution and at the same time suggesting to the consumer that no further procedural steps are possible.

Mrs. Sue Neville was dissatisfied with the quality of medical care provided by a doctor in Philadelphia. She complained to the Philadelphia County Medical Society Grievance Committee, which followed its own procedures and decided that the complaint did not merit action against the doctor. Its letter reporting this decision to Mrs. Neville did not mention that an institution of greater authority exists—the Board of Censors—to which a dissatisfied complainant may appeal a decision of the Grievance Committee. In fact, the Grievance Committee letter is couched in language which suggests the decision is final and unappealable.

Conflict of Interest

Institutions which accept complaints from consumers usually convey the impression that their actions are intended to secure the fair resolution of as many disputes as possible. However, the goals of some third-party institutions conflict with providing impartial and efficient dispute processing.

Mrs. H. A. Cosey, who pressed her complaints about poor service by a car dealer strongly enough to prompt a state agency to suspend two of the dealer's business licenses for short periods of time, also complained to a local association of automobile dealers. Rather than explain that they do not really offer an impartial complaint service, an employee of the association discussed Mrs. Cosey's case and offered aid. Mediation efforts by the association did not lead to a resolution, and when she complained about this failure to the organization's employee, Mrs. Cosey was told, "What do you expect me to do? I'm not a prosecutor!"

Prompted by the federal Office of Consumer Affairs, manufacturers of major appliances and some other commonly purchased items have organized complaint-handling groups known as consumer action panels. MACAP, the Major Appliance Consumer Action Panel, is the oldest of these groups and is generally regarded as the most effective.[2] Yet it relies on staff members of industry associations to conduct its investigations, and refuses to let the public know which manufacturers have the best (or worst) records of compliance with its recommendations, even though members of MACAP have reported privately that manufacturers vary greatly in their willingness to accept MACAP decisions. Moreover, since MACAP is sponsored by the companies with which it deals, it has no power to compel acceptance of decisions. Consumers would be better served if MACAP provided manufacturers with a strong incentive to comply with its decisions, such as publicizing instances of noncompliance. And beyond the level of individual complaint resolution, open record keeping by MACAP would let consumers know which manufacturers receive the fewest complaints per numbers of appliances sold, and allow them to compare the complaint resolution records of various manufacturers.

Better Business Bureaus are most often mentioned by consumers who are surveyed about the help they would seek in disputes with businesses. A study by Congressman Benjamin Rosenthal in 1971 described generally poor performance by Better Business Bureaus in complaint handling, and related that poor performance to the institution's support by dues from its member businesses.[3] Better Business Bureaus usually accept at face value whatever statements businesses make in response to complaints. In many of the case studies, Better Business Bureaus are seen acting in accordance with this description in the Rosenthal report: "It is almost always true that when a firm contests a consumer's claim (either because of a dispute over the facts or because the firm does not believe itself responsible), the BBB quickly steps out of the picture." Further, the report quotes BBB officials to the effect that there is no aggressive soliciting of replies from businesses, in order to avoid antagonizing members, and that a primary function of BBB complaint handling is "cooling down" the tempers of customers.

Some case studies discussed earlier highlight the generally probusiness orientation at Better Business Bureaus. For example, Mr. and Mrs. Harrison asked a local Better Business Bureau for help in obtaining a replacement wheel for their newly purchased baby buggy. The Bureau accepted a statement by the seller that the manufacturer was at fault and that the seller had done everything possible to help Mr. and Mrs. Harrison. Dick Meagher received no benefit from contacting a Better Business Bureau about his dispute with a truck-driving school. Ben Zeller similarly was not helped by a Better Business Bureau when he had a dispute with a bulk meat and freezer sales company. It is obvious, as well as supported by our data and past studies, that Better Business Bureaus can help individuals whose complaints concern businesses operating in good faith and involve simple misunderstandings or other failures in communication. This pattern is consistent with the original BBB purpose of shielding established businesses from government intervention as well as from consumer complaints that might be deemed unreasonable. In fact, a development at one Better Business Bureau recalls that original orientation. The Better Business Bureau of Eastern Pennsylvania has begun a service to assist *businesses* which have complaints against consumers.[4]

Complaint handlers can have institutional goals or traditional procedures which themselves conflict with professed ideals of swift, fair complaint resolution and problem prevention. One common circumstance is unreasonable slowness in carrying out simple procedures. Helen Thompson complained to the Wisconsin Department of Justice's Office of Consumer Protection (OCP) about the sales practices of a local health spa. The OCP had already received about fifty complaints concerning that particular business, but had decided not to take any enforcement action. Even so, the department allowed more than a month to pass while it made a clearly foredoomed mediation attempt; it sent Mrs. Thompson's complaint to the business, demanded a prompt reply, granted an extension of reply time, received a reply denying the charges, and decided that no other action was warranted. It then contacted Mrs. Thompson to tell her that no action would be taken. Furthermore, after this unnecessary delay, the OCP informed her that it would not provide her with any legal advice.

In another of the case histories, third-party complaint handlers tolerated a slow response by a business in circumstances which placed a consumer at a serious risk of injury. Mercy James, of Bluefield, West Virginia, ordered five tons of coal, but received two tons of coal and three tons of rock and dirt. After two months of appeals to various third parties, a local senior citizens program was able to reach an agreement with the company to deliver three additional tons of "good coal." Because of a coal shortage, however, the additional coal was not delivered for over a month. Mrs. James had a limited income and could buy only small amounts of coal from another dealer; there was a real danger of her running out of coal in a cold winter. Yet the only third party that had intervened thought the company was being reasonable. Mrs. James did not run out of coal, but the issue in this case is still valid: The time that it takes to resolve a complaint can be far more important to the consumer than it is to third parties.

Third parties may also be biased in favor of easy actions. Thus, the Postal Service may allow a large mail order business, such as the Longines Symphonette record clubs, to continue improper service. Such businesses may learn that prompt attention to the relatively small numbers of complaints relayed to them by law enforcement institutions can ward off any general investigation by the government unit. In fact, resolving complaints quickly may even enhance the reputation of the business in the eyes of the enforcement agency. Even though its activities produce many complaints, such a business helps the agency compile an apparently good record of satisfactorily completed investigations.

Similar reasoning partly explains the way the New York City Department of Consumer Affairs handled Sidney Berger's complaint about having been charged for unauthorized car repairs. A fine was imposed, but no action was taken to seek restitution for Berger or others who might similarly have been improperly charged for repairs. In *Counsel for the Deceived*, the department's first consumer advocate, Philip Schrag, describes how limits of time and money quickly precluded the department's litigation of any more than a handful of cases.[5]

The manner in which the New York State Department of Motor Vehicles supervises automobile repair establishments may also reflect a preference for easy actions. Although the department may, under authority of a statute that is subject to varied interpretations, have the power to order refunds to wronged consumers, it chooses instead to collect fines that become a part of the state's revenue. The deputy commissioner in charge of repair-shop supervision told a newspaper reporter that "The law does not mandate in any way that we get a repair done or get a refund, or get the customer satisfied. The law gives us the power to clamp down on a shop for violations, and if we do enough of that, we'll clean up the industry over a period of time."[6] It is arguable that the department could decide that a repair shop's failure to offer a refund directly to a customer is itself, in certain cases, evidence of improper conduct. This interpretation of the statute would produce refunds for consumers, but would lead to more appeals by businesses. The department's refusal to seek refunds may keep down the number of complaints that New Yorkers present to the Motor Vehicle Department. In the first eighteen months of the program, ten thousand complaints were received instead of the sixty thousand that had been predicted.[7] Since a consumer will receive no direct benefit for complaining (and possibly taking the time to participate in a hearing), it is not surprising that few complaints are made.

Institutional Problems of "Official" Third Parties

The institutions usually considered to have the most power to prevent consumer abuse—government agencies such as regulatory bodies, attorneys general, and district attorneys—have special institutional problems. Whether these agencies should devote substantial resources to consumer complaints is problematic. The FTC, for example, has been aptly criticized in the past for relying on its mailbag for planning the priorities of its investigations.[8] With voicing of complaints to third parties as limited as studies have indicated, third parties must draw two lessons: particular complaints offer at best an impressionistic guide to consumer victimization; and, government agencies must do a better job of soliciting and facilitating complaints. Law enforcement agencies typically try to mediate disputes,[9] but this may not help prevent future problems, and may even hurt that effort, if significant resources are devoted to case-by-case work on the few complaints that reach the third party. On the other hand, the Massachusetts attorney general's office has attempted to reduce its ordinary complaint-handling activities by encouraging the establishment of local voluntary groups, while relying on computerized record keeping to derive planning data from those complaints.[10]

Recent analyses of ways that federal agencies treat consumer complaints have stressed the utility of complaints in identifying possible widespread problems. To make this process work better, a U.S. Senate study on federal regulatory agencies endorsed a proposal for a central federal complaint office. The proposal itself highlights some of the current shortcomings of official complaint treatment.

A concerted effort should be made to increase public awareness of the existence of Federal Central Office complaint-handling systems. The public should be informed of the scope of these complaint-handling systems' jurisdiction and authority. Informed consumers would reduce the percentage of complaints that are sent to inappropriate complaint-handling systems. The time now spent referring misdirected complaints could be more profitably spent on jurisdictional complaints. Mass media should be utilized to increase the level of public awareness. Further, promotional material should be made available to the consumer at the point of product performance/service delivery. . . .

There is a need to elicit cómplaints from the disadvantaged. Most complaint-handling systems do not make special efforts to seek out such complaints. Where appropriate, such efforts should be initiated.[11]

With particular reference to individual treatment of complaints, state and local prosecutorial agencies are relatively inactive. The consumer affairs units in the attorney general's offices of nearly every state litigate only a comparatively small number of cases each year.[12]

An illustration of federal agency use of complaints is provided by a study of five federal entities charged with regulating the work of financial institutions. It shows that their handling of consumer complaints is unsatisfactory to 70 percent of complainants, and is generally limited to asking the business that is the subject of the complaint to furnish its version of the problem. The report, covering the Federal Reserve Board and four other units of government, describes typical failures to obtain clarifications of consumers' points of view, to publicize complaint-handling procedures, or to conduct educational programs.[13]

A broader study of twenty-two federal agencies, including virtually all of the largest complaint recipients, was conducted by the federal Office of Consumer Affairs, beginning in 1974. At the end of 1979, it was found that most of the agencies had improved their work, measured according to criteria such as adequacy of record keeping, follow-up, reporting, evaluation, accountability, and public awareness. Problems still were said to exist at many agencies, however, with handling of telephone calls, coordination of central and field offices, assignment of skilled employees, and careful understanding of the functions complaints can serve.[14]

Arbitrary Case Selection

Arbitrary selection of cases by some third-party complair handlers clearly limits their usefulness to consumers. For instance an Illinois consumer affairs bureau operated by the state attorne general was found to screen out complaints that would probabl be difficult to resolve.[15] These difficult complaints probably ir volve significant personal and societal costs. As a matter of policy Better Business Bureaus stop their work on cases if it become clear that they involve disputed facts. So, too, most state attorne general's offices avoid disputed consumer cases. For example Louise Meadows, of Charleston, Indiana, bought a suite of livin room furniture from Value City furniture store. She and her hus band were told that it was "one of a kind." When a panel fell ot an end table, the store sent a repairman to the Meadowses' hom to fix it. This marked the beginning of a dispute. The repair di not seem adequate; furthermore, the repairer mentioned that th suite was identical to many other suites of furniture sold by Valu City. Mr. and Mrs. Meadows asked Value City to exchange th furniture, and the store refused. The Meadowses wrote to thei congressman and their state attorney general. When the attorne general's office learned that there was a dispute over wha representations the store had actually made, it dropped the case By coincidence, soon after the Meadowses learned that the at torney general's office would not act in their behalf, they receive a letter from the federal Office of Consumer Affairs (to whic their congressman had sent their letter) recommending that the send the complaint to their state attorney general.

On the other hand, agencies may sometimes place unwarrante emphasis on the fact that a complaint is received from anothe complaint handler rather than from a consumer. Unless an agenc knows that such referrals are the result of a reasonable analysi procedure, there is no reason for complaints referred in this way t receive special treatment. Yet sometimes that is exactly what the do receive. Roxanne Lewis, a resident of New Jersey, received dunning letter from Magazine Collection Bureau, in Illinois. Sinc she had already paid her bill, she complained about the letter t the attorneys general of Illinois and New Jersey. The Illinois at torney general replied that the complaint would be forwarded

with no promise of any action, to a regional attorney general's office. The New Jersey attorney general's reply was that her complaint would be sent to the Illinois attorney general. And then
another letter came to Mrs. Lewis from Illinois. Without referring
o her own earlier direct letter to the office, the Illinois attorney
general's office wrote that based on the referral from New Jersey,
an investigation would definitely be conducted.

Selective Perception of Complaint Topics

Just as some complaint handlers may reject requests for help for
irrelevant reasons, or reasons inconsistent with their own professed
goals, it is clear from the case studies that selective perception
may occur when third parties deal with even the complaints they
do accept. For example, the Pennsylvania State Board of
Optometrical Examiners has the power to revoke licenses of
optometrists; its standard complaint-handling procedure, according to our interviews of its members, is to ignore charges of
unethical practices made by patients and to concentrate on effect-
ing concrete solutions, usually by dealing with the issue of fees.
When patients complain about poor service and simultaneously
mention the cost, the board assumes that cost is the real issue.

Selective perception of issues also operated when a Washington,
D.C., resident complained to a Better Business Bureau that a local
television repair business had kept his television set in its shop for
more than two months, after promising that repairs would take
only four or five days. The BBB considered the case closed, with a
satisfactory resolution, when it passed the complaint on to the
seller and learned that the seller had repaired and returned the set
just prior to hearing from the BBB. No consideration was given to
the implicit broader criticism contained in the complaint: two
months is too much time for a five-day repair job, and a business
which treats a consumer this way ought to be called upon to
explain its actions and to provide the complaint handler with a
reasonable basis for believing that such circumstances will not occur again.

The case of Ethel Koenig discloses another kind of mispercep-
tion of a complaint. When the refrigerator in Ms. Koenig's
Milwaukee apartment stopped working, a lengthy dispute ensued
between Ms. Koenig and her landlord. After several months, she

began to withhold a small amount of each monthly rent payment; eventually she moved out under threat of eviction. Prior to moving out, she contacted the Better Business Bureau, a local tenants union, and the Milwaukee Legal Services Office. None of these third parties provided useful advice or mediated the dispute. Yet when representatives of the third parties were interviewed about the case, a frequent comment was made that this was a problem of "poor communications." In fact, the communications were clear: Ms. Koenig wanted a working refrigerator, and the management company wanted full rent payments. Rights and obligations were perhaps unclear in the case, but the third parties, retrospectively, tended to avoid perceiving the case that way. They preferred to characterize it as a human relations and communications problem.

Similarly, Frank Baer, of Crown Point, Indiana, was injured in an accident related to his employment as a truck driver. Making a delivery, he slipped on ice and suffered a cerebral concussion. He was deemed temporarily disabled, and received workmen's compensation payments for forty weeks. Then, although he was still unable to work, the payments were terminated. He had a right to a hearing concerning future benefits, and after more than a year of delay, such a hearing was held. It led to a decision that for a maximum of 500 additional weeks, Baer should be paid compensation. Yet during the time before the hearing, Baer and his family were supported by their life's savings and charity. They complained to the state and federal legislators, and to newspaper action lines. Without exception, each third party perceived the case as a problem relating to Baer only. The broader issue of the efficacy of the bureaucratic procedures, which worked so harshly in this case, was ignored.

Legitimizing Business Responses

When third parties engage in mediation (the only action most third parties take), they transmit replies from businesses to complainants. Unfortunately, this repetition of the business side of a story can sometimes be misconstrued by a consumer as an endorsement of a business contradiction of his or her point of view.

Mr. and Mrs. Ben Zeller, of Buffalo, New York, were visited in their home by a salesman for ABC Meats, Inc., a food and freezer sales company. They were persuaded to buy a freezer and a large supply of food, and to sign a waiver of the state's mandatory cooling-off period (a period of time in which the customers of door-to-door salespeople may cancel contracts). The Zellers became dissatisfied with the transaction very quickly. The food they had bought did not last as long as they had expected, and the freezer itself, they decided, was too expensive due to the cost of financing its time purchase. Mr. Zeller offered to pay whatever ABC might lose on resale of the freezer. As he told our interviewer, "I just wanted it out of my house." ABC Meats refused to accept return of the freezer, and the Zellers complained to the local Better Business Bureau. What they wanted to know, they told the Bureau, was whether they could reasonably ask ABC Meats to take back the freezer and cancel the time payment agreement. The Bureau's decision in this case, based on representations from the seller, was that no real dispute or grounds for investigation existed. The BBB construed the consumer's dissatisfaction as outside the scope of its activity. The Zellers took no further action. While the BBB did not overtly endorse the ABC company position, the effect of participation by the BBB may have been to lower the Zellers' notion of what kind of resolution may be fair or obtainable.

While the Zellers may have accepted the BBB position, other consumers have regarded such decisions as evidence that they should not try to press their complaints any further. When a BBB told Kevin Partyka that it would not rule in his favor in his dispute with a dry cleaner about the ruined vinyl trim on his jacket, Partyka decided not to take any further action. He thought the BBB was wrong, but that further action would be futile.

This phenomenon of perceiving a third party's withdrawal as evidence of weakness on the buyer's side of a dispute also shows up in the health care cases in the study. When medical societies have said no action is warranted, consumers seemed prone to accept such decisions as final.

Substitution of Symbolic Rewards

As Albert Hirschman has suggested in *Exit, Voice and Loyalty*, some people derive satisfaction from the act of complaining, independent of results achieved, because of the positive feeling they derive from striving to see justice done.[16] Our case studies show that this leaves some people with unfounded beliefs about the efficacy of third-party complaint handlers.

Martha Dudek joined a Cleveland group, Consumer Action Movement (CAM), and worked with it for several months. In addition to helping fellow members press their complaints, she had CAM attempt to resolve a conflict she had with a local dentist. Dentures he had made did not fit her properly; after he refused to furnish a replacement set, Mrs. Dudek was treated by a second dentist who provided her with a comfortable set. As a result of her complaining to the local Dental Society, a compromise was offered: the first dentist would refund about a third of her total payments. Mrs. Dudek rejected the offer. Several months of CAM action then followed, with members of the group and Mrs. Dudek picketing the dentist's office on a number of days. In the end, the dentist refused to change his position, and Mrs. Dudek decided to accept the partial refund. Yet she enjoyed being a member of CAM and told our interviewer, "I would definitely take another serious problem to CAM," even though there was no objective benefit from the CAM actions.

When individuals present consumer complaints to senators or representatives, it is almost a certainty that their letters will be answered. In several case studies, consumers took satisfaction from having received uninformative acknowledgments or reports of referral of their letters to federal agencies or to the businesses that were involved in the disputes.

For instance, Alan Knudson, of Lancaster, Ohio, paid $10,000 to Success Motivation Institute (SMI), a company which had been the subject of an FTC cease and desist order for deceptive sales practices. The payment gave Knudson a franchise to sell additional SMI courses and products. Shortly after he entered into his agreement with SMI he realized that the huge profits he had been promised would not likely be forthcoming. He requested a refund, which SMI turned down. Knudson then wrote to his congressman, and hired a lawyer. The lawyer's efforts produced a refund. The congressman sent Knudson an acknowledgment, referred the letter to the FTC and the Securities and Exchange Commission, and subsequently sent Knudson materials from the FTC and the SEC. The lawyer had produced the refund, but Knudson gave great

redit to his congressman. "He's beautiful," he told our interviewer, "he really kept me informed." A North Carolina
consumer in one of our case studies was delighted with a response
from then Senator Sam Ervin which merely said that as a federal
legislator he could do nothing of direct help to a consumer who
was involved in a dispute with a local business.

Modes of Consumer Participation in Third-Party Processes

Many of the shortcomings of third-party complaint-handling institutions occur because their procedures place complainants in
passive roles. Consumers who present complaints to such organizations cannot observe the effects of conflicts of interest, arbitrary
case selection, or distorted perceptions of complaint subject matter. Similarly, people are likely to develop misconceptions about
institutions which place them in passive positions. Since consumers are not involved in the ordinary handling of cases by Better
Business Bureaus, for example, at any point beyond their registering of their complaints, it is not surprising that they misperceive
the nature of BBB complaint handling.

For consumers who want quick and direct resolutions of
disputes with sellers, many obstacles typically prevent third-party
complaint handlers from being particularly helpful. This may
partially explain why consumers typically avoid such institutions
in complaint disputes. Third parties should evaluate their programs in the light of their mediocre records of resolving consumer
disputes and of consumers' general rejection of the agencies as
sources of help in individual cases. It is easy for individuals who
administer such institutions to believe that processing large numbers of cases indicates that they are serving their constituencies
well. A more accurate perception, however, would view those cases
in the context of the greater numbers of cases that are never
presented to the third parties. Where attention to resolving individual cases prevents agencies from addressing the need for
broadly applicable enforcement or education programs, and
particularly where the results in cases that are treated may be no
better than the results that could be obtained through other means,
agencies should reorient their work.

Third-party institutions such as neighborhood or small claims
courts, or small scale mediation and arbitration programs, can

provide dispute management that includes active participation by the complainant. This participation is the best means of avoiding problems such as the substitution of symbolic rewards for actual resolutions, the legitimizing of business responses, and the confusion about powers of remedy agents, which mark the operations of most complaint-handling institutions. Personal involvement with the handling of a consumer's dispute serves an educational function for the individual consumer and for his or her family and friends. And if neighborhood courts or other public institutions are used, the possible educational benefit can be derived by many members of the community.

Six

Surveying Consumer Troubles and Obstacles to Redress

A QUANTITATIVE EXAMINATION of the consumer complaint process can provide a context for the qualitative descriptions and analyses of impediments to problem perception, complaint voicing, and distribution of redress that have already been presented. Logic requires that problems exist before reasonable complaints can be made. So the initial inquiry must be whether *problems*—distinct from *complaints about problems*—occur, how often they occur, what they are like, and who suffers them. Ascertaining the incidence of problems, however, has been a difficult task for researchers, in part because such information has been kept secret by businesses that have collected it.

A 1979 national survey asked, "Have you (or your family) ever been cheated or deceived in regard to any product or service that you have purchased in the last year or so? People representing 14 percent of the sample, or about 10 million households, replied that at least once in the past year they had been victims of consumer cheating or deception. An earlier version of the survey asked respondents in what way they had been cheated or deceived, and categorized their replies broadly: the concerns most often mentioned, in descending order of frequency, were defective products or services, overcharging, false or misleading advertising, purchases not measuring up to expected standards, and misrepresentation of financial arrangements. Asked to name the specific product or service involved in the cheating or deception, at least 3 percent of the respondents named each of the following: automobiles, appliances, consumer electronics, food and groceries, homes and home furnishings, insurance, clothing (including shoes), telephones,

home repairs, and gasoline. These data indicate that some hal
million households a year are cheated or deceived in transactio
involving each of the named products and services; for automotiv
transactions the number of such fraudulent transactions is about
million; for homes and home repairs, about 3 million. These a
reports of fraud, not merely of serious dissatisfaction. That so man
such experiences would be reported to interviewers suggests th
consumers indeed have a large need for prompt and fair resolutio
of complaints.[1]

Specific information on consumers' difficulties is hard to com
by. Manufacturers often study consumer satisfaction, but the
typically keep their research results secret. For example, a surve
was conducted by Ford Motor Company, seeking data fron
buyers of 1974 model year automobiles on perceived problems re
lated to the cars' mechanical performance and body durability
Ford purported to reveal some of the survey results in magazin
and broadcast advertising in the fall of 1975, but its ads did no
contain any specific data; rather, the survey results were referre
to only in relative terms. One of the claims was that the owners o
Ford Mustangs noticed fewer of certain kinds of problems thar
General Motors Chevrolet Nova owners noticed. The ad depictec
a bar graph with no scale; the Ford bar was smaller than the GM
bar, but the actual difference in terms of numbers or percents is a
secret. When the Center for Study of Responsive Law asked to se
the entire survey, Ford rejected the request.[2]

Even though sellers are in an ideal position to monitor
consumer satisfaction with purchases, and ought to consider such
monitoring obligatory to ascertain whether the products they sel
measure up to their claims about them, sellers are often ignorant
of levels of consumer satisfaction. Food manufacturers and food
chain-store executives were surveyed in 1974, and a majority indicated that "they have no idea what the true consumer dissatisfaction rate is relative to the frequency of the consumer complaints
received."[3]

The public faces numerous obstacles to finding out how
widespread consumer problems have become. And it is true, too,
that sometimes manufacturers and chain stores, the businesses
that should have the best access to this kind of information, do not
themselves have any useful data. Furthermore, they do not ordi-

arily share the data they do have with government or the public. The federal Office of Consumer Affairs (OCA) itself does not possess this kind of information. It monitors the numbers and subjects of *complaints* it receives, but it has made only slight progress in quantifying the existence of *problems* that constitute grounds for possible complaints. Research sponsored by OCA supports the general conclusion that consumers suffer many serious problems. Unfortunately, it has used a methodology that does not lead to findings on the more difficult issue of how many such problems occur in the lives of individuals with various patterns of buying. OCA research has utilized a survey in which people were asked whether they or members of their households had experienced "a consumer problem" during the past year. When problems were mentioned, the survey elicited additional information about them. This methodology was able to produce a description of problems people recalled, but it does not relate the frequency of problem perception to the number of purchases made in the household. Furthermore, asking about "problems" will not produce replies about experiences that people have repressed or avoided acknowledging.

The most prevalent problems reported in the OCA survey were (1) unsatisfactory performance or quality, involving workmanship or ingredients, (2) unsatisfactory repair, (3) unsatisfactory service (unrelated to a repair), and (4) unavailability of a product advertised for sale. The respondents were asked to estimate the possible financial loss they would suffer if their most serious problem were not corrected. The replies ranged from $1 to $3,000, with the average loss estimated at $142.[4]

Other statistical data from OCA may suggest an answer to the question of how many problems households perceive. OCA receives about 30,000 complaints in a typical year. Complaining to any third party is a relatively uncommon consumer action. And complaints made to OCA are only a small fraction of all complaints presented to third parties. One calculation shows that 30,000 complaints made to OCA may represent 75 million instances of perceived purchase shortcomings.[5]

An American Bar Association project has collected data on the incidence of disputed complaints. Obviously, disputed complaints represent only a portion of total complaints. And the total *com-*

plaints people present are themselves only a small selection of a greater number of *problems* people incur. Nonetheless, the ABA finding is noteworthy. In the context of interviews covering such serious subjects as disputed titles to real estate, bankruptcy, and being charged with injuring another person, respondents representing 24.5 percent of the public reported having had disputes with sellers of personal property, home builders or repairers, or creditors. Describing the data preliminarily, the ABA Special Committee on Legal Needs stated that although respondents were asked about their total lifetime experiences, they were likely to report recent events more readily than events of the relatively distant past.[6] Thus, this showing that a quarter of the population has reported consumer disputes, in survey interviews that were clearly focused on serious legal problems, amounts to additional evidence that consumer problems of all kinds are a significant part of most people's lives.

The studies already described do not offer detailed examinations of consumer problems in particular consumption categories. A U.S. Department of Agriculture (USDA) study concerning foods and food sellers suggests that comprehensive analysis of consumers' experiences with almost any kind of purchases is likely to uncover a high incidence of problems.[7] The study shows that 34.3 percent of consumers are "rarely or never satisfied" with the reliability and truthfulness of information in advertisements sponsored by food manufacturers. Over 16 percent of consumers are "rarely or never satisfied" with the freshness of perishable food products available at the stores where they do most of their shopping. And 14 percent of consumers are "rarely or never satisfied" with the price information available at those stores. These data add up to a substantial number of potential complaints. Multiplying the number of people represented by 34.3 percent of all consumers by the number of times those people see the ads they nearly always deem unsatisfactory produces an astronomical total of instances where there are grounds for complaints.

The empirical data suggest that people suffer many problems across a whole range of products and services. A survey specifically designed with a broad point of view was conducted in February and March, 1975, by the Center for Study of Responsive

aw (CSRL) in association with Call for Action, a citizen's help
and action organization affiliated with radio and television sta-
ions in about forty cities.[8]

The CSRL Survey

The hypothesis of the CSRL survey was that businesses and
hird parties are wrong to believe that dealing with voiced complaints fairly discharges their responsibilities towards the public.
The survey examined the following propositions: consumer
dissatisfaction is widespread; many problems are never complained about and are therefore never remedied by sellers; sellers
monopolize the handling of voiced complaints; third parties play a
very small role in consumer complaint handling; third parties are
thus hindered in planning their own activities; third parties currently allow sellers nearly complete freedom to select standards of
dispute resolution; throughout the complaint process people of low
education, income, and social status are underrepresented; and
problems that involve relatively low cost purchases or depend
upon ideas about general improvements in products and services
are underrepresented among complaints.

The survey interviewed by telephone 2,419 respondents in thirty-
four cities in February and March 1975. They were asked about
their experiences with thirty-four typical consumer products and
services (see Appendix).

Perceiving Problems

One limitation of this research should be mentioned at the
outset. Many serious deficiencies in products and services are virtually impossible for consumers to discern; examples are automobiles designed with inadequate safety provisions; foods or drugs
containing harmful substances; and unnecessary surgery. The reaction of consumers to this broad class of problems is outside the
scope of this research. Nonetheless, considering only problems
within the ordinary range of consumer knowledge and perception,
it seemed reasonable to suppose that consumers observe many
problems after purchasing products and services. A further
hypothesis was that perception of problems is hindered by such
factors as the buyer's lack of interest in consumer issues, low

socioeconomic status or the complexity of certain types of problems, and the feeling of some buyers that it is wrong to suffer consumer problems.

Respondents were asked if they or anyone in their households had purchased each of thirty-four products and services in the last year or so. For each item that had been purchased, the respondent was asked a general question, "Was it satisfactory, somewhat satisfactory, somewhat unsatisfactory, or unsatisfactory?" Next, a follow-up question was asked about each item purchased to obtain more detail and to make sure all dissatisfaction that could be recalled was reported. The wording of the follow-up question depended on the response to the general satisfaction question. If a respondent said that a member of the household had found a purchase to be unsatisfactory or somewhat unsatisfactory, the follow-up question was "What was the problem?" If a respondent reported that a purchase had been satisfactory or somewhat satisfactory, the follow-up question was the probe inquiry "How could it have been better for your household?" Often, people answered this probe question with simple statements such as "No way it could be better," or "It was fine." However, in about one out of every six cases, respondents who had rated a purchase as satisfactory or somewhat satisfactory did report problems that were similar to the problems mentioned in response to the question "What was the problem?"

In subsequent discussion, it will sometimes be desirable to treat these two broad classes of responses separately. Problems mentioned in conjunction with an unsatisfactory or somewhat unsatisfactory rating will be called "strong problems," since they were mentioned without a probe. Problems mentioned after a probe will be called "weak problems." A second issue with respect to the definition of problems is how to deal most fairly and accurately with comments about cost. The spring of 1975 was a time of high inflation and high unemployment. Thus, it is to be expected that when respondents were asked "How could it have been better . . . ," a substantial number would reply that any purchase would have been better had it cost less. This expectation is borne out in the data. To separate problems about the specific nature of products and services from the more general problem of the nation's economy, problems will be characterized as either "price-only" or "nonprice." Price-only problems are defined as problems whose subject is limited to price or cost. Problems that do not refer to price or that refer to price along with a comment on a nonprice subject are called nonprice problems.

Data on the frequency with which purchases lead to perceptions of price-only and nonprice problems are shown in table 6.1. Additionally, the table reports these problems as either "strong" or "weak." Three summary categories are established: services, infrequently purchased products, and frequently purchased products, distinguishing between the latter two by estimating whether a household would be likely to make more than one purchase of the product in a single year. Some products were easy to categorize, such as food, clothing, washer-dryer, camera, and vacuum cleaner, but categorization of others was difficult and arbitrary. Although our interviewers were trained to ask respondents about their single most recent purchase of that item, some respondents may have reviewed many recent purchases and reported whichever one involved a problem, particularly in response to the probe question. Presentation of these data separately allows the reader to keep this possible overreporting in mind.

The table shows that about four out of five purchases of infrequently purchased products were perfectly satisfactory; nonprice problems appear in 20 percent of purchases. Only two-thirds of purchases of frequently purchased products were perfectly satisfactory, but as can be seen in the column 1, this is because the probe question generated a large number of price-only problems. This was particularly the case for groceries, which were experiencing rapid and well-publicized price inflation at the time of the survey. Setting these aside, 20.1 percent of frequently purchased products generated nonprice complaints, a figure virtually identical to that for single purchase products. Services have a similar nonprice problem rate, 20.9 percent.

Despite the stability in the nonprice problem figures across the major purchase groupings, there is considerable variation within groups. Several categories have nonprice rates of 30 percent or more, including cars, mail order purchases, toys, and car repairs. Several other categories exceeded 25 percent, including vacuum

Table 6.1   Price-Only and Nonprice Problems by Purchase Category and Strength of Problem
(in order of strong nonprice problem within each group of items)

| | Weak | | Strong | | Other | |
	Price only	Non-price	Price-only	Non-price	and no answer	(N)
Infrequently Purchased						
Products	%	%	%	%	%	
Denture/hearing aid	2.8	7.7	0.7	14.8	0.7	14˙
Car	3.0	18.5	0.5	13.8	0.7	82˙
Vacuum cleaner	2.5	14.4	—	12.4	0.3	35˙
Eyeglasses	3.2	8.6	0.7	12.2	0.9	83˙
Tape/stereo	1.2	9.9	0.2	11.0	0.2	56˙
Washer/dryer	0.8	12.2	—	10.6	0.8	25˙
Camera	1.4	6.5	0.3	10.5	0.3	35˙
Bicycle	1.6	14.9	—	10.0	0.9	43˙
TV set	1.6	11.1	0.2	9.7	0.2	49˙
Calculator	2.0	7.9	0.2	9.1	0.4	49˙
Floor covering	2.3	10.7	—	7.8	0.4	52˙
Air conditioner	1.1	12.0	—	7.4	1.2	17˙
Tires	4.7	6.2	0.5	5.8	0.2	104˙
Radio	2.2	8.0	—	5.1	0.7	41˙
Lamps	1.2	5.9	—	2.6	—	34(
Total	2.5	10.4	0.3	9.5	0.5	724˙
Frequently Purchased						
Products						
Mail order	0.9	11.7	0.2	19.4	1.7	53˙
Toys	1.9	14.8	0.1	15.9	1.1	104˙
Clothing	5.5	14.9	0.6	13.2	1.4	213˙
Jewelry/watch	0.9	7.8	0.4	12.7	1.1	803
Furniture	3.5	12.2	—	11.2	0.6	69C
Grocery items	28.1	15.2	8.1	10.6	2.7	2402
Pots/pans	2.1	7.0	—	9.4	—	71C
Book/record	2.5	6.9	0.1	5.8	1.0	1566
Blanket/sheets	3.5	6.3	0.1	5.3	0.3	1069
Tools	2.2	6.8	0.3	4.2	0.5	65C
Cosmetics	4.7	5.7	0.4	3.5	0.5	1939
Total	7.7	10.5	1.6	9.6	1.2	13550
Total products	5.9	10.5	1.2	9.5	0.9	20791
Services						
Car repair	5.8	13.5	1.4	21.5	2.2	1277
Appliance repair	5.2	9.6	2.3	19.9	2.1	563
Home repair	4.4	9.8	0.4	18.6	1.2	537
Car parking	10.3	8.2	6.0	15.2	3.1	683
Film developing	3.8	9.4	0.7	9.1	1.2	1250
Legal services	3.6	7.2	3.1	8.2	1.0	388

Table 6.1   *(Continued)*

| | *Weak* | | *Strong* | | Other | |
	Price only	Non-price	Price-only	Non-price	and no answer	(N)
Medical/dental care	6.4	8.3	1.5	6.6	1.2	1910
Credit	5.5	4.6	2.0	6.0	1.6	1191
Total Services	5.7	8.9	1.9	12.0	1.6	7783
Total products and services	5.8	10.0	1.4	10.2	1.1	28574

NOTE: Percentages represent fraction of total purchases of item that fall within that category of response.

cleaners, clothing, grocery store items, and appliance and home repairs. The conventional belief that consumers suffer frequent problems with purchases is amply supported by the survey data.

To produce an estimate of national annual instances of consumer victimization would require knowledge of the individual failure rates of all purchased items and of the entire population's annual number of purchases of each item. Such data are not available. Our survey provides failure rates for only thirty-four items. And data on total annual purchasing of consumer goods is available only in part. The Bureau of Labor Statistics (BLS), of the U.S. Department of Labor, completed a survey of consumer expenditures in 1972 and 1973, based on purchase diaries maintained by panels numbering 10,000 families in each year. Its publications reporting the survey contain some information that can provide a context for the CSRL survey.

The BLS reports that 41 percent of American families buy furniture in a typical year, with an average expenditure of $286 (in 1972–73 dollars) per buying household.[9] Our survey shows that 11.2 percent of these purchases have serious perceived problems. Thus, it is clear that large numbers of Americans have significant costly problems with furniture purchases. Taking as a further example one of the items that showed the best performance in the CSRL survey, blankets and sheets, 5.3 percent of purchases involved serious nonprice problems, and the BLS survey shows that 74 percent of households make purchases in that category each year, with an average expenditure of $63 (in 1972–73 dollars) per household.[10] So, even though only about 5 percent of the purchases have serious discernible nonprice problems, that low percentage must be applied to huge numbers of households with typical expenditures that are far from negligible. The arithmetic here shows $23 million in unsatisfactory blanket and sheet purchases in a single year.

A final example is possible, with our survey data on automobiles (new or used) and BLS data on vehicles. According to the BLS, 30 percent of families and single consumers purchased cars in the survey year, at an average cost of $2,249 to each buying household (the average cost of new and used cars is, of course, significantly higher at present).[11] Our data show that consumers experience serious nonprice problems in 13.8 percent of automobile purchases. Considering all grounds for complaint (problems that were strongly perceived, were mentioned in connection with the survey's probe question, that involved price only, and that involved issues other than price alone), our survey shows that 35.8 percent of car purchases led to perception of problems. In light of the numerical and dollar volumes of automobile purchasing seen in the BLS report, our survey findings constitute yet another proof that millions of important purchases lead to significant problems for American consumers.

If complaining about purchase shortcomings can be assumed to carry significant economic and psychological costs, it might be expected that households of low socioeconomic status and low interest in consumer affairs would voice complaints relatively infrequently. This expectation leads to a further hypothesis which can be tested with our data: Households of low socioeconomic status and low consumer interest may perceive problems with their purchases less frequently than do other households. To explore this possibility, each respondent household was assigned an index of socioeconomic status (SES) based on a combination of its income and the household head's education and occupational prestige.[12] By means of this index households were grouped in four categories, from lowest to highest status. A problem perception rate was then calculated for each respondent household. This rate is defined as the ratio of products and services with nonprice problems to total products and services purchased, expressed as a percentage. For example, a household that reported purchases in ten categories and reported nonprice problems for two purchases would have a problem perception rate of 20 percent.

The data in table 6.2 show that problem perception rates are lowest for households with low socioeconomic status. The table also shows an effect of race: in the highest SES category, households in which our respondent was black have a problem perception rate of 15.4 percent, while households in the same SES category in which our respondent was white have a rate of 21.8 percent.

It is not known whether households in all SES categories purchase goods and services of similar quality. But it would strain credulity to explain the relatively low rate of problem perception in low SES households by suggesting that the products and services they buy give better performance than the purchases made by higher SES households. Indeed, it is more likely that these households deliberately purchase less expensive goods and services, which are of poorer quality than those purchased by higher SES households, and contain more defects. The lower problem perception rate in lower SES households is thus not a mirror of reality but an exaggerated underreporting of defects. There are two possible explanations for this phenomenon: lower SES households, and black households compared with white, may expect the goods and services they purchase to be shoddy, and fail to perceive such shoddiness as a defect; and those households may see themselves as abused by the system and powerless to protest a defect they perceive.

To test the hypothesis that households showing interest in issues related to consumerism would be especially prone to perceive defi-

Table 6.2   Mean Problem Perception Rates by Socioeconomic Status and Race

Race	Low		Lower middle		Upper middle		High	
	%	(N)	%	(N)	%	(N)	%	(N)
Black	16.8	143	17.4	47	18.1	56	15.4	46
White	15.7	418	18.0	346	20.2	574	21.8	652
Black, white, and other	15.8	586	17.9	400	20.1	646	21.6	714

Table 6.3　Mean Problem Perception Rates by Socioeconomic Status and
Number of Consumer Issues Discussed

Number of Issues Discussed	Socioeconomic Status							
	Low		Lower middle		Upper middle		High	
	%	(N)	%	(N)	%	(N)	%	(N)
0	10.6	49	15.9	16	11.0	24	11.9	14
1	16.1	54	13.2	16	16.2	32	13.9	29
2	16.8	90	18.3	69	14.6	81	19.8	95
3	17.0	132	16.1	104	19.8	156	22.6	175
4	14.8	146	18.1	120	22.6	217	22.2	213
5	16.7	123	20.0	85	21.2	151	23.0	203

ciencies in their purchases, the respondents were asked if there had
been discussion of five topics at home: shopping for bargains,
quality of car servicing, cost of electricity, ingredient labeling on
foods, and consumer protection laws. Table 6.3 reports the relationship between problem perception rates and the consumer
interest of households. The number of consumer topics discussed
in a household is positively related to the household's problem perception rate for all SES categories. The effect of the consumer
interest measure is more marked, however, for households in the
two highest SES categories. Comparing households that discussed
none, one, or two of the topics with households that discussed
three, four, or all of the topics shows a general pattern of higher
problem perception by the households more interested in consumer issues.

To inquire into the possibility that perception of problems might
be related to general attitudes towards consumer problems,
respondents were asked "Do you think you and your household
have more, less, or about the same number of problems as other
households have?" If replies show fewer than average consumer
troubles this may indicate the resistance of people to identifying
themselves as having many of the problems they do, presumably,
encounter.

The middle of the road reply, "about the same," was given by
62.7 percent of respondents, 32.3 percent said "less," and 3.4
percent said "more" (1.6 percent did not reply). Even though the
mean problem perception rates of various groups of households

vary, as shown in table 6.2, and many individual households have problem perception rates well above average, 95 percent of households believe that, compared with other households, they experience fewer or about the same number of consumer problems. Certainly many more than 3.4 percent of our sample would have been correct to reply that they suffer more problems than do other households. These data show that many households are either ignorant of how their consumer experiences compare with those of their neighbors or are unwilling to state that they do, in fact, have more trouble as consumers than many of their neighbors. Both possible explanations could well be related to feelings that it is wrong or illegitimate to be a victim of unsatisfactory purchase transactions.

The very nature of the deficiency in a product or service may affect people's perception of the deficiency as a problem. The shortcomings of a purchase can be clear-cut or manifest, and thus easy to identify and acknowledge. On the other hand, deficiencies can be complicated or ambiguous, and therefore relatively difficult to perceive and state clearly. Manifest problems would be breakage of a product or improper initial performance of a service, for example. From the case studies, Kevin Partyka's problem with a dry cleaner, the damage to the vinyl trim of a cordoroy jacket, would be an example of a manifest problem. Problems that may involve judgment would include observations about product design or the kinds of procedures a provider of a service uses in its business. An example of a judgmental problem would be Richard Warren's dispute with a correspondence school concerning the truthfulness of an assurance that he would have adequate mathematical aptitude to succeed in the course.

Since our survey data contain reports of both strongly perceived and weakly perceived problems, it is possible to calculate for each type of problem a percentage representing the number of times the problem was strongly perceived, expressed as a proportion of all the time it was mentioned. If a problem was most frequently mentioned in response to the probe question, this suggests that it is a problem people are reluctant to express. Table 6.4 presents data on problem types, their total mentions, and percents of mentions as strong problems. The problems with the highest percentages of strong mentions are those that can be thought of as generally unambiguous, such as breakage, loss of customer's property, or furnishing of a wrong product or service. In contrast, problems with low percentage of mentions as strong problems involve the exercise of more individual judgment, such as cost, design, selection of materials, durability, and ease of use.

In summary, the data concerning the initial stage of the complaint process, problem perception, tend to show that many purchased products and services have deficiencies that their buyers observe. Further, certain households seem to be hampered in perceiving problems with purchases. And for consumers in general, the data show a disinclination to be identified as victims of consumer problems, and show that complicated problems are perceived less strongly than simple problems.

Complaint Voicing

The costs of presenting complaints to sellers or to other potential complaint processers might be expected to discourage people from speaking up. It has already been seen that many people who have suffered purchase shortcomings do not perceive or acknowledge them. If the problem is recognized, possible responses include inaction, voicing the complaint to a seller, consciously deciding to transfer patronage (exit), and presenting a dispute to a third-party complaint handler. If it is true that complaining is difficult, and that many complaints are unvoiced, then the most common response would be inaction or, when buyers do take action, presentation of complaints to the seller. The other possible active responses, changing purchase patterns and using third parties, would likely be made less frequently.

Once respondents in the CSRL survey indicated that they had perceived a problem in a purchase category, they were asked, "Did you or anyone in your household do anything about it?" If the answer was "yes," the respondents were then asked, "What was done?" The interviewers recorded replies verbatim. Up to three actions per purchase were coded for analysis.

The actions consumers took in response to perceived shortcomings in purchases are reported in table 6.5. Some kind of action was reported to our interviewers in 39.7 percent of perceived problems. The most common action (taken in 30.7 percent of the problems perceived) was to voice a complaint to a seller (either a local

Table 6.4   Intensity of Problem Perception by Problem Type

	Total Mentions	Percent of Mentions as Strong Problem
Total breakage	316	72.8
Loss of customer's property	75	69.3
Wrong product or service furnished	167	68.9
Service required more than once	451	64.5
Irritation or allergic reaction	41	61.0
Partial breakage	828	59.7
Shrinking or fading	81	59.3
Misrepresentation	334	58.1
Workmanship	606	57.9
Clerical error/improper billing	102	57.3
Fit or size	185	56.2
Human relations	92	55.4
Too slow, late, or not received	402	54.2
Durability	562	50.7
Stitching	162	49.2
Freshness	189	47.1
Ease of use	138	47.1
Safety	25	44.0
Other (related to quality of item or service)	919	42.7
Selection of materials	271	42.4
Design of item or way of providing service	810	38.1
Other (not related to quality of item or service)	184	35.3
Cost	2609	25.8

retailer or service outlet, or a manufacturer). In their communications with sellers, consumers asked for refunds, replacements, repairs; sometimes they refused to pay or delayed payment. Of all the techniques consumers used in voicing complaints to sellers, returning the item was the action most frequently specified (about one-third of consumers' contacts with sellers). Consumers delayed or refused payment in 2.3 percent of the instances in which they voiced complaints.

Exit, changing the seller patronized or brand purchased, was the exclusive response to 6.2 percent of the purchase shortcomings perceived. In about half of these exit actions, consumers switched brands or service providers. In the remaining instances of exit, they changed buying habits to avoid the purchase that had caused

Table 6.5   Responses to Perceived Problems by Purchase Category
(in order of likelihood of some action within each group of items)

	No Action	Exit Only	Seller Voice Only	Third Party Voice Only	Other Voice	Other	(N)
Infrequently Purchased Products	%	%	%	%	%	%	
Denture/hearing aid	32.4	5.4	62.2	—	—	—	37
Tape/stereo	41.3	1.6	55.6	—	—	1.6	126
Bicycle	41.7	8.7	47.0	—	0.9	1.8	115
Car	41.8	5.7	46.8	1.0	3.3	1.3	297
TV set	42.9	3.6	48.2	0.9	4.5	—	112
Air conditioner	43.2	—	51.4	—	—	5.4	37
Eyeglasses	48.1	4.8	44.8	—	1.9	0.5	210
Washer/dryer	49.2	4.9	44.3	—	1.6	—	61
Camera	53.0	1.5	45.5	—	—	—	66
Calculator	55.2	1.0	42.7	—	—	1.0	96
Tires	63.9	3.9	31.1	—	0.6	0.6	180
Vacuum cleaner	65.4	6.7	26.9	—	—	1.0	104
Floor covering	68.2	—	30.0	1.8	—	—	110
Radio	78.1	1.6	20.3	—	—	—	64
Lamps	78.8	10.2	9.5	—	—	1.4	285
Total	51.8	4.1	41.6	0.4	1.3	0.8	1648
Frequently Purchased Products							
Mail order	40.9	1.1	55.1	2.3	—	0.6	176
Furniture	44.4	3.7	48.1	1.6	2.1	—	189
Jewelry/watch	50.0	4.9	44.5	—	—	0.5	182
Book/record	52.2	2.8	43.4	—	0.8	0.8	251
Clothing	65.8	7.0	26.0	0.1	0.9	0.1	757
Tools	68.2	3.4	28.4	—	—	—	88
Grocery items	70.7	11.0	16.5	0.3	1.2	0.3	1541
Toys	76.8	1.7	21.0	—	0.3	0.3	353
Cosmetics	78.9	10.2	9.5	—	—	1.4	285
Pots/pans/utensils	79.5	3.8	15.9	—	0.8	—	132
Blankets/sheets	81.8	1.2	15.8	—	0.6	0.6	165
Total	67.0	7.1	24.3	0.1	0.8	0.4	4119
Total Products	62.7	6.2	29.3	0.3	1.0	0.5	5767
Services							
Home repair	36.9	4.0	46.0	6.3	5.8	1.1	176
Car repair	38.9	8.7	48.4	0.7	2.9	0.4	550
Appliance repair	42.1	0.5	51.4	2.3	2.8	0.9	216
Credit/charge accounts	55.2	7.4	34.3	0.4	1.7	0.9	230

Table 6.5 *(Continued)*

	No Action	Exit Only	Seller Voice Only	Third Party Voice Only	Other Voice	Other	(N)
Film developing	60.9	8.2	29.9	—	0.6	0.3	294
Medical/dental care	63.7	9.3	22.5	0.2	0.9	3.5	454
Legal services	68.6	7.0	20.9	1.2	1.2	1.2	86
Car parking	77.9	3.4	15.5	0.3	1.4	1.4	290
Total services	54.4	6.8	34.4	1.0	2.1	1.3	2296
Total products and and services	60.3	6.4	30.7	0.5	1.3	0.7	8063

NOTE: Percentages represent instances of this response as a percentage of all responses to a particular item.

the problem. For example, exit in response to problems with grocery store items could be a decision to stop shopping at a particular store or to buy a different brand of a particular product.

The overall totals in table 6.5 show that about one in six of all actions taken in response to problems is an exit action. However, exit actions are not evenly distributed among various purchase categories. Since exit is a forward looking action, we might expect it to be employed in situations where the perceived problem can be tolerated in the present and avoided in the future; where the immediate problem is more serious, and avoiding it in the future is not a realistic alternative, exit should rarely be chosen. Of consumers who observe problems with cosmetics, for example, table 6.5 shows that about half of those who take action voice complaints, and about half simply exit. Of consumers who have problems with home repairs, about nine out of ten who take action report voicing, and only one reports exit. An unsatisfactory cosmetic can be thrown away with small financial loss. An unsatisfactory home repair, however, has failed to remedy a problem that was serious enough initially to require professional attention.

Table 6.6 reports instances of exit as a percentage of consumer responses (other than inaction) to problems with all products and all services, distinguishing between strong (price-only and nonprice) and weak (price-only and nonprice) problems. Exit constitutes 10 percent of the actions in response to strong nonprice

Table 6.6   Exit Actions as Percentages of All Actions by Type of Purchase and Type of Problem

| | Weak Problems | | Strong Problems | | |
	Price-only	Non-price	Price-only	Non-price	All Problems
Products	79.6	14.5	67.1	10.0	20.4
Services	33.7	26.5	32.4	16.6	19.7
Products and services	68.0	14.3	52.5	12.6	20.2

problems with products and 79.6 percent of actions in response to weak price-only problems with products. Price-only problems can readily be remedied by exit: to change seller or brand is to solve the problem (if only in the short run, for the individual buyer).

The third major classification of action in response to perceived problems is voicing a complaint to a third party. Households used third parties as complaint handlers in 1.2 percent of all cases in which consumers perceived problems with purchases, and 3.7 percent of all instances in which they voiced complaints. Table 6.7 presents the distribution of complaints among third parties. More than half of these complaints to third parties had not previously been presented to businesses, but were brought to third-party complaint handlers in the first instance. People used complaint handlers this way in circumstances where the seller was inaccessible, for instance, where it had gone out of business, was a mail order company that did not ship merchandise ordered, or was a doctor or hospital. In some cases, people with a general problem, such as a price believed to be excessive, contacted third parties without discussing the matter with any seller.

Even if all appeals to third parties represented instances of consumer dissatisfaction with the way the seller treated the complaint, businesses would have little to fear from third-party intervention, given the small number involved. But in fact the data show that only 45 percent of cases brought to third parties can be so interpreted. Thus sellers have a near perfect monopoly on complaint handling. They can impose their own standards for complaint resolution without significant fear that consumers will request third-party mechanisms to review their actions.

The data on the choice between voice and exit may provide a partial explanation of how individuals choose to employ the most difficult and specialized kind of voicing, the use of third parties. Where the lingering effects of a problem are significant, use of a third party is most likely. Table 6.5 shows that purchase categories with relatively high use of third parties include home repairs, cars, appliance repairs, furniture, floor covering, legal services, and mail order items. With the possible exception of mail order items, these purchases are significant enough to require a retrospective remedy for perceived problems rather than a forward looking technique of exit or avoidance.

Medical/dental care problems are also voiced to third parties relatively frequently, although their voicing rate in general is low. Analysis of the particular cases presented to third parties supports two notions. The general importance of a purchase is related to voicing, and people are generally reluctant to complain directly to doctors about their work. When consumers complain about health

Table 6.7   Distribution of Complaints Among Third Parties
(multiple mentions permitted)

	Number of Cases
Better Business Bureau	22
Consumer affairs department	16
Lawyer or court	16
State or local agency not an attorney general or consumer affairs department	6
Doctor[a]	6
Professional association	5
Elected official	4
Federal agency	4
Attorney general (state)	4
Post office	2
Social worker or welfare agency	2
Media-related complaint handler	2
Single issue pressure group	2
Utility company	2
Police department	2
Union	1
Bank	1
Insurance company	1
Total	98

[a] Doctors mediated between patients and hospitals or insurance companies.

care to third parties, they will often do so *directly*: intermediaries
such as additional doctors or a medical society are often used.

Consumers know that complaining can be difficult and costly.
This suggests that factors associated with a greater probability of
complaint voicing include high cost of product or service, high cost
of the deficiency in the purchase, and importance of the purchase.
Where high cost or particular importance of a purchase is at
stake, complaining may seem most worthwhile. Also, the sim-
plicity of complaint voicing should be related to variations in voicing rates. If one impediment to complaining is difficulty in ascertaining who is responsible for the problem, it might be
predicted that services will have higher rates of complaint voicing
than products. When a product is not satisfactory, a buyer may be
unaware of whether the seller, manufacturer, or distributor is at
fault, but when a service is improperly performed, it is easy to
identify the service provider.

The effects of purchase type on complaint voicing are indicated
in table 6.8, which reports voicing rates for weak and strong
nonprice problems for the three major purchase groupings. The
range of variation is wide: people voice complaints about 71.9
percent of the problems they perceive in the denture/hearing aid
category but only about 14.3 percent of the problems they perceive
with cosmetics/toiletries. Complaints about services are voiced at
a higher rate than complaints about products. Among the latter,
complaints are voiced more often for infrequently purchased
products (49.5 percent) than for frequently purchased products
(35.3 percent). The service categories with the most problems are
repairs of appliances, homes, and cars, perhaps because such
repair services usually are costly and their quality can be judged
easily in most cases.

The effect of ease of complaining, suggested as a partial explanation of the relatively high rate of complaint voicing for repair
services, may also be seen in the low levels of voicing for
medical/dental care and legal services (32.7 and 28.8 percent,
respectively). People are twice as likely to complain about faulty
appliance repairs as they are to complain about faulty medical or
legal work. The low voicing rates may reflect the often
hypothesized reluctance of individuals to antagonize doctors and
lawyers. Consumers may feel that doctors, dentists, and lawyers

must be treated with deference, and that it is therefore inappropriate to complain to them.

It was noted above that infrequently purchased products have a higher voicing rate than frequently purchased products. This may be a reflection of the generally greater cost of infrequently purchased products. To study costs more directly, the purchases reported were divided into two categories, usually expensive and usually inexpensive. Types of problems were also divided into these two categories. Table 6.9 classifies purchase and problem types by these two cost categories. Table 6.10 reports voicing rates by cost of purchase and cost of problem. Both variables—cost of purchase and cost of problem—affect the rate of voicing directly and significantly.

To explore further the effects of ease of complaining on the likelihood that people will voice complaints, the distinction already discussed between manifest deficiencies and deficiencies that are matters of judgment can be examined in the context of the voicing stage of the complaint process. Manifest problems, such as clerical errors resulting in furnishing the wrong item or service or partial and total breakage of products, do not usually involve differences of judgment between buyers and sellers. In these unambiguous situations a buyer can present the manifest facts to the seller—the item is broken, or it was not delivered—and can reasonably expect redress. Where judgment is required, however, buyer and seller may agree on some facts but differ on whether they indicate poor design or poor workmanship. Furthermore, some of these problems can be caused by buyers as well as sellers. What seems to the consumer to be the low durability or poor design of a toy may be inherent in the product but may also have been caused by a child's misuse of the toy. An illustration of this concept was reported by a household that had voiced a clothing complaint, "You wear it once or twice and it falls apart," and was told by the clothing store, "The kids could have ripped them up themselves." For judgment problems, then, a disappointed buyer might reasonably anticipate that mere presentation of the facts may not establish the right to redress.

It is generally easier to speak up about manifest problems than about differences of judgment. Therefore, if ease of complaining influences complaint voicing, the rate at which manifest com-

Table 6.8   Voicing Rates for Nonprice Problems by Strength of Problem and Purchase Category
(in order of voicing rate for all problems; complaints voiced as a percentage of problems perceived)

	Weak Problems		Strong Problems		All Problems	
Infrequently Purchased Products	%	(N)[a]	%	(N)	%	(N)
Denture/hearing aid	54.5	11	81.0	21	71.9	32
Air conditioner	50.0	20	76.9	13	60.6	33
Tape recorder/ stereo	47.3	55	70.5	61	59.5	116
TV set	44.4	54	72.9	48	57.8	102
Car	50.0	151	67.6	108	57.1	259
Eyeglasses	45.1	71	63.7	102	56.1	173
Bicycles	44.4	63	61.9	42	51.4	105
Camera	43.5	23	54.1	37	50.0	60
Washer/dryer	41.9	31	53.8	26	47.4	57
Calculator	21.1	38	68.9	45	47.0	83
Tires	31.3	64	62.7	59	46.3	123
Floor covering	23.2	56	52.5	40	35.4	96
Vacuum cleaner	12.0	50	47.8	46	29.2	96
Radio	24.2	33	23.8	21	24.1	54
Lamps	0.0	20	55.6	9	17.2	29
Total	37.6	740	62.5	678	49.5	1418
Frequently Purchased Products						
Mail order items	34.9	63	74.5	102	59.4	165
Furniture	40.5	84	77.6	76	58.1	160
Book/record	42.9	105	61.1	90	51.3	195
Jewelry/wristwatch	34.9	63	53.0	100	46.0	163
Grocery store items	32.5	360	41.6	250	36.2	610
Tools	15.9	44	63.0	27	33.8	71
Clothing	26.2	312	40.4	280	32.9	592
Toys	16.1	155	28.3	166	22.4	321
Blankets/sheets	12.5	64	31.6	57	21.5	121
Pots/pans/utensils	10.0	50	23.9	67	17.9	117
Cosmetics/toiletries	11.0	109	19.7	66	14.3	175
Total	26.9	1409	44.6	1281	35.3	2690
Total products	30.6	2149	50.8	1959	40.2	4108
Services						
Appliance repair	45.3	53	75.0	112	65.5	165
Home repair	51.0	51	72.3	94	64.8	145
Car repair	55.2	172	63.0	273	60.0	445

Table 6.8   (*Continued*)

	Weak Problems		Strong Problems		All Problems	
Credit/charge accounts	48.1	54	58.0	69	53.7	123
Film developing	29.3	116	43.4	113	36.2	229
Medical/dental care	28.3	152	38.3	120	32.7	272
Legal services	25.0	28	32.3	31	28.8	59
Car parking	14.3	56	29.0	100	23.7	156
Total services	38.6	682	54.6	912	47.7	1594
Total products and services	32.5	2831	52.0	2871	42.3	5702

[a] N's represent bases for percentages.

plaints are voiced should be higher than the rate at which differences of judgment are asserted. The classification of problems as manifest or judgmental and the voicing rates for each class of problems are given in table 6.11. The expectation that manifest problems will be voiced more frequently than judgmental is confirmed for all combinations of product/service, product and service, and strong and weak complaints. Furthermore, the differences are more marked where reinforced by other factors—where problems are weak rather than strong, and where they involve products, responsibility for which may be uncertain, rather than services.

We might expect the difficulty of complaining to be reflected in our data in another way. A consumer who perceives a problem might be more inclined to complain if there is reason to anticipate a favorable response. This hypothesis can be tested in two ways. First, we can see whether voicing rates are related to rates of favorable response by complaint handlers. Second, assuming that individuals who have arranged to pay for purchases with long-term credit perceive themselves as possessing the bargaining tool of nonpayment or delayed payment, we can examine whether they voice complaints more readily than consumers who pay cash.

Employing a generous definition of satisfactory resolutions, manifest complaints are settled to the satisfaction of consumers in 61.6 percent of cases and judgmental at the lower rate of 50 percent. It should be recalled that manifest problems are also voiced more often.

Table 6.9   Classification of Purchases and Problems as Usually Expensive and Usually Inexpensive

Usually Expensive	Usually Inexpensive
Purchases	*Purchases*
Car	Radio
Tape recorder/stero equipment	Lamps
Tires	Blankets/sheets
Air conditioner	Pots/pans/utensils
TV set	Tools
Vacuum cleaner	Toys
Washer/dryer	Book/record
Furniture	Clothing
Floor covering	Cosmetics/toiletries
Calculator	Grocery store items
Camera	Mail order items
Jewelry/wristwatch	Film developing
Bicycle	Car parking
Eyeglasses	
Hearing aid/dentures	*Problems*
Car repair	Partial breakage
Home repair	Ease of use
Appliance repair	Selection of materials
Medical/dental care	Design of product or procedures
Legal services	for furnishing service
Loans/credit cards/charge	Human relations
accounts	
Problems	
Total breakage	
Slow/late/not furnished	
Wrong product or service furnished	
Misrepresentation	
Clerical error/improper billing	
Loss of customer's property	
Safety	
Irritation/allergy	

The survey asked respondents whether payment for each purchase was made "in cash, or within about a month, or with longer payments." The clearest evidence of the effect of credit on complaint voicing can be found by looking at purchases of usually expensive products as defined in table 6.9 (thus controlling for the interrelationship between the use of credit and purchase cost), made by households in each of the four SES categories (see text accompanying table 6.2). As table 6.12 shows, use of credit leads

Table 6.10   Voicing Rates by Problem Cost and Purchase Cost

	Usually Expensive Problems	Usually Inexpensive Problems	All Problems[a]
	%	%	%
Usually expensive purchase	58.1	48.9	52.7
Usually inexpensive purchase	41.5	31.7	35.7

NOTE: All rates are computed on bases greater than 275.
[a] Includes only problem types categorized in Table 6.9.

to a greater probability that a perceived problem will be complained about. This pattern holds for all four SES categories. Credit purchasers are in a continuing relationship with sellers, which may make communication easier. And obviously people who have not yet paid the full price may reasonably believe that their problems will be treated with greater consideration.

Decisions by consumers not to complain when they perceive problems with purchases may also be explained by a general at-

Table 6.11   Voicing Rates for Manifest and Judgmental Problems by Strength of Problem and Type of Purchase

	Weak Problems		Strong Problems	
	Manifest	Judgmental	Manifest	Judgmental
	%	%	%	%
All products	55.9	20.9	66.6	40.5
All services	42.6	35.4	64.8	46.5
All products and services	52.2	23.5	66.1	42.2

Manifest Problems
Partial breakage
Total breakage
Freshness
Slow/late/not furnished
Wrong product or service
  furnished
Loss of customer's property
Clerical error/wrong billing

Judgmental Problems
Workmanship
Design of product or
  procedure for furnishing
  service
Ease of use
Selection of materials
Durability
Stitching
Fit or size
Shrinking or fading
Misrepresentation

Table 6.12   Voicing Rates for Nonprice Problems with Expensive Products by Method of Payment and Socioeconomic Status

Household Socio-economic Status	Method of Payment							
	Cash		Short-term credit		Long-term credit		Cash and all credit	
	%	(N)	%	(N)	%	(N)	%	(N)
All SES categories	48.4	1058	55.4	175	59.0	383	51.7	1616
Low	42.2	154	46.4	28	55.6	72	46.5	254
Lower middle	46.4	153	—[a]	—[a]	60.0	75	52.7	245
Upper middle	47.2	345	53.3	45	53.2	124	49.2	514
High	52.5	406	55.3	85	66.7	112	55.6	603

[a] Base is fewer than 25 cases.

titude toward complaining, an attitude that may vary with household characteristics. Households were even more reluctant to characterize themselves as "complainers" than they had been to acknowledge that they perceived problems and thus might be thought of as carpers or sticklers. Respondents were asked: "Do you think you and your household make more, less, or about the same number of complaints as other households make?" Only 9.1 percent believed that they voiced complaints more often than most, whereas more than half insisted that they complained less often (compared with the third who claimed that they *perceived* fewer deficiencies). Since many of these responses must be empirically incorrect, Americans must have other reasons for preferring to think of themselves as encountering, and complaining about, bad products or poor services no more often than their fellows. This is a surprising finding, in light of the conventional wisdom that Americans are a highly litigious people.

If voicing complaints is generally disfavored, it is likely that households would be even more reluctant to complain to third parties, an inference confirmed by the very low rate at which third parties are actually used. We would expect to find that those households that do overcome the obstacles of cost, difficulty, and image are distinguishable in terms of political leanings, education, and consumer consciousness. To explore this expectation, we asked respondents to characterize themselves as radical, liberal, middle-of-the-road, conservative, or strong conservative. As table

6.13 shows, politics do not appear to influence the decision to voice a complaint; there is no significant difference in the distribution among political affiliations of those who experience problems and those who voice complaints. But there does appear to be a significant difference between those who complain in any fashion, and those who complain to third parties: consumers at the middle or toward the right of the spectrum decline in proportions, and consumers toward the left of the spectrum increase. To make this clearer, we calculated a ratio of complaints to third parties divided by any complaints, for each political category (see table 6.14). And once again, a significantly higher proportion of those with radical or liberal convictions complain to third parties when they do complain. If we compare the same ratio (complaints to third parties divided by all voiced complaints) across educational categories, we find a direct relationship: 6.1 percent for high school or less; 8.4 percent for college graduates; and 10.6 percent for postgraduate education. Interest in consumer affairs, as measured by this study (see discussion of table 6.3), also related directly to third-party use.

The data indicate that third-party complaint-handling mechanisms, as they now operate, disproportionately serve the better educated, better informed, and politically more liberal households. Furthermore, the relationship of these social characteristics to third-party use suggests that, throughout the complaint process, people with less education and less knowledge of consumer affairs press sellers to respond to their grievances less often than our mar-

Table 6.13 Perception of Nonprice Problems, Voicing of Complaints, and Voicing to Third Parties, by Political Views of Respondent

	Households		
Political View of Respondent	With any nonprice problems	That have ever voiced	That have used third parties
	%	%	%
Radical	2.6	2.4	4.4
Liberal	22.3	23.6	31.1
Middle of the road	45.8	45.2	36.7
Conservative	26.7	26.0	25.6
Strong conservative	2.6	2.8	2.2
(N)	(1717)	(1191)	(90)

**Table 6.14   Likelihood That a Consumer Who Complains Will Complain to a
Third Party, by Political Views of Respondent**

| | Households | | Ratio of Third Party Use to Total Complaints (%) |
Political Views of Respondent	Number that have ever voiced	Number that have used third parties	
Radical	29	4	13.7
Liberal	281	28	10.0
Middle of the road	538	33	6.1
Conservative	310	23	7.4
Strong conservative	33	2	6.1
(N)	(1191)	(90)	

keting system requires. The disproportionate use of third parties
by liberals and radicals may reflect public belief that complaining
to third parties (and perhaps forceful complaining of any kind) is a
form of left-wing political activity.

For all the reasons just indicated, and because of the data
presented earlier on perception of problems, we would expect the
voicing of complaints to be related to socioeconomic status and
race. Table 6.15 confirms this expectation: whites complain more
than blacks within each SES category; and within the white population, complaints vary directly with SES (though it is anomalous
that among blacks, those in the lower middle SES category complain the most frequently). It has already been shown that
socioeconomic status is directly related to *perception* of consumer
problems (see table 6.2). If we combine the effects of socioeconomic status on perception and voicing, then for every 1,000

**Table 6.15   Complaints Voiced as a Percentage of Problems Perceived by
Socioeconomic Status and Race**

| | Socioeconomic Status | | | | | | | |
Race	Lowest		Lower middle		Upper middle		Highest	
	%	(N)	%	(N)	%	(N)	%	(N)
Black	35.4	81	45.0	30	41.5	40	41.9	34
White	39.8	262	37.8	261	42.2	457	46.1	571
Black, white, and other	38.4	356	38.7	298	42.5	508	45.8	620

purchases, households in the highest status category voice complaints concerning 98.9 purchases, while households in the lowest status category voice complaints concerning 60.7 purchases.

Another discrepancy between the troubles consumers perceive and the complaints they voice involves the nature of the deficiency: voiced complaints overreport some topics and underreport others. Table 6.16 shows the distribution of types of perceived problems and voiced complaints. Here we see, for example, that design is the subject of 11.6 percent of perceived problems, but only of 6.4 percent of voiced complaints. In general, the principal discrepancy between perceived problems and voiced complaints is the underrepresentation of complaints requiring the consumer to assert a difference of judgment, e.g., about the selection of materials, design, durability, and ease of use, and the overrepresentation of complaints about defects that can be proved objectively and easily, e.g., clerical errors, furnishing incorrect items or services, and breakage and loss of customers' property.

Table 6.16   Discrepancies Between Nature of Perceived Nonprice Problems and Nature of Voiced Complaints

	Perceived Problems	Voiced Complaints
	%	%
Clerical error/wrong billing	1.5	2.5
Wrong item or service furnished	2.3	3.3
Partial breakage	11.7	16.9
Total breakage	5.2	7.1
Loss of customer's property	1.0	1.4
Slow/late/not furnished	5.9	7.0
Freshness	3.0	3.4
Fit/size	2.7	3.1
Workmanship	9.2	9.4
Misrepresentation	4.9	4.2
Shrinking/fading	1.2	0.9
Stitching	1.8	1.5
Ease of use	1.9	1.4
Durability	7.9	4.6
Design of product or method of furnishing service	11.6	6.4
Selection of materials	3.9	2.0
Other (except price)	24.4	25.0
Total	100.1	100.1
(N)	(7227)	(3227)

The discrepancy in the rates at which complaints are voiced is more profound than the small percentage differences Table 6.16 indicates. In our data, *all* problems perceived by a respondent regarding a purchase are deemed to have been voiced if *any* complaint is made about the purchase. Thus our analysis considers both a design problem and a clerical error as voiced if the respondent states that the seller was contacted, even if the respondent only complained about the clerical error to the seller It is therefore likely that there is an upward bias in our figures for the voicing of judgmental problems, and that the discrepancies revealed by our data indicate larger differences. This suggests that business and government are currently deprived of a good deal of firsthand information about desired changes in products, services, and marketing practices.

Results of Complaining

The hypothesis that a great deal of consumer trouble currently goes unremedied is borne out by the CSRL data on rates of problem perception and complaint voicing. Even if all complaints led to satisfactory resolutions, the bulk of consumer problems would not be redressed. However, it is not realistic to suppose that all complaints lead to acceptable corrective action. Common experience suggests that many complaints are rejected by their recipients. Discovering what happens to voiced complaints is fundamental to understanding the consumer complaint process. To probe this issue we asked each respondent who described any action in response to perceived problems, "What was the result?" with respect to each purchase.

Replies were recorded verbatim by the interviewers, and up to three responses for each result were coded for analysis. Results were categorized as full satisfaction, full dissatisfaction, or mixed. In general, factual reports of concrete events were supplied by the respondent; in some instances, though, respondents merely said that a result was "satisfactory," or "not good." Table 6.17 enumerates the results that were classified as satisfactory and unsatisfactory.

Of those complaints presented to third parties, a small subgroup of all voiced complaints, about one-third of all resolutions were satisfactory (see table 6.18). Pending cases equal about one-fifth of

Table 6.17   Results Classified as Satisfactory and Unsatisfactory

Satisfactory	Unsatisfactory
Item repaired	Seller or manufacturer denies
Item replaced or service	responsibility
performed again	Nothing was done
Money refunded	Problem has recurred
Money partially refunded	Bought new item
Seller or manufacturer adopted	Paid for repair
suggestion	Respondent states that result
Respondent states that result	is unsatisfactory
is satisfactory	

all resolved cases, an indication that many cases may remain unresolved for substantial periods of time.

Overall satisfaction with complaint resolution by purchase category, for all voiced nonprice problems, is reported in table 6.19. A sharp distinction can be seen between products and services. Results for infrequently purchased products were somewhat worse than for frequently purchased products. Not only do service complaints more often lead to unsatisfactory resolutions, but as compared with product complaints, they also take longer to resolve. Ten percent of all voiced service complaints were pending when the respondents were interviewed, compared to 7.6 percent of complaints about products.

Comparing the rates at which different types of problems lead to satisfactory resolutions for both product and service purchases

Table 6.18   Results of Complaints Handled by Third Parties, by Identity of Third Party
(numbers of cases)

	Satis-factory	Unsatis-factory	Pending	No Specific Request Made[a]
Better Business Bureau	4	18	—	—
Consumer affairs department	4	5	6	1
Court or lawyer	5	5	6	—
Others	13	23	4	4
Total	26	51	16	5

[a] E.g., a general complaint about high prices.

Table 6.19   Results of Nonprice Complaints by Purchase Category

	Satis-factory	Unsatis-factory	Mixed	Other	(N)
Infrequently Purchased					
Products	%	%	%	%	
Washer/dryer	80.8	15.4	3.8	—	26
Camera	71.4	21.4	7.1	—	28
TV set	61.1	13.0	22.0	3.7	54
Tires	59.3	25.9	14.8	—	54
Calculator	57.9	18.4	15.8	7.9	38
Tape/stereo	57.4	19.7	16.4	6.6	61
Car	56.4	30.5	8.3	4.5	133
Bicycle	56.4	27.3	14.5	1.8	55
Eyeglasses	54.3	19.6	20.7	5.4	92
Vacuum cleaner	48.0	36.0	12.0	4.0	25
Floor covering	46.7	36.7	6.7	10.0	30
Total[a]	57.5	24.3	14.5	3.7	649
Frequently Purchased					
Products					
Clothing	75.3	18.7	4.0	2.0	198
Book/record	75.2	17.1	2.9	4.8	105
Toys	69.4	14.3	9.7	5.6	72
Cosmetics	69.2	26.9	3.8	—	26
Mail order	67.5	18.8	2.5	11.3	80
Grocery items	60.1	32.3	4.4	3.2	248
Furniture	59.2	14.5	15.8	10.5	76
Tools	58.3	25.0	16.7	—	24
Jewelry/watch	57.7	22.5	14.1	5.6	71
Blankets/sheets	56.0	40.0	4.0	—	25
Total[a]	65.8	23.1	6.5	4.7	944
Services					
Home repair	52.6	29.5	12.8	5.1	78
Car repair	49.8	36.0	9.2	5.0	261
Credit	49.3	29.0	2.9	18.8	69
Film Developing	45.2	38.1	8.3	8.3	84
Appliance repair	35.5	43.9	15.9	4.7	107
Medical/dental care	34.5	46.4	8.3	10.7	84
Car parking	29.8	63.8	4.3	2.1	47
Total services[a]	43.9	39.7	9.2	7.2	746
Total products and services[a]	56.5	28.7	9.5	5.3	2339

[a] The following purchase categories each have fewer than 13 resolved complaints; they are not listed in the table, but their values are included in the totals: radio, air conditioner, lamps, pots/pans/utensils, hearing aid or dentures, legal services.

Table 6.20   Satisfactory Result Rates by Problem and Type of Purchase
(in order of satisfactory results for products and services)

	Products	Services	Products and Services
	%	%	%
Freshness	81.5	—	81.5
Stitching	76.7	—	76.7
Partial breakage	67.9	37.7	64.0
Total breakage	66.5	—[a]	63.4
Shrinking/fading	62.1	—	62.1
Fit/size	61.3	—[a]	61.0
Clerical error/wrong billing	—[a]	62.5	60.3
Durability	59.3	—[a]	57.1
Workmanship	63.4	50.0	55.8
Slow/late/not furnished	62.2	47.8	53.8
Other (except cost)	57.1	48.3	53.3
Wrong item or service furnished	65.4	34.8	51.0
Selection of materials	45.1	—[a]	41.8
Ease of use	45.5	—[a]	41.5
Misrepresentation	41.3	31.0	38.8
Loss of customer's property	—[a]	35.9	38.3
Design of product or procedures for furnishing service	39.8	31.3	36.2

[a] Base less than 25 cases. Reported rates have bases ranging from 29 to 826 cases.

suggests that type of purchase is more significant than type of problem in overall effect on the outcome of voiced complaints (see table 6.20). In all but one category, problem topics lead to satisfactory results less often for services than they do for products. The two manifest problems that are most frequently voiced as complaints, partial and total breakage, show relatively high rates of satisfactory resolution: 64 percent and 63.4 percent, respectively. Among judgmental problems, only 36.2 percent of the design complaints lead to satisfactory resolutions. Judgmental problems, collectively, lead to satisfactory resolutions in 50 percent of instances in which they are voiced; the comparable figure for manifest problems is 61.6 percent.

We also investigated whether the complainant's socioeconomic status is related to satisfaction with the resolution of the complaint. Although the complaints satisfied, averaged within the four socioeconomic categories, ranged from 59.3 to 65.4 percent, there was no statistically significant correlation with SES. Yet this lack of bias at the terminus of the complaint process should not obscure the fact that households in the lower socioeconomic strata perceive fewer problems and complain less often, so that even a completely unbiased response to their complaints would not provide them with a fair share of problem resolutions.

CSRL Survey Summary and Conclusions

Consumers perceive deficiences in many of the products and services they buy. About one in every five purchases leads to observation of a nonprice problem and for some items, notably cars and some services, the rate of problem perception is considerably higher (about one in three purchases). How troublesome this distribution of purchase shortcomings is cannot easily be measured, because no useful historical comparison exists.[13] It is apparent, however, that consumers have a lot to complain about. And although we cannot be sure whether the survey findings represent an improvement or a worsening of business performance, it is possible to pose a rhetorical question: Would any business advertise "Satisfaction provided to four out of five customers?"

The widespread incidence of purchases with problems is quantitative proof that the consumer complaint process can fulfill an important function in compensating the consumer for defective performance; it also suggests that the complaint process can furnish a great deal of information about purchase failures. Unfortunately, the data tend to show that there are significant differences between the problems people notice and the complaints they voice. Consequently, the complaint process is seriously deficient in compensating the buyer and informing the seller. At the problem perception stage, individuals of low socioeconomic status notice fewer problems. Similarly, low household interest in consumer affairs is linked to low problem perception rates. For all households, simple manifest problems are perceived more strongly than judgmental problems. And almost all consumers are reluctant to acknowledge that they have suffered more than an average amount of trouble with purchases.

At the complaint voicing stage, buyers suppress complaints concerning about two-thirds of the problems they perceive. Not all suppressed complaints are associated with complete inaction. In ome instances, buyers may exit; however, these exit actions serve neither to compensate the buyer for the loss incurred nor to inform the appropriate business about its failure.[14] Buyers do present roughly one-third of perceived problems to complaint processors, but these do not accurately represent the full range of consumer problems. Compared with perceived problems, voiced complaints overrepresent problems that are simple, that involve high cost, and that are experienced by high socioeconomic status households. The data show, too, that third parties deal with only a small segment of the problems people perceive and the complaints people voice. Because of the pattern of third-party use, businesses are able to impose their own unreviewed standards for decision-making on almost all the complaint cases they handle.

The data show that, overall, somewhat more than half the complaints are resolved to the satisfaction of consumers. Complaints concerning services do not produce as many favorable outcomes as those concerning products, and there is a similar disparity between complaints about judgmental and manifest problems.

Buyers thus provide business with a subsidy in the form of up to a two-thirds discount on requests for redress, and many voiced complaints are not resolved to the buyer's satisfaction. Our analysis allows a close examination of the discount customers currently provide in the marketplace; it shows that it is given to business through the systematic suppression of complaints involving personal judgment, complaints involving relatively low cost items, and complaints about purchase failures suffered by people of low socioeconomic status.

The survey data are consistent with the patterns drawn from our case studies.[15] The complaint process is fundamentally unfair to all customers, because its breakdowns exact an economic cost to all who buy goods and services. It is further unfair because in some ways it appears to favor people who have relatively high status and who are able to articulate judgmental problems, a group of consumer "haves" over "have-nots."[16] Ultimately, a swift and sure process for correcting business failures may lead to better design and quality control by manufacturers, and to better procedures and supervision by suppliers of services. Thus, a decrease in the amount of consumer troubles can be the end result of efforts to improve the treatment of particular troubles that befall buyers currently.

PART THREE

Prospects for Improvement

Seven

Consumer Initiatives for Improving Treatment of Complaints: At the Buyer-Seller Stage and Beyond

NO ONE can live a life free from consumer trouble. At present, problems with goods and services are common occurrences and often expensive or otherwise vexatious. This study shows, moreover, that most of these problems, voiced and unvoiced, are not redressed. The pattern of unremedied consumer injury clearly suggests that changes are needed to promote fairness to individual purchasers and to encourage improvement in the quality of products and services and in the marketing process. In considering proposals for change, it is important to bear in mind the hindrances to consumers at the various stages of the complaint process.

The goals of change in complaint handling can be stated simply. Fundamentally, improved complaint processing should lead to better performance by business. This means that products and services should more often match the express and implied representations sellers make about them; procedures used in selling goods and services should more often be free of fraud, deception, and misunderstanding; and a higher proportion of buyers of unsatisfactory products and services should receive redress. These benefits can be brought about by procedures that identify groups of problems and treat them collectively, and by the cumulative effect on businesses of responding fairly to large numbers of individual complaints. To achieve those goals, a significant reduction must first occur in the numbers of problems consumers fail to perceive or fail to complain about. Also, sellers and third parties must be made to deal with voiced complaints with greater speed and fairness. Although the obstacles to redress may each be difficult to overcome, one reason for optimism is the likelihood that reforms will have cumulative effects. When results of complaining, for example, are perceived as satisfactory, people may be encouraged to make further legitimate complaints in later instances of deficient purchases. In general, any increase in voicing should lay the foundation for additional increases, since members of communities will learn from positive examples.

Increases in problem perception and complaint voicing will come about as part of generally better complaint processing. Some specific actions, however, may directly affect perception and voicing rates, and this chapter will examine them. These actions involve: rights consciousness of consumers; treatment of complaints at the intial buyer-seller stage; consumer access to third parties; and treatment of complaints by third parties, in terms of single disputes, classes of disputes, and programs of preventive action.

Encouraging Perception of Genuine Problems and Voicing of Complaints

Programs designed to encourage consumers' awareness of their rights will undoubtedly increase problem perception and the complaint voicing. In New York City, the Consumer Law Training Center program at New York Law School has trained representatives from community groups and social service agencies to teach and advise clients on wise consumer habits and basic consumer law.[1] The National Street Law Institute has produced materials that are used in high school courses in forty-nine states; in Washington, D.C., law students participate in high school classes that concentrate attention on consumer issues.[2]

Complaint-handling institutions can help to increase rights consciousness by making themselves more accessible to the communities they serve. For example, the Consumer Fraud Unit of the San Francisco district attorney's office has used a mobile complaint office—a remodeled delivery van—to facilitate the complaint process.[3]

Dissemination of information from this study and other similar works may help to increase awareness of the near universality of consumer problems. This knowledge may awaken some consumers to their tendency to repress voicing of complaints and to adopt expectations which impair their ability to perceive problems. The desirability of including consumer education topics in elementary and high school curricula is reinforced by evidence in the case studies that even people who have secured third-party help in consumer disputes have great difficulty in identifying their rights as buyers and in making skillful use of third-party resources. Undoubtedly many forces not explicitly related to the complaint process can also work to increase consumers' awareness of problems and their incentive to voice complaints. Foremost among these forces is inflation: As it becomes harder for people to afford to correct purchase shortcomings they will be more inclined to seek compensation from sellers and manufacturers. Regressive taxation burdens, such as increases in Social Security taxes, may also have this effect.

Tactics for Full Participation in the Complaint Process

The first step in obtaining the full benefit of purchasing any product or service is to take careful note of how well the product performs or the service accomplishes its purpose. This means that a consumer should be alert to all aspects of a purchase's performance, its initial quality, its durability, and whether it meets claims made for it by salespeople or advertisements. When determining the facts or the buyer's rights in a particular situation is difficult, a first step is to refer to the seller's claims about the product or service at the time of sale. Comparing the reality to what was promised is a technique favorable to sellers, since it merely adopts the seller's own standards of acceptable performance; it may, however, help in initially defining the rights and duties of buyer and seller. Another way to obtain guidance on the performance of a product or service of course is to get advice from friends or consult the magazine *Consumer Reports*. Finally, people should become aware that consumers in general have unrealistically low expectations about purchases and seem to feel that having problems is somehow wrong. Awareness of these phenomena may help a person with a problem to avoid falling prey to either of these two distortions.

How to complain about the problems is not easily decided. The rules of many third-party complaint handlers reinforce the course of action most people choose automatically: returning to the seller and asking for repairs, replacements (or in the case of unsatisfactory repairs, new efforts to furnish the service), or refunds. Obviously, the first action should be a request that the seller make things right. When a seller refuses to do so, the best response is to use a single mediating third-party complaint handler, and then if there is still no resolution, to use a small claims court or other kind of legal pressure. It is generally not useful to involve more than one complaint-handling institution in a dispute. If a seller's refusal is caused by a failure of communications, the intervention of any single mediating institution will usually promote a resolution.

Where a mediating effort does not produce resolution, a consumer's most efficient action is to use a court or arbitration to bring legal accountability to bear on the seller. Where small claims courts or arbitration are not available, however, a consumer may be powerless to force sellers to apply neutral and equitable standards to the problem. Of course, a variety of approaches to complaining can be tried, subject to the limitations of money, time, and emotions. On balance, though, the two-step procedure outlined is probably the most efficient for cases in which a seller's original response to a complaint is not satisfactory. First, present the problem to the seller for resolution one more time through a mediating group and second, apply the force of law to require a further evaluation of the justness of the consumer's point of view.

Improving the Complaint Process

Citizens can improve the complaint process in a number of ways. They should work to implement a federal program of aid for state small claims courts, and for the establishment of neighborhood courts where such courts are unavailable. They should also press for adoption of local, state, and national requirements for fair and expeditious procedures of complaint handling. Consumers should seek to publicize the complaint-handling records of local businesses. This can be accomplished through consumer groups or the press, by advocating that sellers maintain accurate and open records of complaint handing, and by evaluating and publicizing the data from such records. The crucial factor is accountability for decisions. Publicity can make businesses suffer the proper consequences for unfair complaint handling; legal actions can force individual review of a business resolution of a dispute.

Without fair complaint handling, every consumer spends hundreds and sometimes thousands of dollars each year on products and services that do not meet fair standards of performance or that do not measure up to the claims sellers make about them. Lack of adequate complaint handling leaves those individual consumers as victims without relief. The absence of practical and predictable recourse for aggrieved buyers insulates business from responsibility to individual customers, and from important knowledge about product and service performance. In the past, for example, safety regulations for X-ray machines have been seriously delayed, and indisputably important modifications to increase the safety of passenger airplanes have been avoided by interest groups shielded from significant consumer reaction.[4] As technology grows, this lack of accountability may lead to serious injuries to the nation's economy and environment, to people's health, and to confidence in our political system.

The Buyer-Seller Stage of Complaining

Justice, efficiency, and convenience make the store or service establishment the sensible initial contact point for a customer with a problem. For this reason, efforts to improve handling of complaints should begin with attention to this basic buyer-seller relationship.

The preference of most individuals for handling problems by dealing with sellers rather than manufacturers, in combination with a reasonable assumption that most sellers will act in good faith and fairness, can be a basis for a practical modification of current legal controls of complaint handling. A procedure which compels a decision to be made in all buyer-seller disputes and which publicizes the existence of a simple process which can lead to such a decision, would encourage more voicing of complaints and better treatment of complaints once they are voiced.

The Federal Trade Commission, state legislatures, or consumer affairs departments could require sellers of consumer goods and services to establish formal complaint-handling systems.[5] These systems would designate a single individual or department responsible for answering complaints within a brief period, perhaps two or three business days. Consumers would also have access to a single higher level employee charged with reconsidering lower level decisions which consumers found unacceptable. This individual would be required to communicate a decision to the buyer within two or three business days. Sellers would also be required to keep a simple record of complaints received and their resolutions. This record, perhaps a single notebook in the case of a small store, would be open to public inspection. Adherence to these rules would be encouraged by a further rule: if a seller failed to establish or follow these procedures, such a failure could be a complete defense for any buyer sued by the seller for nonpayment of a debt related to the disputed transaction. Additionally, fines or penalties might be imposed for failures to adopt or follow the required procedures.

The public record requirement would add the force of competition as an incentive for compliance by sellers. Individual buyers or representatives of public interest groups could monitor and publicize the complaint-handling practices of businesses. Broad-based consumer groups specializing in the treatment of consumers by particular industries or kinds of services would be particularly well suited to carry out this function.[6] Since this record-keeping technique would allow comparison between competing sellers, it might promote fairer treatment of complaining customers. Knowledge that such a complaint system exists might also encourage buyers to register grievances even in instances when they anticipate rejection by the seller, since they would have the satisfaction of knowing that their report would be available to other buyers, consumer groups, and officials.[7]

The record-keeping system would also improve the ability of law enforcement agencies to act against sellers whose complaint-handling practices show a pattern of unfairness. Wide discretion is available to regulatory bodies in defining fair complaint-handling policies.[8] Even criminal sanctions, though usually ignored in consumer abuse cases, might be used against sellers with especially poor records.[9]

The proposed rules would have numerous benefits for the handling of individual complaints. The very existence of such complaint procedures, given adequate publicity (perhaps including explanatory signs posted in stores), might minimize some of the present obstacles to complaining. For instance, the notion that having problems or complaining about them is wrong might be modified by this evidence that stores clearly expect people to complain about unsatisfactory purchases. The process in which problems change as time passes and thus become more difficult to perceive and articulate might occur less often with the availability of an easy means for prompt complaint. Clearly, the proposed rules would reduce the apparent costs of complaining by eliminating wasteful, misguided efforts. To some extent, they would also counteract the imbalance of power between buyers and sellers because putting complaint handling on the public record would expose it to market pressures. And lack of knowledge about third parties would become less serious, since more complaints would be resolved to the satisfaction of buyers at the buyer-seller level.

Improving the treatment of individual complaints is a change that focuses on single, specific problems. Thus, it works primarily towards fulfilling only one of the goals of the complaint process: delivering compensation to victims of consumer trouble. Its impact on the other important goals of the process, developing solutions to recurring problems and encouraging prevention of recurring problems, is indirect but important: when sellers and manufacturers face greater likelihood that they will have to pay for product and service deficiencies they will probably make greater efforts to prevent such shortcomings. Currently, because the marketplace offers sellers a discount on the redress they ought to provide, the economic force of accountability for deficiencies is muted. Better responses to individual problems will, therefore, reduce the incidence of individual problems.

It is likely that even with an ideal mechanism for grouping problems for uniform and preventive treatment, individual circumstances would sometimes make individual treatment of complaints desirable. This is a necessary consequence of the existence of two broad classes of potential problems: deficiencies in production, design, or delivery of products or services that can be prevented at a reasonable expenditure; and deficiencies that can be prevented only at an expenditure that would raise the sale price of each product or service by an unreasonable amount. Deficiencies in the first class ought to be identified and corrected through the pressure of repeated resolutions of individual complaints or through processes that take advantage of complaints as prods for group solutions. But for those deficiencies that could be prevented only at a very high cost, it may be more efficient to tolerate occasional lapses (except those related to health or safety) and to remedy them with a system of refunds or replacements that places the costs of the lapses on the sellers instead of on the unlucky consumers who happen to purchase particular flawed products or services. Improved treatment of complaints at the buyer-seller level is therefore needed to reduce the incidence of shortcomings that can be prevented at reasonable costs, and to motivate sellers to provide fair treatment to buyers whose purchases have deficiencies that could have been averted only by unreasonably costly quality controls.

Eight

Mediation

THIRD PARTIES play an important role in complaint handling. Even without their intervention, individual businesses treat many problems fairly, and there are forces that prompt consumers to assert their rights vigorously.[1] But for complaints that sellers do not settle in the first instance, an array of third-party institutions exists; they are mediators, arbitrators, and coercive dispute-settlers. This chapter describes the spectrum of third parties and examines mediators in detail. To attempt to prove that any one kind of third party is ideal would be futile. Furthermore, the attempt would be impractical, since it is likely that a variety of third parties will continue to operate for the foreseeable future. Therefore, an effort should be made to explore the strengths of all third parties.

The Range of Third-Party Intervention

Third parties can be classified as either judicial or nonjudicial. Judicial third parties are courts and mechanisms associated with courts, both formal and of the small claims or neighborhood format. The crucial distinction between courts and other third parties is that the decisions of courts are enforced by the state. An order, for example, that requires a seller to pay money to a buyer can be enforced by judicial officials if the seller does not comply. Nonjudicial third parties may have no coercive power or nearly as much coercive power as courts.

Among nonjudicial complaint mediators are Better Business Bureaus, newspaper and broadcast "action line" services, local and state consumer affairs departments, and voluntary assistance agencies. Most government consumer affairs agencies deal with consumer complaints by attempting to mediate them. Some trade associations in particular industries operate mediation services that deal with problems related to the members' products. In general, mediation consists of an effort to stimulate the disputants to reach a mutually satisfactory resolution. Arbitration programs, discussed in chapter 9, are a form of third-party mechanism that relies on an initial agreement by the parties that they will abide by the decision reached in the arbitration process; some arbitration programs include a mediation phase as a required first step prior to actual arbitration.

The Significance of Coercive Power

The case studies and the survey are consistent with the conclusion that most sellers respond favorably to complaints when it seems to them fair or expedient to do so, and that they probably reject many complaints in which there is a real disagreement over facts or the legal implications of undisputed facts. These cases of real disagreement are the least likely to be amenable to non-coercive processes such as mediation, since facilitating communication will not help where the parties already know what their dispute involves. Therefore, the most useful third parties for consumers with these "real disagreement" disputes would be those empowered to decide the facts and enforce the remedy. Despite this theoretical indication that courts and programs of binding arbitration would likely be the most efficient third parties, many disputes that are capable of being resolved in coercive institutions can also be resolved through negotiation or other forms of mediation. And although the coercive third parties may be the most efficient in terms of achieving definite results, the less formal institutions can provide other benefits, such as lower cost and a greater sense of self-reliance and self-determination for the parties to the dispute.

Substitutes for Coercive Power in Mediation

Consumer problems do not usually present the parties with the risk of suffering criminal sanctions. Nor, usually, do they involve parties who have significant interest in continuing a relationship after their dispute has been resolved. The exclusion of these factors from the context of most consumer disputes indicates that consumer disputants may be particularly unlikely to submit to mediation. As an alternative to a jail sentence or the loss of a prized relationship, mediation can seem worthwhile. But with these risks not a part of the typical consumer dispute, mediating institutions have sought substitutes for real coercive power. Industry associations, for example, claim that the threat of expulsion may motivate their member companies to abide by the results that they recommend, although the largest of these groups do not require that member companies carry out the recommended settlements. Other institutions, such as media-related complaint handlers and government agencies, allow themselves to be perceived as having elements of coercive power; thus, although they may not be able to act against a business that refuses to accept their recommendations, they allow themselves to appear as though they do have the ability to act forcefully.

The success that media-related institutions have achieved may well be related to perceptions by sellers that bad publicity may harm them. Local organizations that lack significant power nonetheless may present themselves to sellers with calculated efforts to appear powerful. For example, a local group in Massachusetts prominently prints on its stationery the phrase "Working with the Attorney General of Massachusetts," although its affiliation with the state is loose and it is unlikely that the organization could subject a seller to criminal liability. A student group at the University of Pennsylvania operated a mediation service under the name "Pennsylvania Consumer Board," and may have allowed businesses to assume incorrectly that it was a state agency.

Mediation efforts carried out by actual state and local government entities are always accompanied by implicit threats of formal action. The New York City Department of Consumer Affairs is an example of one such agency; it mediates thousands of complaints each year, but takes concrete legal actions such as lawsuits or license revocation actions only against fewer than one out of every hundred companies complained about. An analysis of that agency's complaint mediation highlights the kinds of results other such agencies and nongovernmental complaint handlers may achieve.

Local Government Mediation: The New York City Example

The New York City Department of Consumer Affairs has analyzed its complaint-handling performance by studying a sample of its cases processed in 1977 and 1978.[2] The complainants were contacted in approximately half the cases studied, and in all cases a detailed review was made of the department's records. The data show that simple mediation, carried out by a unit of municipal government, can achieve satisfactory resolutions in a significant number of cases. Specifically, 60 percent of the cases studied led to successful settlements. For cases involving less than $100, a 70 percent success rate was achieved. Some cases were handled with personal visits to the businesses by department personnel, while others were handled by mail and telephone. No significant difference in resolution rate was found, comparing the two modes of treatment. Thus, for mediation, the simple acts of restoring communication between the disputants and asserting the interest of a governmental unit seem to produce worthwhile results in many cases.

Tabulating the likelihood of success in terms of the amount of money involved in the dispute, the Department of Consumer Affairs found that it was less and less successful as the amount in controversy rose. Similarly, in cases where the department was able to resolve a case quickly, its ratio of success was far higher than in cases where, because of complicated details or business intrasigence, the numbers of contacts between the department and the business were greater.

Other Examples of Mediation Efforts

Mediation by groups such as trade associations and media-sponsored complaint handlers will likely show signs of the same influences at work on the mediation efforts of government groups, although some additional factors may be present. Newspaper or broadcast station services may become less effective as businesses resist their implicit threats of publicity; by resting firm on their rejections of a buyer's request, businesses may actually avoid publicity, if the newspaper or broadcast station does not want to appear ineffective. Further lessening the long-range effectiveness of these services is the fact that they can sometimes stop their operations entirely. In early 1976, there were seven such services operating in New York City, while three years later, the number had decreased to three.[3] Lessened interest on the part of publishers or station owners, coupled with the realization that it is very expensive to process the large numbers of complaints that a media-related enterprise will attract, lead to declining prospects, in general, for the action lines. Although about four-hundred newspaper and fifty broadcast action lines are operating it is commonplace for them to work only on a tiny fraction of the complaints that they receive.[4]

The value of business-sponsored mechanisms is also questionable. Single-industry associations are not publicized well; the largest one deals with major appliances, but it is sponsored by associations of appliance manufacturers and is structured so that it cannot exert any pressures against companies that reject its proposed settlements. Better Business Bureaus have widely varied quality, since they are locally administered and supported by local businesses. One Better Business Bureau advised prospective members that it was able to establish that 90 percent of complaints raised by consumers were invalid. This kind of promotional claim indicates a bias that would be fatal to effective mediation.

A federal program has established experimental neighborhood justice centers in Atlanta, Los Angeles, and Kansas City, Missouri. Their early results demonstrate the importance of some kind of compulsion in mediation. Most of their cases have involved possible criminal charges (or have been referred to the centers directly from the criminal justice system), or have been disputes between parties who participate in and wish to continue ongoing relationships. The programs, thus, have concentrated on matters other than consumer abuse. For buyer-seller matters that the centers do treat, their power to promote resolutions derives only from the indirect threat of future complainant action in small claims court or through other official third parties. In most consumer disputes, the seller has no significant interest in maintaining a relationship with a single buyer. Therefore, the desire to restore peace and equilibrium that can influence mediation of family disputes, for example, does not operate in typical consumer cases.[8]

Variables Related to Successful Mediation

Although the case studies cannot determine the legitimacy of the complaints they examine, they seem to show that factors such as lack of ambiguity in the subject of a complaint, the kind of business involved, and the apparent cost to the business of resolving the complaint in favor of the buyer all influence the likelihood of success. These same effects are seen in the New York City Department of Consumer Affairs complaint-handling study, as well as in reports from other third parties.

For example, cases in which third-party mediation was of no help to the buyer involved an appliance store, a health spa, a truck-driving school, and the sale of low cost furniture, enterprises that are frequent sources of consumer trouble (although generalizations of this kind are subject to error in particular cases).[6] Sylvia Klein's washing machine problem (involving the destruction of some of her clothing) involved a complicated runaround and no worthwhile results, even after a local Call For Action complaint handler attempted mediation. Helen Thompson gained no benefit from contacting her state's Office of Consumer Protection in a dispute with a health spa; the basis of her complaint was that the seller had sold a contract identical to hers to a friend of hers for half the price it had charged her. Dick Meagher's dispute over a diploma from a truck-driving school remained unresolved even after mediation efforts by a Better Business Bureau and Action 3, a media-related complaint handler. Louise Meadows sought help from the federal Office of Consumer Affairs in the dispute concerning living room furniture that had been described as unique but was in fact identical to other furniture the store had sold. In all of these cases, the facts were in dispute.

Another ambiguous case, concerning a seller with perhaps a greater stake in his reputation, had a different result. Sue Neville's problem involved a doctor whose record-keeping was apparently haphazard. The Pennsylvania Health Rights Advocate, an experimental program, sought to mediate. The doctor would not agree to a settlement or admit that he had been wrong, but as time passed it became apparent that he had decided not to deposit a check from Ms. Neville representing her disputed payment to him.

Ideally, mediation is a kind of peaceful negotiating process but in practice, situations abound in which agreement simply cannot be reached. In the case of John Zygoria, furniture was delivered with a defective finish. The seller offered an exchange or refund, but Zygoria wanted the furniture repaired. Mediation by the Montgomery County, Maryland, Office of Consumer Affairs could not modify the position of either party, and so no resolution was achieved.

Situations of imperfect communications between disputing parties may be best suited for mediation. William Devon's problem with the incorrect nap on the upholstery of a sofa became complicated when the seller and the manufacturer began to blame each other for the defect. Under pressure to respond to inquiries from several mediating third parties, the manufacturer and seller suspended their own dispute to make a settlement offer to Devon. Harold Lowry bought carpeting from a high volume retailer and it was installed with an ugly, poorly sewn seam. When he complained to the seller, no resolution was offered. But Lowry continued to complain, and discovered that a low-ranking employee had misrepresented his claims. He became angry and contacted a consumer affairs department. That department's inquiry broke through the internal communications problem within the seller's organization and led to a satisfactory settlement.

Values Served by Mediation

Mediation, like all dispute-resolution processes, may overcome some of the obstacles consumers face in perceiving problems merely by its availability. People who are aware that a neighborhood justice center or a newspaper action line is available to deal with consumer problems may be less inclined to feel that having problems or complaining about them is wrong. Mediating institutions that take complaints only in writing may not make complaining less burdensome for people who find writing difficult. However, where the institutional process includes a conversation between a complainant and a mediator, certain desirable effects may occur; the buyer may be able to clarify his or her request for relief, and will thus be helped to avoid wasted efforts, such as presenting an unduly complex complaint to a seller or carrying the complaint to another inappropriate third party.

Results can be expected to vary depending on the apparent power of the mediating institution, or on the degree to which the buyer and seller anticipate maintaining a relationship. Programs such as those administered by single trade associations or Better Business Bureaus are not likely to be perceived by businesses as

coercive. Disputes mediated by these entities will most likely be resolved if they involve only a misunderstanding or if the parties
have a desire to remain in a continuing relationship. Mediation
conducted by government prosecutional agencies or media-related
services does possess an implicit threat of coercive action. These
groups may have the most success in countering business responses
such as the runaround, victim blaming, and use of legal gimmicks.

Nine

Arbitration

ARBITRATION IS a dispute-resolution technique with a history
hundreds of years old.[1] In arbitration, the parties to a dispute
agree to permit an impartial third person or panel of third persons
to render a final binding decision. If one of the parties tries to
disobey the decision after such an agreement has been made,
enforcement of the arbitration ruling can be obtained virtually automatically through the courts. Arbitration can take place between
any two parties who agree to carry it out. Commonly, third parties
such as trade organizations or service organizations administer ongoing programs offering the opportunity for arbitration to the
general public. Also, some court systems incorporate arbitration
procedures.

Applying arbitration to consumer disputes is a recent phenomenon. The American Arbitration Association has engaged in
consumer arbitration and conducted various consumer programs
in the past two decades. For example, the Cleaning and Dyers Institute in New York has for a number of years included a standard
arbitration clause in the claim check forms of member cleaners
and dyers. When disputes cannot be resolved informally, the customer may, without having to pay a feee, submit the dispute to
binding arbitration before a volunteer arbitrator appointed by the
American Arbitration Association. The association has arbitrated
various other kinds of consumer disputes, such as those between
architects and their customers, in the course of its commercial arbitration activities.

With the growth of the consumer movement in the 1960s, there
was increasing demand for more consumer arbitration. In 1969,
for example, the Report of the Task Force on Appliance War-

ranties and Services advocated use of informal mediation and ar
bitration to resolve consumer grievances. In 1968, the America
Arbitration Association established the National Center fo
Dispute Settlement under a Ford Foundation grant, in order t
apply mediation and arbitration techniques to consumer dispute
and other areas of community conflict.

Relative Unavailability

Despite some increased interest in consumer arbitration, curren
programs have had very little success. Their failures indicate som
of the obstacles to development of effective and widesprea
consumer arbitration programs. For example, the National Cente
for Dispute Settlement (now known as Community Disput
Services, or CDS) at first concentrated on obtaining advance com-
mitments from businesses to submit disputes to arbitration. This
effort was unsuccessful because of lack of pressure on businesse
to settle disputes with consumers. Businesses do not contend with
significant organized opposition from consumers, in contrast to
the pattern of business-labor relations that has led to major use o
arbitration in employment disputes.

The CDS subsequently tried to establish a consumer arbitration
system in Washington, D.C., in which a consumer advocate organization staffed by Howard University law students would refer cases
to arbitrators. Again, the local business community was an-
tagonistic; they perceived the arrangement as biased in favor of
consumers. Next, the CDS established an Advisory Council which
was supposed to assist in soliciting business participation in
consumer complaint arbitration. At the same time the CDS created
the Consumer Arbitration Service, for the Washington, D.C., area,
which was to be operated on a trial basis until two months had
elapsed or one hundred cases had been handled, at which time it
would be evaluated. Due to inadequate publicity and staff and
budget constraints, among other reasons, not a single arbitration
was held in the two-month period. For similar reasons, other pilot
projects established in various cities have been unsuccessful.[2]

In 1974 and 1975, seven Montgomery Ward stores in the Albany, New York, area experimented with precommitment to arbitrate any disputes which could not be resolved through their own
grievance procedures. Although the project was presented as a

major development in consumer arbitration, due to the precommitment, not one case was arbitrated during the one-year experiment, and only fifteen or twenty were settled prior to arbitration. The project suffered from inadequate staff—it was administered by one person serving on a part-time basis—and was insufficiently promoted, so that relatively few consumers were aware of it. According to the former administrator, the project "never really took hold in the community."[3]

The most comprehensive consumer arbitration program now in existence, the National Consumer Arbitration Program, operated by the Council of Better Business Bureaus, has reached only a small number of individuals. This program was launched in 1972 and is administered by local bureaus throughout the country. Although BBBs in more than 100 cities participate in the program, actual usage by consumers has been relatively slight. In the first four years of the program, only 2,300 cases were arbitrated.[4] In 1977, 4,600 cases were arbitrated.[5] This would amount to about 4 cases per bureau per month if the cases are distributed evenly in terms of time and geography. Even when one takes into account that a large number of cases are settled before arbitration, the number of complaints handled by this program is a minuscule portion of the total volume of consumer complaints. The majority of the cases involved home improvements, appliances, and automobiles.[6]

Some few additional avenues to arbitration are available. The National Association of Home Builders, the American Society of Appraisers, and a handful of other trade and professional associations have established consumer arbitration mechanisms for members. In the Washington, D.C. area, the Automobile Owners Action Council (AOAC), a nonprofit organization, has prepared a "dealer recourse agreement" whereby an automobile sales or service establishment agrees to submit disputes with AOAC members to arbitration. Only signatories to such agreements may advertise in the AOAC publication and present themselves as AOAC approved.[7]

A few government units have launched consumer arbitration projects. Fairfax County, Virginia, is administering a voluntary program of consumer arbitration which uses trained volunteers from the community as arbitrators. The American Arbitration

Association helped conduct training sessions and establish arbitra
tion procedures for this program. Fairfax County operates a
similar arbitration program for landlord-tenant disputes. In a
number of states, arbitration mechanisms annexed to courts ca
treat consumer complaints.[8] In the Pennsylvania court system, ar
bitration is compulsory for most claims for damages under $5,000
the parties subsequently have an opportunity for a *de novo* trial
New York State has tried compulsory arbitration on a pilo
project basis in Monroe County (Rochester). In New York City
plaintiffs in small claims court can choose to submit disputes to
arbitration rather than a small claims proceeding.[9]

Potential Value

To judge the value of increasing the use of consumer arbitration, it is necessary to examine arbitration's characteristics and
advantages. Since arbitration of consumer disputes has been
conducted primarily through the fledgling BBB program, that
program's procedures can serve as an example. Before a consumer
dispute proceeds to BBB arbitration, attempts are made to resolve
the problem through mediation and other informal means, and
many complaints are settled at this point. If such efforts prove
unsuccessful, both parties may agree in writing to submit the
dispute to binding arbitration. Some businesses precommit themselves to arbitration.[10]

Where the dispute goes to arbitration, the first step is to select
the arbitrator or arbitrators. The Better Business Bureau usually
sends the parties a list of five arbitrators drawn from the community's arbitrator pool. Each party lists the arbitrators it finds
unacceptable, and an arbitrator is selected from among those
persons who are mutually acceptable. The arbitrators are volunteers who serve without pay and who undergo a training session
of several hours. Usually they include lawyers, educators, retired
persons, experts in various fields, and members of community organizations.

If the parties cannot agree on an arbitrator, each side selects a
person of his or her choice from the pool of arbitrators, and the
two so chosen select the actual arbitrator. Some BBBs use preselected panels of three for certain types of cases, such as those
involving low monetary amounts. The parties agree on a mutually

convenient time and place for the arbitration session. Both parties are usually required to prepare written statements of their positions and furnish each other with a copy of the statement prior to the session. This often leads to settlements before the arbitration session, since the statements provide a clear indication of the parties' positions.[11]

The sessions themselves are relatively informal. The parties are provided information on the arbitration procedure in advance so that they have some idea of what to expect. Each party presents evidence, has witnesses testify, elaborates on the written statement, and cross-examines the adversary and the adversary's witnesses. Formal rules of evidence do not apply, and parties are rarely represented by attorneys, although they may be. No individual who lacks direct interest in the case may be present at the session without permission from the disputants.

Where appropriate, the arbitrator conducts an inspection of the disputed merchandise or property, usually with both parties present. In fact, the arbitration sessions themselves are frequently held at the locale of the dispute, a practice which accentuates the informality of the hearings. For example, a hearing concerning an automobile repair may be conducted at the garage where the work was performed.[12] Besides inspections, BBBs provide independent experts for arbitration hearings and inspections involving technical matters, and products are sometimes sent to testing laboratories. The costs of inspections, technical experts, and testing are borne by the bureaus, as are administrative costs generally. However, the parties bear the costs of attorneys' fees, witnesses, and transcripts of the arbitration proceeding, and in some instances the parties will be required to post refundable performance bonds to assure their presence.

The arbitrator must promptly issue a written award (within ten days of the hearing, in the bureau programs). Usually the decision is rendered at the end of a hearing. About 40 percent of the arbitration decisions in the bureau program are in the consumer's favor, 40 percent are in the business' favor, and the remainder are split.[13] Decisions are filed in court and have the final status of a judgment or court order.

Arbitration has a number of distinct advantages as a means of resolving consumer complaints. The first is its possible swiftness.

In the Better Business Bureau programs, the average length of time between the initial request for arbitration and the making of the arbitration award is only twenty-one days.[14] Some longer delays might occur, however, if the BBB program handled a larger number of cases. Some court-related arbitration programs involve significant delays.[15] Generally, however, arbitrators can be selected immediately after the parties request arbitration, and the proceeding can be held promptly.

One of the great advantages of arbitration is its informality. Parties do not have to contend with procedural complexities or the laws of evidence, and in the majority of cases they are not represented by an attorney. The fact that the hearings are often held in familiar or ordinary surroundings, or, in many instances, the locale of the dispute, also contributes to the informality. And an arbitrator is less formidable than a judge, especially since he or she is usually drawn from the community and selected by the parties.

Arbitration can be accessible to consumers because of its low cost as well as its informality. Usually, parties need not hire a lawyer or incur other costs associated with litigation. As noted above, the Better Business Bureaus bear the costs of operating arbitration programs, and the arbitrators are volunteers. Other programs, however, have charged fees, ranging from $3 for cases under $500 in one program to a splitting of a $25 fee in another, that may discourage small meritorious claims.[16]

While arbitration is voluntary, it is also characterized by finality.[17] As noted above, the arbitrator's decision is not only enforceable but is also nonreversible unless fraud, corruption, prejudice, or a similar gross impropriety can be demonstrated. Errors of law or judgment by the arbitrator generally do not suffice for reversal, so that the arbitrator has considerable discretion. The consumer does not have to worry about subsequent proceedings which could involve added costs and delays. However, if the arbitrator is partial to business or to consumers but is not guilty of such gross misconduct as to justify reversal, the element of finality can work against one of the parties. It is therefore important to ensure that arbitrators make their decisions solely on the merits of the case, an issue which shall be discussed below.

A final characteristic of arbitration is its privacy. Both the business and the consumer might be reluctant to fight a dispute in public. The business might be fearful of adverse publicity, and the consumer might be intimidated by the public attention given his or her complaint. Since arbitration proceedings are held privately, with no outsiders present except by mutual consent of the disputants, there is no possibility of adverse credit reports, undesirable precedents, or other similar consequences. Again, these aspects may make arbitration more attractive to individual participants, but at the same time, they make the process far less capable of contributing to preventive measures.

Improving Quality and Accessibility

The obstacles this study describes that hamper perception of problems and voicing of complaints also work in an ironic fashion to impede the development of consumer arbitration. For example, because consumers rarely litigate their buyer-seller disputes, there is little pressure on businesses to develop or submit to programs of arbitration. Yet such programs are needed for many of the reasons which explain the lack of consumer litigation. If businesses experienced more extensive challenges from consumers, they would be far more likely to participate in arbitration programs.

Several solutions have been proposed for this problem. One is that arbitration be made compulsory for disputes which cannot be resolved through grievance procedures or mediation. In order to protect the parties' right to trial, it would be necessary to provide an opportunity for a judicial proceeding subsequent to the arbitration. This requirement would remove some major advantages of the arbitration procedure, however; the speed and finality of the arbitration process, for example, would be forfeited.

In some situations, a combination of voluntary arbitration and proceedings in small claims courts may prove more advantageous than compulsory arbitration. In New York City, small claims court plaintiffs can choose to have their cases arbitrated rather than decided by a judge. This is a practical example of how arbitration and small claims proceedings could be connected. Businesses would be encouraged to opt for arbitration by such factors as the confidentiality of the hearing and its flexibility as to time and place, and because such arbitration would not present the constant possibility of an automatic subsequent trial, as in compulsory arbitration. The success of such a procedure, however would depend on the willingness of consumers to use small claims courts if businesses refused to arbitrate.

In order to encourage participation in arbitration, organizations such as trade associations can employ a number of sanctions. Where they are comprised of member businesses, they can make membership conditional on willingness to submit to arbitration. Several Better Business Bureaus impose such a requirement on their members, although the Los Angeles bureau recently dropped its requirement that members precommit themselves to arbitration.[18] Consumers can be encouraged to transact business with establishments that submit to arbitration, and such businesses can indicate in their publications and broadcast announcements that they consider participation in arbitration programs an essential feature of fair dealing. Those businesses, for example, which have precommitted themselves to participation in the Better Business Bureau consumer arbitration program are authorized to use in their advertising a national arbitration logo prepared by the Council of Better Business Bureaus.

As businesses and trade associations become involved in consumer arbitration programs, reluctance of additional businesses to participate should decrease. There are two reasons why this should be so. First, businesses would likely conclude that the arbitration process provides some benefits, or else so many other establishments would not be participating. Second, they would perceive that participants in the program have a competitive advantage over nonparticipants, since the former can advertise their involvement in the program and in some cases hold themselves out as approved by certain consumer or trade associations.

Until consumers, too, are familiar with consumer arbitration programs and willing to redress their grievances through arbitration, the growth of consumer arbitration will be curtailed. Thus far the existing programs have been inadequately publicized among consumers as well as businesses.[19] Despite the fact that Better Business Bureaus operate programs in virtually every major city, most consumers with substantial unresolved grievances have not used the programs. All sellers that rely on complaint processing to ulfill their obligations to deliver full value to their customers should recognize an obligation to facilitate presentation of complaints; part of this obligation should be educating customers about the availability of arbitration programs.

The limited consumer participation in arbitration is part of the larger phenomenon of consumer recognition of the obstacles in the consumer complaint process. To the extent that lack of action results from a feeling that efforts would prove fruitless, publicity about arbitration might change such attitudes. Consumers would perceive that even if the business initially neglected or failed to resolve the complaint, the subsequent step of arbitration would be available. The existence of arbitration would mean that a definite resolution of the problem could be obtained with relatively little effort, time commitment, or cost to the consumer.

If consumer arbitration is to attract businesses and consumers, it is important to reinforce the fairness and impartiality of the arbitrators. The use of volunteer arbitrators drawn from the community, as in the Better Business Bureau's programs, appears to promote this objective. The arbitrators disclose pertinent personal and financial data, and parties can object to arbitrators they find unacceptable. Also, the parties must usually agree on the choice of an arbitrator. However, the Better Business Bureaus (which receive most of the funding from the business sector and are closely tied to the business community)[20] maintain a number of controls over the selection and training of arbitrators which call into question their claim that the arbitration process is conducted independently of the bureaus. They are responsible for training prospective arbitrators and for some cases they use preselected panels of volunteer arbitrators.

In one of the case studies, for example, a consumer whose dispute involved dry cleaning decided not to accept an offer of arbitration in a BBB program, because all of the proposed arbitrators had connections with dry cleaning businesses. It would be preferable for training to be handled by a more independent body such as the American Arbitration Association or conducted with more participation by community organizations other than the bureaus. Also, parties should be given the option of selecting the more highly trained arbitrators in the American Arbitration Association's panels of arbitrators as well as those in the BBB's

volunteer pool. In cases involving technical matters, an arbitrato
with expertise would be likely to make a rational assessment of th
merits due to his or her familiarity with the issues. Although a
expert is always available for assistance, a party might feel mor
comfortable if the arbitrator who makes the final decision had ex
tensive knowledge of the issues in dispute, in cases where pre
selected panels have been required.

The need for careful selection of arbitrators is highlighted i
another of our case studies. A poorly trained arbitrator in the Buf
falo, New York, BBB arbitration program produced a decisio
that satisfied neither party in a dispute between a home improve
ment contractor and his customer. The customer's complaint wa
that the metal siding installed by a contractor on his house wa
unsightly. The contractor said that the siding appeared uneven because the walls of the house beneath the siding were uneven. The
arbitrator ruled that the customer was entitled to a gamble: he
could have the contractor remove *all* the siding; then, if the customer and contractor agreed that the underlying walls were
smooth, the contractor would have to reinstall the siding at his
own expense, but if the parties agreed that the underlying walls
were uneven, the customer would have to pay the contractor for a
second complete installation of siding. The customer rejected this
gamble, and the dispute remained unresolved.

If consumer arbitration is to serve large numbers of consumers
and businesses, substantial government funding of consumer arbitration programs is needed. Such funding is, of course, currently
provided in compulsory arbitration programs such as in Pennsylvania, in small claims/arbitration combinations such as in New
York City, and in government-administered voluntary arbitration
programs such as in Fairfax County, Virginia. Thus far voluntary
programs have relied on foundations, businesses (whose contributions to Better Business Bureaus partly defray the costs of administering consumer arbitration programs), and on arbitration fees.
Funding from private groups often tends to be unpredictable, since
it depends on special interests, and would likely be inadequate to
support extensive consumer arbitration programs. Fees may
dissuade consumers from pursuing valid claims. Government funding, on the other hand, would provide steady support for arbitra-

ion programs and would enable consumers to arbitrate disputes at
no cost or at a minimal fee. Since widespread consumer arbitration would ease the burdens on courts and consumer agencies and
would reduce hostilities between consumers and businesses, the
government would itself benefit from supporting, sponsoring, or
administering arbitration programs.

Ten

Courts for Consumer Cases

BELIEF IN the legitimacy of the legal process is a basic element in our social structure. It would contradict a fundamental sense of American democracy if victims of consumer trouble were denied the opportunity to use the legal system.[1] Yet legal resources are scarce and access to law is limited. Small claims courts attempt to resolve this dilemma. Ideally, the development of these courts has shown our society's basic commitment to equal access to law and has recognized the advantages of simplified procedures for certain kinds of cases.

Small claims courts are coercive institutions. If a consumer chooses to have a dispute resolved by a small claims court, and if the business decides not to participate in the process, the dispute will almost always be decided in favor of the consumer. Small claims courts usually do no require the use of lawyers, as ordinary courts do. Cases are heard promptly, without the long delays typical of other courts, and the ordinary rules of evidence and other procedural rules are applied informally. In sum, creators of these courts intended them to be dignified and friendly forums where people of all backgrounds could present problems themselves to a judge who would help in the process of developing the facts and would decide the case quickly.[2]

Support for courts that would meet this ideal is still widespread. The National Institute for Consumer Justice (NICJ) placed highest priority on recommendations for encouraging the availability and fairness of small claims courts.[3] The Chamber of Commerce of the United States has advocated the same goals.[4] Federal legislation, to be discussed below, has the potential to support local small claims courts. One particularly detailed proposal by he Association of the Bar of the City of New York calls for establishment of "neighborhood consumer courts," where informality, accessibility, and accountability for constituent communities would be a matter of policy, strengthened by procedural ules and geographic dispersion. The proposal calls for locating one court in each state assembly district, and for even more courts n crowded areas, using community school board districts as a geographic measure.[5] By having courts serve small constituencies, there is a greater likelihood that monitoring by neighborhood citizens will encourage fair treatment of plaintiffs. Also, neighborhood residents may come to feel relatively unfearful about making use of the court. An experimental court of this type began operations in San Jose, California, in 1977.[6]

Unfortunately, the conception of an ideal small claims court has rarely been realized. In the places where courts do exist, they are often inaccessible, as a practical matter, because of their location or hours of operation. Some small claims courts are dominated by business-initiated cases, so that clerks and judges appear to be unsympathetic to consumers. And about half of all successful plaintiffs are unable to collect the money they have settled for or been awarded by the judge.[7]

Establishment of Small Claims Courts

Around the time of the World War I, legal writers began to discuss the high cost of litigation. New procedures such as arbitration were being developed; it was known that in Denmark and Norway conciliation tribunals were successful in settling disputes without lawyers.[8] Reformers considered the difficulty working class plaintiffs would experience in trying to use conventional procedures to collect payment for work they had performed; fairness was thought to require some simple and inexpensive forum for this kind of problem. By the mid-1920s about eight states and a dozen cities had established small claims or conciliation courts.[9] By 1939, nine more states and the District of Columbia had established small claims court systems.[10] As of 1972, small claims courts could be found throughout thirty-three states and in metropolitan areas of eight additional states.[11]

Suggestive of the general inaccessibility of small claims courts is the fact that some of the most basic information about even the existence of small claims courts is hard to come by. For example, reliable information on what states have what kinds of courts is difficult to find. When the NICJ sponsored a study of small claims courts, the report was detailed in its examination of policy issues but it relied on the only other recent comprehensive study of the courts, the Small Claims Study Group's *Little Injustices*, for data on where the courts really are. Thus, the NICJ report concluded that many states and parts of states do not have small claims courts.[12] Yet a researcher for Consumers Union produced a listing of forty-seven states and the District of Columbia has having small claims courts.[13] A popular guidebook, *Sue the Bastards*, claims that forty-nine states and the District of Columbia have small claims courts.[14]

Recently, the National Center for State Courts published a statutory survey of the states indicating that specialized small claims courts are present in forty-two states.[15] Some of these states make small claims procedures available only in urban counties.[16] The survey shows great variety in court formats and monetary limits on claims. For example, Montana has small claims courts in a few counties (with jurisdiction for cases involving up to $1,500), Mississippi uses a justice of the peace system (for cases that involve up to $200), and Pennsylvania has small claims courts in Philadelphia but justices of the peace in other parts of the state. Limits on the maximum amount of money that can be involved in a small claims court case vary from state to state, from $150 to $3,500. A county by county analysis of the availability of small claims procedures has never been undertaken. Without such a tally, only estimates can be made. In 1974, a Senate committee published a report estimating that 41 million Americans have no effective access to small claims courts.[17]

The discrepancies among various studies may be caused partly by differing definitions of small claims court. They do, however, lead to startlingly different conclusions. The *Little Injustices* report, and the press conference at which it was released, maintained that small claims courts are either unavailable, unusable, or invisible to most consumers.[18] *Sue the Bastards* asserts that most Americans can find justice quickly and easily at small claims courts. The weight of fact supports the conclusion that small claims courts are actually often beyond the reach of consumers.

But this conflict illustrates the confusion that bedevils understanding of small claims courts.

Universe of Users

Even in the 1940s, it was predicted that businesses might make substantial use of the simple, small claims procedures that had been devised primarily to aid individuals.[19] This pattern has in fact developed in a number of places. Studies have analyzed small claims court caseloads to see what percentage of cases is attributable to business and governmental use of the courts: such uses represent from 44 to 90 percent of court caseloads, in fourteen past studies.[20] A recent scrutiny of one small claims court in California shows that twenty-six particular business enterprises are involved in one-third of all of that court's completed cases.[21]

Individuals who bring cases to small claims courts have highly diverse backgrounds in terms of education, occupation, and income. At the Rochester, New York, small claims court, about half of the litigants are white collar workers, small business owners, or salaried laborers.[22] In 1972, the income distribution of consumer plaintiffs in the Philadelphia small claims court included 25 percent with less than $5,000 per year, 40 percent between $5,000 and $10,000, 23 percent between $10,000 and $15,000, and 13 percent over $15,000.[23]

Types of Cases

Empirical studies of various small claims courts have shown that consumer plaintiffs present problems as diverse as the consumer experience itself.[24] To provide a qualitative sample of kinds of cases in which consumers succeed in small claims courts, volunteers from a University of Pennsylvania student-organized consumer help agency monitored and wrote descriptions of cases in the Philadelphia court during 1974 and 1975.[25] Their brief descriptions of cases indicate the range of disputes in which small claims courts can provide satisfactory resolutions to aggrieved consumers:

A home improvement contractor installed aluminum siding with poor workmanship. Some of the siding had holes in it, in some places it had cracks or lacked insulation, and the installation caused a formerly sound roof to leak. The judge's decision called for the seller to repair the work to the buyer's satisfaction within two days or pay the buyer $499, the maximum amount possible for the court to award.

An automobile transmission costing $280 was sold with a ninety-day guarantee. Within a short time, it stopped operating properly, but the seller refused to repair it. The judge ordered the seller to refund the buyer's total payment.

In a dispute involving a television set repair, the consumer reported that a repair establishment had taken six months to repair a set, and that the repair itself was inadequate. The judge awarded the consumer plaintiff a total refund.

A consumer complained five times to a store about a bicycle which had cost $111.30. Something was wrong with the gears, and the wheels were not aligned. Although the seller wanted to continue to make repair attempts, the judge ordered a complete refund.

A consumer was dissatisfied with carpeting that was installed in a large room; a line was evident across the middle of the floor. Although the seller said the line would blend in after vacuuming, the buyer believed that it remained visible after repeated vacuuming. The judge awarded the plaintiff $340, which was approximately one quarter of the purchase price.

A woman sued a dry cleaning store for seventy-two dollars, the cost of a dress damaged by the store; its sequins and its sleeves were discolored. The judge awarded fifty dollars to the plaintiff, in the face of statements by the cleaning store operator that the most careful work possible had been done.

In a case involving an alleged fraud, the plaintiff had paid $600 to a company which advertised employment services. The company furnished a counseling service, but did not produce offers of jobs, as its advertising had convinced the plaintiff it would. The company refused to give the plaintiff a refund. The judge ruled that it should refund $200.

These cases show that disputes about services and products, involving disagreements about physical evidence or intangible matters such as promises, can be treated to the satisfaction of consumers in small claims courts.

The Business Overload

In many places, the kinds of consumer cases described above are relatively rare, in comparison to vast numbers of cases filed by businesses suing their customers. This imbalance distorts the original purpose of small claims courts, because consumers may come to view a particular court as a place where businesses carry on their work. Seen as an extension of the facilities of stores, such small claims courts are less likely to be used by consumers than would be the pattern if the reputation of the courts were more balanced.

This problem of business domination of small claims courts can be treated as one of jurisdiction. That is, the claims of creditors can be defined as out of the jurisdiction of the courts. For example, in some states small claims courts are not open to corporate plaintiffs or collection agencies. An annual limit on the number of cases that may be brought by any single plaintiff can be imposed; in the Conciliation Division of the Detroit Common Pleas Court, individuals and businesses are allowed to begin no more than four cases in any single twelve-month period.[27]

Since businesses deserve access to fair and efficient means of vindicating their rights, it might be desirable to find ways of controlling business abuse of the courts other than by excluding businesses or limiting the number of cases that a single business can bring. One such approach would be to tighten controls on default judgments, the judgments given to one party when its opponent does not appear at court for the trial. Studies in various courts show defaults as representing from 10 to 90 percent of all judgments.[28] Typically, business plaintiffs obtain default judgments against consumer defendants who are never notified of the lawsuit or who have been notified but do not appear in court. Automatic granting of judgments in these situations encourages businesses to bring suits that may not be fully justified, in the expectation that many of the consumer defendants will default. Where this occurs, consumers can be expected to lose confidence in the court. A remedy for this abuse is simple, however; judges can make an independent examination of the validity of the plaintiff's claim before entering a default judgment.[29] This would not eliminate default judgments in situations where a plaintiff might have proved he or she was not liable, had he or she appeared in court, but it would help to reduce the business incentive to file weak lawsuits, and might thus increase the apparent fairness of the small claims court. Remedies are also possible for the problem of failure to notify defendants that they are being sued. "Sewer service," where process servers throw summonses away rather than deliver them to defendants, is avoided to some extent by provisions in some jurisdictions which require that defendants be notified of the suits against them by registered mail.[30]

Another solution to the problem of frequent suits by businesses against consumer debtors would be the imposition of a rule of law requiring lenders to be prudent. Debts that result from extensions of credit in circumstances where a reasonable businessman would not have sold goods or made a loan could be cancelled by the court. This "prudent lender" concept, along with judicial willingness to permit nonpayment of debts for inadequate merchandise, would clear the courts of much of their overload of collection cases.

A Consumers Union report on small claims courts argued that barring creditors from small claims courts might lead to the trying of these suits in more formal higher courts where it is even harder for individual defendants to succeed. A counterargument is that public pressure would lead to free legal aid for such defendants, resulting in better protection for them.[31] *Little Injustices* held that collection suits ought to be kept in small claims courts where they are most visible and are most susceptible to the moderating influence of community advocates or advisors.

Of course, the imbalance between consumer as plaintiff and consumer as defendant currently typical of caseloads at many small claims courts might also be modified by increasing the number of consumer-as-plaintiff cases. At present, businesses know about small claims courts and routinely use them to collect debts. The number of these cases presumably would not change much if small claims courts were to receive publicity or were made more accessible; that number of cases, though, could be submerged in a vastly increased flow of consumer plaintiff cases.

Plaintiff Domination

On an overall basis, plaintiffs do very well in small claims courts. In various studies of success rates, typical reported percentages of plaintiff victories range upwards from 80 percent.[32] In one study, plaintiffs showed a 100 percent victory rate.[33] The reasons for these rates include the number of defaults entered for plaintiffs, higher plaintiff motivation, and the claim evaluation process most plaintiffs go through before deciding to file a complaint. More widespread knowledge of this pattern can encourage consumer use of small claims courts. For example, community outreach programs at the New York City Harlem small claims court have increased usage of the court through speeches that lay advocates make at community meetings.[34] A Columbus, Ohio, television station presented a weekly program dramatizing small claims courts cases; it led to a marked increase in the number of cases instituted in the courts.[35]

Actual Trial of Cases

Most small claims court judges analyze evidence, decide what the truth is, and apply appropriate law to the facts very quickly. In a study of a Philadelphia court, about half of the hearings took less than five minutes.[36] How close is that to the conceptual ideal of deliberative justice? What effect can this have on the apparent legitimacy of court proceedings? Certainly, some cases can be treated well in only a few minutes, but analysis of time spent can yield a rough idea of the quality of justice.

Use of Lawyers

The original conception of small claims courts, by Roscoe Pound and Reginald Heber Smith, among others, excluded the use of lawyers, consistent with the notion of maintaining a people's court.[37] Eight states bar lawyers from small claims courts currently.[38] But in many jurisdictions, lawyers are commonly used by both plaintiffs and defendants. It has been established that representation by a lawyer is not a very important determinant of probable victory.[39] Presence of a lawyer is not, however, totally without effect. One study that attempted to analyze kinds of lawyer participation found that all plaintiffs who obtained particular help from lawyers about exactly how they should *prepare* for trial or settlement negotiations were satisfied with the results of their cases; plaintiffs who received other kinds of legal help and plaintiffs who received no legal help at all reported about the same results—victories in about 80 percent of their cases.[40] In general, it may be that the presence of an attorney on the plaintiff's side cannot dramatically increase the plaintiff's already overwhelming rate of victories, while an attorney's presence for a defendant can improve the ordinarily weak showing of defendants, if only by introducing valid defenses that a defendant without a lawyer might fail to identify.[41] Prospective users of small claims courts are of course not ordinarily aware of the actual impact of lawyers, and would probably consider it a great disadvantage to appear without one.

It should be acknowledged that many businesses which appear frequently in small claims court do not need to hire lawyers because they can obtain the supposed benefits of representation by counsel through the technique of using the same one or two employees time and again to present their cases. Those individuals quickly learn the skills of small claims court litigation by trial, error, and practice.

Judges

Judges in small claims court have a role unlike that of judges in any other part of our court system. Perhaps because of this, there is wide variation in their styles. Some are strict, some lenient, some are serious in demeanor, some consider small claims as subjects for jokes and ridicule. Better understanding of what is expected might help judges perform in a more uniform manner. The fact that most small claims courts make no record of the proceedings adds to the difficulty of assuring high standards of judicial conduct. One typical arrangement for staffing the small claims court bench is rotation of all the judges of the lowest level trial court in a jurisdiction, so that each judge hears small claims cases for some part of each week, month, or year. This system may incline some judges to think of small claims work as an unpleasant burden. It would be desirable for court administrators to handle small claims court assignments with greater flexibility, so that judges who seem interested in small claims cases could be given more responsibility for them. Another method of selecting judges should be adopted to increase the dignity and apparent importance of the courts. This method would require the judges of all of a jurisdiction's higher courts to preside in small claims courts periodically. Their presence in the small claims courts might provide an example, and perhaps an inspiration, to judges who regularly serve there. Undoubtedly, higher court judges would learn from the experience as well.

Settlements

Small claims court judges are famous for forcing settlements. In an old joke, a plaintiff who has been ordered to step outside the courtroom with the defendant to try to compromise looks around at the crowd of other plaintiffs and defendants and says: "In the halls of justice, the only justice is done in the halls." When a judge advocates settlement, plaintiffs may feel coerced.

In some courts, however, procedures exist to prevent this pressure for settlement from working to the disadvantage of the plaintiffs. In New York City, at the Harlem small claims court, community advocates (who are lay employees of the court) assist plaintiffs and defendants in deciding whether to go to trial or to accept the New York City option of a hearing before an arbitrator. The arbitrators have the reputation of being careful and considerate. Using the rough measure of time spent on cases, it is interesting to note that arbitrators—who seek to reason with the parties—take about forty-five minutes to decide each case.[42] Some small claims courts offer the services of conciliators, court officials who attempt to help litigants settle their differences without a trial. Because the conciliator is not the individual who will rule on the case if agreement is not reached, this procedure reduces the risk that plaintiffs will accept unsatisfactory settlements out of fear of antagonizing the judge.

Judgment Collection

After winning in court, about half the victors never collect their judgments. This is perhaps the worst problem of small claims courts. A study of this problem in New York City showed that 82 percent of plaintiffs who agree to settlements collect their money, but only 50 percent of plaintiffs who win at trial are able to collect.[43] The main categories of defendants who do not pay judgments reflect the range of common consumer concerns: a wide assortment of sellers of merchandise, and the following services—parking garages, dry cleaners, moving and storage companies, electronics repair shops, automobile repairers, and airlines and travel agents.[44]

Resolving the Problems

The hope for improving small claims courts is in recognizing their imperfect nature and making the best of it. The courts are meant to be small and informal, yet they are impersonal and located centrally in cities. This can be corrected by moving them to neighborhoods, either as permanent fixtures, as scheduled part-time occupants of public buildings, or in mobile offices. Evening and Saturday sessions must be maintained for both trials and filing claims. In the San Jose, California, experiment with a neighborhood branch small claims court, usage has been slow to develop, even though the court has a convenient location and evening sessions. This points to the complexity of designing a well-functioning court.[45] In some places, evening hours may be considered dangerous times for people to travel to a court. Furthermore, it takes time for a gradual dissemination of favorable reports about an institution such as a court to produce an increase in its usage.

Domination of the courts by business plaintiffs in many jurisdictions can be remedied by better publicity about the courts and more sympathetic service to individuals by clerks. Paralegal assistants at the courts can help citizens formulate their complaints and prepare to present their cases in court, which might increase usage of the courts by individual plaintiffs. A successful program of this kind is operated by the Toledo, Ohio, small claims court. Originally begun as part of a University of Toledo Law School clinical program, the Small Claims Assistance Project is now operated directly by the municipal court. Law students are employed to advise unrepresented individuals on preparing their claims for presentation at the trial, and on preparing defenses. The student employees are supervised by the court administrator, who is a member of the bar.[46]

Trials are sometimes confused mixtures of pressure to settle, intimate involvement by the judge, and detached decision making by the judge. This can be corrected by recognizing and separating the different functions. A two-stage procedure requiring litigants to attempt settlement and proceed to a formal trial only if settlement is not reached offers the advantage that the settlement stage does not confuse the trial stage. Further, the official at the settlement stage could be someone with significant human relations skills. Especially prior to a formal trial, small claims courts can take advantage of modern ideas of informality. Even in federal court trials at present, some judges hold court seated at a conference table along with the disputants.[47] Certainly a similar approach can be used in the settlement phase of small claims court proceedings. Indeed, a poster promoting the San Jose neighborhood court illustrates such a meeting at a conference table.[48]

Separating the functions of mediation and judicial decision making could also help remedy the issue of the presence of lawyers at small claims court. The Small Claims Study Group took a flexible position on the role of lawyers in small claims courts, a stance which reflects the confusing multifunction aspect of the courts. The group advocated barring lawyers eventually, with replacements for lawyers coming from the community and performing functions similar to those of the Harlem small claims court community advocates. Perhaps another solution would be to bar lawyers from the settlement stage but to permit them in the unambiguously adjudicative stage.

For judgment-collection problems, a number of remedies are possible. New York State has enacted two imaginative statutes that may improve plaintiffs' chances of collecting judgments. The first provides that a judgment against any person or company currently subject to three unpaid judgments can be executed by a sheriff or marshal at three times its value. The intention of this statute is to encourage defendants to make timely payments, and to provide a greater incentive to the commission-earning marshals for the collection of judgments.[49] The second statute requires that unsatisfied judgments be returned to the court and that the court maintain a file of defendants showing their payment history.[50] Thus, a licensing agency can determine if any of its licensees are scofflaws prior to renewing licenses. In New York City, the Department of Consumer Affairs has attempted to use this information to deny license renewals to the enterprises it regulates. Theoretically, the public or the press could also use these data.

Plaintiffs might have better success at collecting judgments if courts gave them more help. In some instances, defendants are

particularly vulnerable to special collection techniques: people who
own real estate, for example, can be barred from selling it if an
unsatisfied judgment is recorded on the title to the property, and
for cases related to traffic accidents, at least one state can suspend
the driver's license of a judgment debtor.[51] In all situations, a winning consumer plaintiff needs assistance to discover what
procedures are required to bring the law to bear against the recal-
citrant judgment debtor.

Of course, the best possible assistance would be a procedure in
which the state carried the entire burden of judgment collection.
For example, in a number of states, a state corporation pays compensation to anyone injured by an uninsured motorist; the state
then seeks repayment from the motorist. Such a fund could be established for small claims court judgments, so that small claims
court winners could be certain of prompt payment. This idea of
swift and automatic compensation in a situation where a consumer's rights are established clearly is in keeping with a more far-
reaching proposal by Maurice Rosenberg. In "Devising Procedures that are Civil to Promote Justice that is Civilized," he advocated establishment of a federal agency which would offer immediate payments to consumers who presented proof that a
product or service had failed, and that the failure was a kind of
failure for which the seller or manufacturer should be responsible
financially.[52] In the Rosenberg proposal, stated simply in an
example, consumers would return defective toasters to the Department of Economic Justice. The Department would pay a reasonable compensation, and at efficient intervals it would obtain mass
repayments to itself from the manufacturers and sellers for whose
failures it had reimbursed consumers. A problem with this proposal is that the Department's decisions regarding which consumers
deserve payments and how much any payment should be could en-
tail the delays and potential for injustice typical of decision making
by administrative agencies. For this reason, the automatic payment
idea has its best applications in circumstances where the right to
payment is absolutely clear-cut; a judgment awarded in a small
claims court case is one example of such an unambiguous right to
payment.

Although small claims courts may resolve single problems well,
it should be asked whether their work can promote any

generalized benefits beyond directing compensation to individual plaintiffs. In two ways, use of small claims courts can be consistent with societal identification and regulation of chronic wrongdoers. First, businesses which engage in improper practices are likely to change those practices if they become unprofitable. So, even though a small claims court must give the same treatment to the fiftieth case involving a particular defendant that it gives to the first case involving the same defendant, that treatment can provide a significant economic penalty and can therefore discourage patterns of abuse.

The case by case limitation on action inherent in small claims courts could also be modified by procedures that would take advantage of information that the courts produce as a by-product of their work. At present, the Consumer Product Safety Commission operates a data-collecting system which receives daily reports from more than 100 hospital emergency rooms about product-related injuries; the concept of this system deserves high marks, since serious injuries related to the use of products are very likely to be observed and evaluated in emergency rooms.[53] In a similar fashion, if neighborhood courts were to become as frequently used a mechanism for serious consumer disputes as hospital emergency rooms are for physical injuries, data could be collected about the types of transactions complained about and the businesses found to have treated consumers unfairly. These data could be used to plan law enforcement priorities, to alert individuals or consumer affairs departments about untrustworthy businesses or consumer deception schemes, and to determine needs for additional consumer protection legislation.

The Potential

For all their faults, currently operating small claims courts demonstrate great possibilities. New adequately structured neighborhood courts could function both as a symbol of the rule of law and as a practical means for citizens to observe the workings of the law and the conduct of businesses. Further, individuals who participated in the proceedings of such courts would benefit from obtaining final resolution of their disputes and from learning more about the consequences of their business dealings.

One dilemma that must be faced is inherent in the operation of the courts as a special forum for so-called small claims. The only definitions of small claim now in use rely solely on the amount of money at stake. The small claims court advantage of informal treatment is offered to all cases involving less than particular stated amounts of money, without regard to the fact that a case involving a very low amount of money might be of crucial importance to an individual and to the community and might involve very complex issues. Support for small claims courts should not work to exclude such crucially important cases from the fullest consideration our judicial system can supply, in cases where the participants seek such consideration. Some lawsuits conventionally considered "large" might receive adequate treatment through small claims court procedures. On the other hand, particularly where an important factor for consideration is the impression the individual obtains of fairness and propriety, some conventionally "small" claims may merit the kind of lavish treatment ordinarily given to large lawsuits between businesses or between businesses and the government.

Well-publicized and accessible small claims courts can potentially help buyers overcome many of the obstacles this study describes. The notions that having problems and speaking up about them are illegitimate can be counteracted by the perception that an important element of government is available to redress consumer wrongs, and that rights without enforcement are no rights at all. A court that is well known in its community can raise the rights consciousness of those who use it and of those who hear about its use. Ready availability of the courts will decrease the cost of complaining. And the courts will likely help to modify the typical business monopoly of access to information needed to voice a complaint fully and clearly.

Federal funding may be available to encourage small claims court development. The Consumer Controversies Resolution Act was first proposed in 1974. A version that became law in 1980 establishes a dispute resolution program within the Department of Justice.[54] A grant program will offer states aid in maintaining small claims courts and other kinds of dispute-settling mechanisms. The statute also provides general goals for application to small claims courts. They emphasize ease of access and an opportunity for settlement. One of the best features of the law requires that courts or alternative institutions be associated with programs of public information to increase their actual accessibility.

When results of complaining are considered, a major advantage of courts (as well as other coercive institutions) becomes apparent. Legal gimmicks, victim blaming, partial redress, and selective perception of grievances can be used freely by businesses when the resolution of a complaint will not be reviewed. Involvement of a court guarantees that neither the buyer nor the seller will have the last word; the court determines the resolution, and though biases may be present, they will not be biases directly determined and controlled by the seller. Compared with other complaint handlers, courts are very powerful institutions. Consumers are not likely to overestimate the powers of the court, since in fact they are quite broad. Courts, unlike some other third parties, cannot engage in arbitrary selection of cases, since they deal with *all* of the cases in their jurisdiction that people present to them. Furthermore, conflicts of interest have not seemed to harm consumer plaintiffs in the courts; the major institutional goal of the courts is quick resolution of cases, not maintenance of any particular balance between plaintiff and defendant victories.

Eleven

Lower Cost Legal Service

JUST AS some people may avoid small claims courts because they think a lawyer's help is necessary and know they cannot afford such help, in other contexts, too, the cost of legal help may inhibit people from acting to enforce their rights. In his famous 1906 address, "The Causes of Popular Dissatisfaction with the Administration of Justice," Roscoe Pound wrote, "Our administration of justice is not decadent. It is simply behind the times."[1] Lack of access to legal help is still a significant difficulty for many people with consumer problems; more than seventy years after Pound's address, it can still be said that lawyers and old fashioned organization of the legal profession are primarily to blame for this lack.

Quantitative evidence of the lack of recourse to lawyers is seen in the American Bar Association's Legal Needs survey. That study shows that people have frequent needs for assistance in will drafting, divorce, real estate acquisition and resolution of disputes involving purchases, but it shows that the rates at which people obtain legal help in these situations are varied. In fact, use of lawyers in purchase disputes is markedly lower than for the other problems mentioned; if people responded to disputes about major purchases by using lawyers as frequently as they do when confronted by divorce or will-drafting, lawyers would handle approximately ten times as many consumer cases as they handle currently.[2]

New mass-market legal service firms do not seem to seek consumer problem cases. Their advertisements are primarily aimed at obtaining cases that deal in simple repetitive tasks like divorce and real estate matters, or at obtaining cases with possibly large financial returns, such as negligence lawsuits. Thus, bringing legal attention to individuals' consumer problems remains difficult. One promising way of directing legal resources to consumer problems has been developed by the prospective beneficiaries themselves: group or prepaid legal services. Since the early 1970s, limited experience has shown that prepaid or group legal practice programs have the potential to overcome low and middle income people's lack of access to law. For the very poor, the federally supported legal services program has the same potential. These new forms of legal practice can be evaluated in terms of their cost, their success in helping their constituencies take advantage of legal assistance, and their ability to educate their constituencies in self-help techniques based on law.

Prepaid legal services plans vary in terms of sponsor, organization, benefits, and techniques of service. Up to the present time, plans have been sponsored by state bar associations, various businesses including insurance companies, and groups of consumers such as unions or student groups. In terms of organization, plans use open panel, closed panel, or mixed open and closed panel groups of lawyers. In an open panel plan, members select any lawyer and the lawyer is paid according to a schedule of benefits provided by the plan. In a closed panel plan, members must use a lawyer designated by the plan. Some closed panel plans employ lawyers on a full time basis. To draw an analogy to health care plans, open panel plans are similar to Blue Cross, and closed panel plans are similar to group health or health maintenace organizations.

Benefits can be extended either to group members or to group members and their families. Of course, the amount of service provided to eligible recipients can vary; some plans cover only employment-related problems while others cover criminal cases, divorce cases, and a range of other services. Finally, plans have different techniques of assuring efficient utilization of benefits. Some plans use publicity within the group to alert members to potential situations where legal help could be useful, and some offer telephone advice service for members who are about to sign consumer contracts, while a number of plans make no appreciable effort to increase utilization.

Early History of Legal Services Plans

Group legal services plans began in the 1900s, with railroad unions and policemen's associations that offered representation to their members, primarily for problems related to employment. In the 1920s, automobile clubs began to offer a wide variety of legal services to their members. For example, a club in Illinois advertised "A Legal Staff At Your Service," and described various benefits in detail:

> If your car is damaged or if someone sues you for property damage, call on the legal department. Attorneys for the club will try to make an adjustment for you, and if necessary will handle your case in court.
> Speed trap operators, fake motoring organizations, swindling concerns selling to the motorists and crooked officials, all find the legal department an able and determined foe.[3]

Here was an enterprise that collected together a large group of people with a common interest and need—protection from abuses associated with automobile ownership—and supplied them with worthwhile services at a reasonable cost. Both this plan and the employment-related plans met with strong opposition from bar associations.

Opposition from the Organized Bar

Under the guise of protecting high standards of performance, bar associations traditionally utilized rules prohibiting "corporate practice of law" and the use of "lay intermediaries" to oppose innovative ways of delivering legal services. According to ethics and disciplinary rules, nothing could be allowed to interfere with the traditional single lawyer and single client practice of law, even though that mode of practice was clearly seen as denying the large majority of people access to lawyers. It has required a series of Supreme Court rulings, beginning in 1963, to counteract resistance by lawyers to innovations in the organization of legal work. The first of these rulings held that the National Association for the Advancement of Colored People could maintain a staff of lawyers to advise individuals about possible lawsuits based on violations of their civil rights. Then three subsequent Supreme Court cases involved labor unions, establishing the rights of unions to set up legal services plans for their members.[4] In the most recent of these decisions, the Court held:

The principle here involved cannot be limited to the facts of this case. At issue is the basic right to group legal action, a right first asserted in this Court by an association of Negroes seeking the protection of freedoms guaranteed by the Constitution. The common thread running through our decisions . . . is that collective activity undertaken to obtain meaningful access to the courts is a fundamental right within the protection of the First Amendment.[5]

Following this decision, a coalition of labor unions, consumer groups, insurance companies, and the ABA supported an amendment to the Taft-Hartley Act to permit labor-management negotiations for legal services as fringe benefits. The ABA supported this change because it was interested in furthering open panel plans. As enacted, however, the amendment allows unions to seek either open or closed panel plans.[6] Most unions have been interested in closed panel plans, which has led to strong ABA attacks on closed panel practice.

The ABA preference for open panel plans stemmed from the fundamental difference between open and closed panel plans in terms of impact on conventional organization of legal practice. With open panel plans, people who have a legal problem within the scope of the plan's coverage may hire any lawyer they choose. That lawyer is paid by the open panel plan. Thus, open panel plans do not change the structural organization of legal work in a community; they only provide a supply of new clients and new fees to established lawyers. Closed panel plans, on the other hand, handle problems with an internal staff or with a limited number of lawyers who belong to the panel. This means that those individuals who belong to a closed panel group are highly unlikely ever to become customers of lawyers who are not members of the plan's panel.

In 1969, the ABA adopted rules of ethics and discipline that approved prepaid legal services if the plans were nonprofit and were incidental to a group with a different primary purpose. In 1974, the ABA hedged its approval of group practice by defining two categories of plans, "Qualified" plans that are open panel and sponsored by bar associations, and "Other" plans, including closed panel and consumer sponsored plans. Attorneys theoretically could participate in closed panel plans, but an ethics rule was adopted stating that ethical risks were involved in participation in any nonqualified plan. Furthermore, the 1974 rules imposed an opt-out provision for closed panel plans; such plans would be obligated to pay a reasonable sum to a nonplan lawyer any time a plan beneficiary chose to be represented by a lawyer who was not a member of the closed panel.[7]

The net effect of these rules was the strong disfavoring of closed panels. This opposition to the clear import of the Supreme Court decisions aroused protests from Congress, some members of the bar, consumer groups, and the Department of Justice. A year later, the ABA withdrew its opposition to closed panels.[8]

The ABA's reluctance to endorse innovative changes in legal practice was also reflected in the organization's traditional support of lawyer referral services. Anyone who calls one of these services will be told the name of a lawyer; however, the competence of the lawyer is not known by the referral service. At present, bar associations operate referral services in most cities. Yet all that the services guarantee is that the lawyer named is a member of the bar. In some places, a further refinement of the service does exist; there is a promise that an initial meeting with the lawyer will not cost more than a specified amount. Referral services obviously do nothing to help people find lawyers of proven competence, nor do they have the potential to provide preventive service to individuals.

There has been tension within the ABA between the general membership and the specialized groups inside the organization set up to study prepaid and group services. Generally speaking, the membership has been reactionary while the specialized groups have sought to implement the line of Supreme Court decisions on group practice.

Costs and Benefits

Of all the reasons for the absence of necessary help, high cost is both the most obvious and the simplest to remedy. High cost is the product of the traditional choice made by lawyers to sell services on a low volume basis. The pattern of high fees and relatively few customers has been so deeply a part of American thinking about legal services that one early analysis outlined the restrictive effects of legal fees and then suggested installment credit as the primary solution.[9] Fortunately, other approaches can lower costs rather than spread them out over time: increasing competition, stimulating the use of paraprofessionals, and increasing the bargaining power of legal services consumers.

Mass bargaining power is the heart of the group practice idea. At first, unions developed ties with particular lawyers who would handle workmen's compensation cases and allow the union to influence the quality of representation and the size of the fee. Now various kinds of prepaid plans represent about 1.5 million people; this massed buying power offers an opportunity for cost cutting through bargaining. Particularly for closed panel plans, it is possible to hire staff attorneys at reasonable guaranteed salaries who can do work that would cost much more than their salaries if it were obtained on a piecework basis from lawyers not affiliated with a plan. Group bargaining power is not limited to discussions of fees; it can also be used to influence the style of representation and the organization of legal work. For example, some plans incorporate twenty-four-hour a day, everyday telephone advice or bail services; a number of plans require that the participating lawyers disclose their incomes.[10]

Particularly when a legal services group uses the closed panel style of organization, significant efficiencies can be obtained. Such plans have the best opportunities to use legal paraprofessionals and nonlegal workers such as social workers, which both reduces costs and improves the quality of work.[11] Where plans develop specialization by individual lawyers, this can also lead to better service at lower costs. A survey of fee-for-service closed panel plans in California showed that some provided services at fees as much as one-third less than state averages.[12]

Education efforts can be a major benefit of group legal practice. A parallel can be drawn to food co-ops and credit unions. These groups have had success in educating members partly because the members have confidence in the motives of the group, and because the members have greater interest in communications from their groups than they would have in communications from other sources.

Client participation is related to preventive education. One of the great values of closed panel plan is the feeling members develop that lawyers need not be feared. Since members think of the lawyers as their employees, they are more likely to participate actively in the work of their cases. This can produce better service for the members and also give them prospectively useful knowledge of their rights. Client participation can be particularly beneficial for consumer problems since much of the legal work in these cases involves simple negotiation with sellers rather than litigation. Members who work closely with their lawyers on a single case can learn how to counter tactics of intimidation used by sellers.

Closed panel plans provide another valuable form of client involvement; as a group, the clients are often the sole employers of the lawyers. Even if a closed panel hires an independent law firm to serve as its panel, the plan is usually one of the firm's largest clients. Where this is true, clients can influence the firm's organization and its procedures. The benefits of this kind of influence are obvious. As an example, a primary goal of the Laborers Legal Service Plan in Washington, D.C., is the abolition of patterns of interaction that its clients, mostly black unskilled workers, used to experience in their occasional dealing with lawyers. The old pattern was one of lawyers treating their clients as though the clients were their servants; in contrast, the plan lawyers are at all times conscious of the fact that they are employees of their clients.[13] Other groups with substantial client control have also adopted innovative procedures. A Maine teachers's group has an attorney who rides circuit around the state to be present where members need help. Evening office hours are a typical feature of some other plans that are responsive to needs of members.

Current Plans

An example of a closed panel plan is Municipal Employees Legal Services (MELS) operated in New York City by District Council 37, American Federation of State, County, and Municipal Employees. This plan currently covers a small percentage of the union membership on an experimental basis, funded partly by the Ford Foundation. It will be expanded on the basis of the experience now being obtained. The members of the union come from a wide range of social and economic classes, yet they have been using MELS in roughly the same proportions they represent in total union membership. This lack of class differences means that no one group of union members is subsidizing the legal care of any other group—a pattern which could have been predicted since virtually all people but the very rich currently have unmet needs for legal services.[14]

Policies of the MELS plan allow relatively low cost even with high utilization. For example, the plan makes extensive use of paraprofessionals, and standard forms of handling repeated problems are being set up. Utilization, in a recent period, was at the rate of about once per year for each six eligible users. Of all the problems treated, consumer matters account for 22 percent. About half of these involve purchase of goods and services, and about a quarter involve debts and bankruptcy. In the opinion of the MELS director, these consumer problems would be particularly unlikely to have been handled by traditional private lawyers, but a significant number of MELS clients were eager to have them dealt with by MELS.

In other ways, MELS has created greater value for its clients than would have been available to them in any alternative. A social worker is a permanent staff member, enabling the program to offer counseling in marital and money-management problems. Also, clients have no reluctance about evaluating the quality of legal help they receive. The director of the MELS program has stated: "Accountability comes by a natural source—people's initial right to go to Victor Gotbaum, head of the union. They consider that this is a union program which they are paying for through collective bargaining . . . They feel quite free to state their feelings about it."[15]

MELS publicizes successful cases in the union newspaper. This may increase utilization of the plan by making union members more aware of the legal implications of consumer transactions, as they read about successful defenses of the rights of fellow members. This may help them deal with some legal problems without any need for direct assistance from MELS. A California plan that carries out similar education-oriented publicity also issues membership cards. There are reports of individuals brandishing the cards during disputes at stores. Members thus prove they really mean it when they say "I'll call my lawyer" and they have, through education, been helped to know when the message is appropriate.[16]

Unions are not the only sponsors of legal service plans. Consumer cooperatives and credit unions also sponsor them, as do students at many colleges and universities. The student plans have special promise. Funded by contributions from students or by grants from charities, they put the legal system to work for a group that usually has had almost no power to oppose landlords or merchants who have taken advantage of their inexperience. Besides this significant immediate aid to students, the plans are by their very nature a future benefit as well. The students they serve are are learning through experience how to use legal principles in consumer problems. For example, a program at Indiana University served nearly 2,000 students in one year of operation. About 40 percent of its cases were landlord and tenant problems, and nearly 25 percent were consumer problems.[17] Such a high level of activity is bound to have influence even beyond the large number of particular instances in which individual legal actions are taken.

Consumers Group Legal Services in Berkeley, California, is operated by a co-op organization. Co-op members can pay an annual fee for participation in the group's legal services program. The plan claims to have been successful in reducing the reliance of its members on lawyers. For example, in simple divorce cases, the group supplies a script and a set of instructions, and briefs the client on the personality of the scheduled judge; the client then goes to court without a lawyer. The group also has evening education programs on topics that have included use of small claims court, wills, lawyers and their fees, and problems with moving companies.

Credit unions are another medium through which individuals can have access to group legal services. The National Credit Union Administration, the agency that regulates federally insured credit unions, has authorized them to offer legal services programs to their members. Participation in the plan must be voluntary, and the plan must be operated by an entity other than the credit union itself. A credit union can publicize a plan to its members and can transfer money from members' accounts to pay their premiums to the plan operator. On the other hand, the generally restrictive effect of the federal rules is highlighted in a provision that forbids credit unions to have any representative of the legal service plan permanently present on credit union premises.[18]

Insurance Company Activities

Insurance companies have so far played a minor role in the spread of prepaid legal services. Finding individual customers has been hard for them primarily because the nature of the need for legal service is far different from the need for other kinds of services that insurance companies traditionally cover.[19] For medical services, for example, everyone has a significant risk of some very high cost occurrence at least once in a lifetime. This is not true for legal services, where high cost services may never be needed for most people, and where high cost is likely to involve far less money than high cost in the medical context. Low cost legal services are likely to be needed by many people, but this is not a pattern that makes insurance protection practical. In fact, paying for low cost but relatively frequent occurrences through insurance will only add the expense of administration to costs that might otherwise have been borne fairly easily through budgeting. This budgeting concept, though, does point out a value of insurance for legal fees. Insurance payments can be a kind of money management, and it may be true that people will use lawyers more freely if they realize that the lawyer's fee will be taken care of by money they have already spent.[20]

When an insurance company takes an active role in designing a legal services plan, its customers are in a position to benefit from the potential cost savings of group practice. Insurance companies already have vast experience in administering closed panel legal plans: although it is not usually so characterized, legal defense provided to beneficiaries of automobile insurance policies can be thought of as such a plan.

Future Developments of Group Practice Plans

One of the major impediments to the growth of legal services plans has been the strict prohibition of almost all kinds of advertising and promotion by lawyers. It was not until the spring of 1977 that a United States Supreme Court decision recognized the public interest in wider and clearer knowledge of legal services, and forbade states and local bar associations from imposing sanctions against all lawyer advertising.[21] The ability to advertise will make it easier for plans to attract members. It will also allow lawyers to organize group practices and market the availability of those group practices to employers, unions, and other groups.

As is often true in the process of modernizing the administration of legal services, some elements in the organized bar resist innovation. For example, the New York State Bar Association and the rules committee of the Maryland Court of Appeals have proposed rules for lawyer advertising that interpret the governing Supreme Court decision very narrowly. The United States Department of Justice criticized both proposals because they prohibited television advertising.[22] Similarly, Ohio rules have forbidden lawyers to use outdoor billboard advertising, and other New York State provisions have precluded direct mail advertisements such as discount offerings for real estate closing work.[23]

In addition to having impact on group legal service plans, new policies on lawyer advertising have also enabled individuals lawyers to offer their services at prices lower than formerly typical, and in styles of practice that are highly original. This attention has centered on legal work this is more easily routinized than the representation of consumers in disputes with businesses, but any increase in the availability of low-cost legal help may ultimately benefit consumers. In 1979, a chain of more than forty law offices spent $1.09 million for television advertising; the amount spent that year for all lawyer advertising on television was $4.52 million.[24] An Atlanta lawyer has rented space at a weekend flea market and posted a fee schedule in his booth.[25]

In the near future, employment-related plans are likely to be the most common prepaid services. Indeed, in a recent one year period, the number of prepaid legal services plans connected wth employment tripled.[26] This suggests that individuals can expect success if they seek to establish legal services plans as benefits of employment. Issues of concern for all kinds of plans will be the continuing development of consumer control, and consumer participation in individual cases.

Experience predicts that substantial numbers of group members will bring their consumer problems to the lawyers. Small but annoying disputes over unfair sales practices or the quality of moderate cost goods and services can now be exposed to legal treatment more often. It remains to be seen whether individual lawyers in private practices will serve consumers in similar ways;

the low fee practices that have developed recently have not fulfilled this potential. Particularly for the more complex cases that lawyers in conventional practices might reject either through unfamiliarity or due to a belief that potential recoveries are too small, group plans represent the most practical means of obtaining legal redress.

A final significant value of group legal plans should be emphasized. The plans can be a resource of preventive law data for state and national planning. As they come to represent more individuals, and as those individuals present more of their formerly ignored injustices to lawyers for remedy, the plans will be important collectors of information that can identify specific individual frauds and general problems that need attention from legislators and regulatory officials.

PART FOUR

Conclusion

Twelve

Product and Service Reliability: A Goal for Consumer Protection

JUSTICE FOR consumers means that ordinary buying and selling must be carried out fairly, and that lapses from that fairness must be redressed quickly and easily. But this justice must be understood as part of the totality of life in America, and the realities of America's economic and social problems must help shape our understanding of how it will work. The increasing scarcity and expense of energy should inform our understanding of consumer justice. If confidence in our institutions is lessening, this, too, should affect how businesses and regulators of businesses think of improvements in complaint prevention and complaint treatment.

During the Hoover administration, at the beginning of the Great Depression, a vast governmental study, "Recent Social Trends," was conducted. The sociologist Robert S. Lynd contributed a study on Americans as consumers. As was typical of analysis of consumer problems at that time, the study described the kinds of things people bought, and suggested that learning how to select purchases was the most pressing need of the consumers.[1] So-called shopping skills are still important. But that study, nearly fifty years old, is relevant to the present in quite another way. Lynd described the function of consuming as "buying a living," and asserted that although members of previous generations had "made" a living for themselves, by actually producing much of what they needed to sustain their lives, Americans in the 1920s were removed from skills and resources which could supply food, shelter, clothing, and other needs. Society had replaced *making* a living with *buying* a living.

At the present time, we are even more dependent on buying

(rather than making) the elements from which we each fashion a way of life. In selecting from perhaps 10,000 kinds of products, made in 360,000 manufacturing plants, and sold in more than 2,000,000 retail establishments,[2] and from services provided in similar magnitude and diversity, our buying of a living is complicated, and yet vital to our survival. The idea that our purchasing amounts to buying a living highlights the fact that a person who cannot acquire purchases or whose purchases have systematic deficiencies faces a kind of loss of life, or a kind of death. A society that faces a severe shortage of energy, that suffers from inflation and other economic ills, and that has acknowledged that environmental resources must be used with great care, cannot tolerate inefficient market transactions. The ultimate theoretical consequence of supplying some people today with substandard products and improperly performed services may well be that in the future no people will be supplied with any products or services.

Treatment of Individual Complaints

Since our country can no longer operate as a high waste, low efficiency society, every possible means must be used to make buying a living work properly. Proper regard for consumer complaints can help achieve the fairness and efficiency in the marketplace that changes in overall social and economic conditions require. When valid complaints quickly lead to compensation to buyers, there will be a great incentive to businesses to do things right the first time. Trial and error as a buyer's method of obtaining proper products and services will no longer be needed—where errors, or deficiencies, occur they will be paid for by the sellers who have caused them. Economic and physical scarcities make it clear that individual buyers cannot afford to pay for purchases that do not yield proper returns. Complaint handling should ensure that those buyers do not have to bear that burden.

Decent and efficient treatment of individual complaints will lead businesses to do better at providing goods and services that perform as well as they are supposed to perform. This may mean performance at a high level of durability and dependability, or (where health and safety are not at issue) may mean performance for short periods of time with less reliability. The value of establishing an expectation of payment for purchase failures is that businesses will have a strong incentive to make their performances match their promises. Thus, treatment of single complaints will lead to general improvements in the way sellers meet their responsibilities.

Treatment of Groups of Complaints

Fair treatment of single complaints will increase the likelihood that complaints will be made—and this is a vital first step in large-scale preventive measures. No group treatment of problems can be undertaken without identification of problems; voicing of individual complaints can be an indicator of appropriate targets for mass actions. Thus, there is a link between resolution of individual complaints and actions that can produce broadly applicable results. Mass actions may seek compensation for large groups of buyers who have been defrauded or injured in other ways, or they may seek to prevent future harm. Each of these benefits from mass actions can be brought into being, in part, through development of pressures for better handling of individual complaints.

As has been noted, some kinds of problems may be highly expensive to prevent, and relatively inexpensive for individual buyers to incur. If expenses are calculated fairly in this analysis, and the total expenses of buyers who seek correction of abuses are taken into account, perhaps only a small category of product and service shortcomings will remain properly describable as cheaper to correct than to prevent. But the existence of problems of this type should be recognized, and considered in proposals for improved treatment of complaints. Prevention of purchase deficiencies in this special class would cause unjustifiable increases in the costs of some products and services. Group treatment of buyers' injuries concerning these purchases should seek compensation to past buyers and guarantees that complaint handling techniques will be developed to compensate future buyers, if necessary. The goal in these cases should not be programs of total defect prevention, but should rather be assurances that future victims will be given proper remedial payments or other service.

New Rules for Sellers

The new rules this study proposes for sellers of products and services are intended to have two effects. By requiring sellers to

keep simple records of the kinds of complaints they receive and
the treatment they give them, the rules would encourage sellers to
treat complaints more quickly and fairly, and to sell products or
perform services that require fewer corrections. Simple market
pressure, perhaps organized through systematic comparisons of
various sellers' complaint records made by journalists or public
interest groups, might discourage sellers from continuing to
operate in ways that generate perceived problems. The records
would also be a help to law enforcement agencies in identifying
kinds of products or services that seem to generate many complaints, regardless of who the seller may be. And, more directly,
the records might also be a guide to locating particular sellers who
fail to maintain adequate standards of complaint handling. Thus,
if the proposed rules are adopted, and if people work to obtain the
informational benefits the rules may make available, two broad
classes of consequences may develop: stores and service providers
may seek to better their records of complaint handling, since
lapses in this part of their business activity would be made apparent to prospective customers; further, businesses would be discouraged from repeating the kinds of transactions that lead to
problems.

Better Participation by Third Parties

Benefits in terms of preventing future problems from occurring
and encouraging better treatment of buyer-seller disputes that do
take place could also be brought about by increased activity on the
part of a variety of third parties, such as mediating groups,
government agencies, and courts. For resolving individual disputes, third parties can sometimes help the buyer and seller agree
on a compromise; in many instances, third parties with real or apparent coercive power can obtain a seller's commitment to meet a
buyer's request. Where block solutions to recurring problems are
concerned, third parties are in a position to monitor whole seg-
ments of commerce, and become aware of types of businesses or
types of transactions that are becoming sources of trouble. To
move in response to these identified trends, government agencies
can enforce existing laws and regulations. Third parties such as
courts do not begin actions themselves, but act only in response to
individual formal requests for rulings or judgments. Yet even these

institutions can play a role in prevention of consumer problems. By making their records easily accessible to the public and organizing those records by type of case and name of defendant, courts can facilitate widespread public use of the data they generate as a by-product of their own endeavor of resolving individual cases. This use of information can help buyers avoid products or sellers that have caused other buyers difficulties.

Class Actions: A Unique Legal Procedure

The goals of complaint handling—directing compensation and identifying opportunities to prevent future injustices—will both be advanced by the accumulated pressure of instances of required fair treatment of individual complaints. This pressure may be created indirectly through record-keeping requirements or other developments that could allow citizens to observe individual sellers' complaint-handling practices. And both goals will also be served by increasing the activity and accessibility of third parties. For certain kinds of problems, however, an additional process is available. These are problems that affect large numbers of people in similar ways; in these situations, class action litigation may allow a single entity to bring a lawsuit that will lead to a ruling requiring the wrongdoer to make amends to all the consumers who have been injured. Class actions can also lead to judicial rulings that require changes in the future operations of businesses. One special aspect of class action procedures is that they can be initiated by single citizens; they do not require the participation (or control) of any third party. Thus, a single public-spirited citizen can accomplish significant preventive work to the general benefit of all consumers.

In class actions, a single individual is allowed to be the plaintiff in a lawsuit against a defendant who is alleged to have acted wrongly against a large group of people. This individual plaintiff represents *all* people who allegedly have been injured by the defendant. The unique aspect of class actions is that most of the people whose rights are determined in the lawsuit do not take any part in its management. Examples of problems handled in class actions include violations by banks of Truth in Lending Law requirements, systematic overcharges by taxi companies, and systematic overcharges by hotels for telephone calls made by guests.[3]

Where the class action plaintiff is successful, past victims receive some compensation, and future wrongdoing is prohibited. It is possible that the availability of this procedure could itself exercise some deterrent force, even if not many class action cases are litigated, as long as enough well publicized consumer victories occur to give business people an accurate perception that such lawsuits are effective.

Currently, a number of obstacles prevent class actions from being used to their fullest potential. Federal courts require the person who seeks to begin the lawsuit to contact all the individuals who can reasonably be identified as being within the class he or she seeks to represent, a potentially expensive process.[4] For lawsuits involving economic harm caused by violations of antitrust laws, state attorneys general are permitted to take the role of plaintiff,[5] but for the bulk of possible issue that could be treated through class actions, significant procedural difficulties remain.

In response to problems in establishing particular people's rights to be class action plaintiffs, and in determining appropriate methods to distribute money ordered to be paid by defendants, the U.S. Department of Justice has proposed legislation to encourage class actions. The proposal calls for defining two kinds of class actions, one involving injuries of not more than $500 each to at least forty people, and another involving larger injuries. For both kinds of class actions, simplified procedures would be employed, intended to cut down on windfall fees to attorneys and speed up the early procedural stages of the lawsuits. For what would be called "public penalty" suits, involving damages to each individual of $500 or less, the Department of Justice would be given an opportunity to take over the prosecution of the lawsuit, upon a finding that the individul who had started it could not handle it as well as the government could, or upon a finding that the government and the person who started the lawsuit should prosecute it together. Any judgment received from the defendant under this procedure would be paid to the Administration Office of the United States Courts, for distribution to its ultimate recipients.[6] The main impediment to current class actions—difficult requirements of notification of potential class members—would be eliminated in this proposal.

If the Department of Justice reforms or other changes aimed at the same corrective effect are adopted, class action litigation may develop into a significant source of preventive pressure.[7] At only a very small cost to the government, the class action procedure can empower individual consumers and consumer advocates to take actions so strong that businesses will ultimately seek to prevent potential class action liability.

Specialized Consumer Action Groups

The specialized consumer action groups, mentioned in connection with possible monitoring of sellers' records of complaint handling, could also serve the preventive function in other ways.[8] For example, these CAGs could act as plaintiffs in class action lawsuits. Their presence in the context of insurance sales, or automobile sales, for example, could be an effective counterbalance in a relationship that is ordinarily weighted drastically in favor of sellers.

Insurance, public utilities, home repairs, and automobiles are typical of enterprises in which massed buyer power could yield significant preventive results. These groups could be funded through procedures authorized by state statutes; sellers would be required to make their record-keeping and money-collecting systems available to the CAG for the purpose of solicitations of *voluntary* contributions.

Each consumer action group would address the full range of issues in its area of concern. At the same time, it would have discretion to determine those issues on which to concentrate at any given time. One of the major activities would be participation in administrative proceedings. These proceedings, which have a profound impact on the public, frequently have been dominated by representatives of industries and other powerful interests. The intervention of the CAG would counter their influence and make regulatory and administrative agencies more aware of consumer needs and concerns. Statutes could require that the appropriate public bodies notify the CAG of proceedings which affect the interests of the CAG constituency. The CAG could intervene in any such proceeding. CAGs would also be authorized to represent the interests of consumers before legislative bodies.

In addition, the CAGs would employ judicial means to redress grievances and pursue reforms. While a CAG would attempt to

redress grievances by informal means before resorting to litigation, its capacity to engage in litigation would give the consumer
movement more leverage in its dealings with industry and government. Not only would CAGs be authorized to intitiate or
otherwise participate in civil actions for the review of administrative decisions, but they would also be permitted to bring lawsuits
and furnish expert witness assistance on behalf of members where
such activity would promote the interests of their constituencies.
An example of allowable lawsuits would be actions against deceptive sales techniques in the insurance and automobile industries.

Many of the day-to-day activities of a CAG would consist of
studies, surveys, and investigations to gain the in-depth understanding of issues and problems which is a prerequisite to effective
consumer advocacy. Furthermore, CAGs would monitor private
entities and governmental bodies operating in their areas of
concern. They could identify problems at a relatively early stage
and attempt to resolve them by negotiations. The collection of
detailed information on industry abuses would enable the CAG to
provide these data to regulatory agencies and law enforcement
units and thereby assist them in carrying out their responsibilities.
Finally, monitoring would increase the visibility and accountability of public and private officials to the citizenry. Officials would tend to be more responsive to consumer needs, where
a public interest organization vigorously scrutinized their actions
and challenged them through judicial and other means.

Since the CAGs would serve particular constituencies, education
of their members in consumer issues would be an important and
vital function, closely related to prevention of victimization.
Activities such as information programs, consumer counseling,
and participation in initiative and referenda campaigns would
further this purpose. Informed consumers would be better able to
understand the problems they experienced and more inclined to
take appropriate measures when aggrieved. In addition, greater
public sophistication about consumer issues would promote broad-
based citizen participation in public interest movements.

Problems, Solutions, and their Interrelationships

In our analysis of consumer troubles, it is clear that what happens at each stage of the process—perceiving problems, voicing

complaints, and obtaining redress—affects each of the other stages. It can be predicted that improvements in the treatment of obstacles to success at any of the stages in the process will produce benefits throughout the complex buyer-seller relationship.

As more complaints are voiced, there will be more successful resolutions. Successful resolutions will increase the incentives for sellers and manufacturers to do their work better in first instances, to avoid the costs of repeat performances. And the total demand for corrective actions will create a sense that buying is a serious endeavor, treated carefully by both buyers and sellers, and that considerate treatment of complaints is an obligation of all who operate in the marketplace. The basic fairness of giving customers what they deserve, giving people their money's worth, is indisputable. The value of facilitating fair complaint treatment is incalculable. Services people pay for will be performed correctly. Products people buy will work or will be repaired or replaced. When manufacturers and retailers are really accountable for what they sell, customers may broaden that accountability to consider issues such as long-term costs, environmental impact, and possible lower cost substitutes for many purchases. In every aspect of participation in consumer complaint making, people will benefit from self-assertion and rights-consciousness. This benefit is fundamental to our democracy.

In an eighteenth-century lawsuit, a judge anticipated an objection that might be raised by some today, that encouraging complaining promotes too many remedies. He wrote: "And it is no objection to say, that it will occasion multiplicity of actions; for every man that is injured ought to have his recompense."[9] Reaching that goal has never been more important than it is now, given our lessening economic strength and our declining supplies of resources. It is true, too, that advances that can be made in various aspects of complaint handling all have the ability to reinforce each other—which makes reaching toward the goal reasonable and practical, as well as fundamentally necessary.

Appendix

CASE STUDY SELECTION

The disputes that were the subjects of the case studies were located with the assistance of the following recipients of consumer complaints (in each instance, the number of cases followed by our researchers is given in parentheses):

Better Business Bureau of Western New York (6)
Center for Study of Responsive Law (Ralph Nader) (29)
Consumer Action Movement, Cleveland (4)
Consumer Education and Protective Association, Philadelphia (2)
Consumer Federation of America (4)
Consumer Product Safety Commission (8)
Federal Trade Commission (7)
Food and Drug Administration (5)
Montgomery County, Maryland, Office of Consumer Affairs (7)
Pennsylvania Health Rights Advocate (3)
United States Postal Service (2)
Washington, D.C. Small Claims Court (13)
Washington Star Action Line (7)
WERE Call For Action, Cleveland, Ohio (6)
Wisconsin Attorney General (12)
WKYC TV Action 3, Cleveland, Ohio (6)
United States Office of Consumer Affairs (11)

Each of these recipients of complaints allowed our researchers to read large numbers of recent complaints, and to select cases for study according to criteria which sought to identify cases in which consumers evinced relatively high degrees of concern and activity. In reporting the cases for this study, the names of consumers have been changed, and the names of businesses and institutions have been revealed.

SURVEY METHODOLOGY

The Center for the Study of Responsive Law (CSRL) survey reported in chapter 6 used random telephone interviews of adult household members in thirty-four cities during February and March 1975. All interviews were conducted by volunteer staff members of Call For Action under the supervision of survey leaders trained at its national convention in January 1975. Call For Action is a national organization, with units in many metropolitan areas, which offers telephone assistance for a wide variety of urban problems. Each local group is associated with a local broadcasting station which provides publicity and pays the group's operating expenses.

Selection of cities for the survey was determined by the location of Call For Action units. All units were asked to participate and to collect as many interviews as staff resources would permit. Naturally, some groups were able to devote more resources to the project than others.

Telephone numbers of households were selected at random from the most recent editions of the white pages telephone directories of the participating cities. In multiple directory metropolitan areas, numbers were selected from each directory according to its proportion of the metropolitan area's total residential telephone number listings. Nonresidential listings were not included. In the largest cities, numbers from a table of random numbers were substituted for the last two digits of each number that was obtained from a directory, to increase the likelihood of reaching households with numbers that are unlisted by request of the household or because the household had moved after the printing of the directory. Up to eight attempts were made to reach each sampled number to increase the chance that an interview would be obtained. Interviews were completed with an adult household member in 80.3 percent of the households contacted. Overall, 2,419 interviews with adults were completed.

At each household contacted the interview was conducted with an adult who served as spokesperson for the entire household, reporting the experiences of all its members. An effort was made to compensate for the greater frequency with which women answered the telephone by asking to interview an adult male in the household and interviewing an adult female only if an adult male was not present or was not willing to be interviewed. This procedure yielded a sample that was 35.5 percent male and 64.5 percent female.

The distribution of interviews by cities is shown in table A1. As a group, the 2,419 households interviewed are closely representative of the Standard Metropolitan Statistical Areas (SMSAs) in which their cities are located; in turn, the population of these SMSAs is a reasonably valid

Table A.1   Distribution of Completed Interviews by City

Albany, N.Y.	14
Altoona	34
Baltimore	47
Birmingham, Ala.	19
Boston	208
Buffalo	48
Chicago	86
Cleveland	148
Denver	32
Durham	19
Little Rock	51
Los Angeles	20
Memphis	49
Miami, Fla.	29
Milwaukee	26
New Haven	34
New York	371
Oklahoma City	238
Omaha	22
Peoria	34
Philadelphia	208
Pittsburgh	50
Providence	46
Raleigh	22
Sacramento	229
San Diego	49
San Francisco	8
Seattle	47
Syracuse	48
Tacoma	40
Tucson	41
Utica	25
Wheeling	26
Youngstown	51
Total	2,419

representation of all the nation's urban consumers. In terms of race and employment, for example, our sample's demographic characteristics are quite close to those of the totality of SMSAs covered in the survey. And although more of the SMSAs are located in the east than would be desirable for perfect geographic balance, there is some evidence to suggest that geography is not of major importance to the subject of this study.

The U.S. Department of Agriculture study referred to in chapter 6 shows that variables such as type of community or geographic location have less effect on consumer reactions than do a number of other variables, such as education and income. The federal Office of Consumer Affairs survey, also referred to in chapter 6, shows that perception of problems is influenced only slightly by region or by urban versus rural residence, except that residents of the South Central states appear aberrant. This study found income to be the variable with the most pronounced effect on the decision to take action on complaints, although the data also show a somewhat higher rate of action for Northeastern households.

In order to test for possible biases introduced by the selection of cities, we examined whether there was substantial stability in the critical variables of our analysis. As the data in table A2 indicate, the results for the key variables, such as number of purchases per household, interest in consumer issues, problem rates, or voicing rates, are generally quite stable.

Twenty-six products and eight services were chosen for investigation in

Table A.2   Differences in Mean Response to Questions by City

	Number of Interviews	Mean Items Purchased	Consumer Interest[a]	Political Efficacy[b]	Mean Problem Rate	Mean Voicing Rate	Mean Satisfaction Rate
		%	%	%	%	%	%
Small cities[c]	326	11.9	3.3	2.3	17.3	36.7	68.2
Oklahoma City	238	10.6	2.9	2.2	18.3	34.9	58.9
Sacramento	229	11.9	3.3	2.1	19.1	41.5	61.2
Other medium cities[d]	249	11.7	3.4	2.3	16.5	55.6	61.8
Cleveland	148	11.9	3.7	2.4	23.1	40.7	66.6
Other large cities[e]	328	12.7	3.3	2.4	18.5	41.2	61.6
Boston	208	13.0	3.7	2.1	21.3	41.2	67.4
New York City	371	11.0	3.6	2.4	21.9	40.6	55.3
Philadelphia	208	11.3	3.3	2.4	16.6	49.1	63.8
Other very large cities[f]	114	12.9	3.5	2.5	18.4	40.1	45.5

[a] Consumer interest measure is the number of "yes" answers to question 1.
[b] Political efficacy is number of "yes" answers to questions 5a through 5d.
[c] Under 150,000 households in SMSA.
[d] 150,000 to 299,000 households in SMSA.
[e] 300,000 to 799,000 households in SMSA.
[f] 800,000 or more households in SMSA.

Table A.3   Purchase Categories Surveyed

Car (new or used)
Tires
TV set
Tape recorder/stereo equipment
Radio
Air conditioner

Vacuum cleaner
Washer/dryer
Furniture
Lamps
Carpeting/floor covering
Blankets/sheets

Pots/pans/cooking utensils
Tools
Calculator
Camera
Wristwatch/jewelry
Bicycle

Toys
Books/records
Clothing
Eyeglasses
Hearing aid/dentures
Cosmetics/toiletries

Grocery store items
Mail order items not already mentioned
Car repairs
Home repairs
Appliance repairs
Medical/dental care

Legal services
Loans/credit cards/charge accounts
Film developing
Car parking

this study. Table A3 lists those items. They were selected from the schedule used by the Bureau of Labor Statistics of the United States Department of Labor in its Consumer Price Index (CPI) survey. The CPI divides consumption into five categories—food, apparel and upkeep, transportation, housing, health and recreation—all of which are represented in this study's purchase categories.

In addition to questions about their purchasing experiences, respondents were asked about their attitudes toward complaining, as well as about their socioeconomic characteristics. The questionnaire is set out below.

QUESTIONNAIRE

Hello, I'm (name). I'm a volunteer with (station) Call For Action, and we are conducting a survey to help consumers. Your phone number was selected at random. (If speaking to a woman:) I have just talked to several women. To help round out the survey, is there a man available I could speak to? (If no:) Let's continue. We would very much appreciate your help. (If speaking to a man:) We would very much appreciate your help.

1. I'm going to read some topics to you. Please tell me if they have been discussed in your home: a) Cost of electricity; b) Quality of car servicing; c) Ingredient labels on foods; d) Shopping for bargains; e) Consumer protection laws.

2a. Did you or anyone in your household buy (name of item) in the last year or so? (If yes, ask 2b. and 2c.)

2b. Was it paid for in cash or within about a month, or with longer payments?

2c. Was it satisfactory, somewhat satisfactory, somewhat unsatisfactory, or unsatisfactory?

2d. (If satisfactory or somewhat satisfactory:) How could it have been better for your household? (If somewhat unsatisfactory or unsatisfactory:) What was the problem?

2e. (If could have been better or if there was any problem:) Did anyone in your household do anything about it? (If yes, ask 2f and 2g.)

2f. What was done?

2g. What was the result?

3. Can you think of any other products or services you or the other members of your household have used in the past year or so that have not been satisfactory? (Write in the first and second items named. Ask questions 2b through 2g about each item.)

4a. Do you think you and your household have more, less, or about the same number of problems with products and services as other households have?

4b. Do you think you and your household make more, less, or about the same number of complaints about products and services as other households do?

Now I'd like to read some of the kinds of things people have said in interviews, and ask you whether you agree or disagree. I'll read them one at a time—please tell me whether you agree or disagree.

5a. "People like me don't have much say about what the government does."
5b. "Voting is the only way that people like me can have any say about how the government runs things."
5c. "Sometimes politics and government seem so complicated that a person can't really understand what's going on."
5d. "I don't think public officials care much what people like me think."

Finally, I'd like to ask you some questions about your background.
6. In what year were you born?
7a. Including yourself, how many people live in your household?
7b. How many are 17 years old or younger?
7c. How many are 5 years old or younger?
8. Are you now married, widowed, divorced, separated, or have your never been married?
9. In what religion were you brought up?
10a. Are you the head of the household?
10b. What is the highest grade of school you (the head of the household) completed?
10c. Are you (Is the head of the household) currently employed, unemployed, retired, a student, a housewife, or what?
10d. What kind of work do you (does the head of the household) do?
10e. What is the job title?
10f. In what kind of business or industry is that?
11. How many years have you lived at your current house or apartment?
12. In politics, as of today, do you consider yourself a Republican, and Democrat, or Independent?
13. In politics, would you say that you are a radical, a liberal, a conservative, a strong conservative, or would you call yourself middle of the road?
14. What is your race—black, white, or something else?
15. Was your family income last year above or below $15,000? (If above, ask:) Was it above or below $25,000? (If below, ask:) Was it above or below $8,000?
16. Subject's sex? (Not read to respondent).
Thank you very much for helping in this survey.

Notes

1. THE UNIVERSE OF CONSUMER TROUBLES

   1. *Washington Post*, Aug. 9, 1977, p. A-10.

   2. Edward M. Swartz, *Toys That Don't Care* (Ipswich: Gambit, 1971), 44–48.

   3. Center for Auto Safety, *Mobile Homes: The Low-cost Housing Hoax* (Washington: Center for Auto Safety, 1975), p. 95.

   4. Philip Boffey, "Death of A Dye," *New York Times Magazine*, Feb. 29, 1976, p. 9.

   5. *New York Times*, Sept. 4, 1977, sec. IV, p. 1.

   6. *Ibid.*, Dec. 29, 1978, p. A-10.

   7. "The Brand-New (Imperfect) Car," *Consumer Reports*, April 1976, p. 196.

   8. U.S. House, Staff of House Subcommittee on Oversight and Investigations of the Committee on Interstate and Foreign Commerce, *Cost and Quality of Health Care: Unnecessary Surgery*, 94th Cong., 2d sess. (1976), p. 30.

   9. See, for example, Mark J. Green et al., *The Closed Enterprise System* (New York: Grossman, 1972).

   10. U.S. Senate, *Regulatory Reform—1975: Hearings Before Committee on Government Operations of the U.S. Senate*, 94th Cong., 1st sess., (1975), pp. 19–23. (Statement of Ralph Nader)

   11. *New York Times*, Feb. 8, 1977, p. B-4.

   12. Arthur Best and Bernard L. Brown, "Governmental Facilitation of Consumerism: A Proposal for Consumer Action Groups," *Temple Law Quarterly* (1977), 50:253, 255–56. See also *New York Times*, Feb. 3, 1979, p. 26.

   13. Julian L. Simon, *Problems in the Economics of Advertising* (Urbana: University of Illinois Press, 1970).

   14. *Warner-Lambert Co. v. Federal Trade Commission*, 562 F.2d 749 (D.C. Cir. 1977).

   15. Upton Sinclair, *The Jungle* (New York: Doubleday, 1906). See Daniel J. Boorstin, *The Americans: The Democratic Experience* (New York: Random House, 1973), p. 632, for a report that "Sinclair later complained that while he had hoped to strike Americans in their hearts, he had only succeeded in hitting them in their stomachs."

   16. Wesley Mitchell, "The Backward Art of Spending Money," *American Economic Review* (1912), 2:269.

17. Stuart Chase and F. J. Schlink, *Your Money's Worth* (New York: Macmillan, 1927); Arthur Kallet and F. J. Schlink, *100,000,000 Guinea Pigs* (New York: Vanguard, 1933); A. Dameron, "The Consumer Movement," *Harvard Business Review* (1939), 17:271.

18. See, for example, U.S. Senate, *Consumer Controversies Resolution Act: Report of the Senate Committee on Commerce on S. 2069 to Regulate Commerce by Establishing National Goals for the Effective, Fair, Inexpensive and Expeditious Resolution of Controversies Involving Consumers, and for Other Purposes*, 94th Cong., 2d sess. (1976).

19. Although proposals for such agencies which were passed by the House and the Senate stressed the agency's use of complaints as a source of information (see, for example, U.S. Senate, *To Establish an Independent Consumer Agency: Hearings before the Committee on Government Operations on S. 200*, 94th Cong., 1st sess. (1975), pp. 24–26), other complaint-handling functions for that Agency were proposed. For example, President Carter referred to the proposed agency in a March 5, 1977, broadcast of conversations with citizens from various parts of the country, saying that "it would let you and I know where to go to register a complaint. . . ." (*New York Times*, March 6, 1977, p. 32).

20. Paul Brodeur, *The Zapping of America* (New York: Norton, 1977).

21. *New York Times*, Aug. 12, 1975, p. 23.

2. PERCEIVING PROBLEMS

1. *Oddo v. General Motors Corp.*, 46 L.W. 2248 (1977). Other similar cases are: *Overland Bond and Investment Corp. v. Howard*, 292 N.E. 2d 168 (Ill. App. 1972); *Jorgenson v. Pressnall*, 545 P.2d 1382 (Ore. Sup. Ct. 1976); and *Tiger Motor Co. v. McMurtry*, 224 So. 2d 638 (Ala. Sup. Ct. 1969). See also W. Clark, "Lemon Aid for Kansas Consumers," *Journal of the Kansas Bar Association* (1977), 46:143.

2. *New York Times*, Jan. 14, 1978, p. 27; *In the Matter of Ford Motor Company*, FTC Docket No. 9105, Jan. 13, 1978; *Advertising Age*, Feb. 25, 1980, p. 2.

3. See, for example, David Caplovitz, *The Poor Pay More* (New York: Free Press, 1963); Jerome Carlin, Jan Howard, and Sheldon L. Messinger, *Civil Justice and the Poor* (New York: Russell Sage Foundation, 1967).

4. David I. Greenberg, "Easy Terms, Hard Times," in Laura Nader, *No Access to Law* (New York: Academic Press, 1980).

5. *Ibid.*

6. Carlin et al., *Civil Justice*, p. 61, 63.

7. *Ibid.*, p. 67.

8. Tibor Scitovsky, *The Joyless Economy* (New York: Oxford University Press, 1976), p. 176.

9. See Austin Sarat, "Studying American Legal Culture: An Assessment of Survey Evidence," *Law & Society Review* (1977), 11:427.

10. Stan Albrecht, "Cognitive Barriers to Equal Justice Before the Law," unpublished, described in Sarat, "Studying American Legal Culture," p. 478.

11. "Legal Knowledge of Michigan Citizens," Michigan Law Review (1973), 71:146.

3. VOICING COMPLAINTS

1. TARP, *A National Survey of Complaint Handling Procedures Used by Consumers* (Washington, D.C.: United States Office of Consumer Affairs, 1976), p. 38.

2. David Caplovitz, *Consumers in Trouble* (New York: Free Press, 1974), pp. 280–83.

3. *New York Times*, Feb. 27, 1976, p. 35.

4. Earl Lomon Koos, *Families in Trouble* (New York: King's Crown Press, 1946).

5. David Caplovitz, *The Poor Pay More* (New York: Free Press, 1963).

6. Eric H. Steele, "Fraud, Dispute, and the Consumer: Responding to Consumer Complaints," *University of Pennsylvania Law Review* (1975), 123: 1107, 1118–19.

7. *Ibid.*, pp. 1183–84.

8. Better Business Bureau Form CBBB R-106, on file at Center for Study of Responsive Law, Washington, D.C.

9. Barbara A. Curran and Francis O. Spaulding, *The Legal Needs of the Public* (Chicago: American Bar Foundation, 1974), ch. 6.

10. Earl Johnson, Jr., Introductory Address, "Proceedings of the Harvard Conference on Law and Poverty," May 17–19, 1967.

11. Barlow F. Christensen. *Lawyers for People of Moderate Means: Some Problems of Availability of Legal Services* (Chicago: American Bar Foundation, 1970), p. 25.

12. Linda R. Singer, "Nonjudicial Dispute Resolution Mechanisms: The Effects on Justice for the Poor," *Clearinghouse Review* (1979), 13:569, 573.

13. See, for example, Albert O. Hirschman, *Exit, Voice and Loyalty: Responses to Decline in Firms, Organizations and States* (Cambridge: Harvard University Press, 1970), p. 260.

14. See Marc Galanter, "Why the Haves Come Out Ahead: Speculations on the Limits of Social Change," *Law & Society Review* (1974), 9:95.

15. Carol Soskis, "Report on the First Six Months of the Demonstration Complaint Service of the Southeastern Region Department of Health" (Commonwealth of Pennsylvania, 1975), p. 29. Mimeo on file at Center for Study of Responsive Law, Washington, D.C.

16. N.Y.U. Consumer Help *Newsletter* (Summer 1976), p. 4.

17. *Wall Street Journal*, Jan. 27, 1978, p. 1.

18. Better Business Bureau, *Consumer's Buying Guide* (New York: Award Books, 1969), p. 10.

19. Ralph Charell, *How I Turn Ordinary Complaints Into Thousands of Dollars* (New York: Stein & Day, 1973); interview with Charles Kraft, New York State Public Service Commission, Sept. 25, 1974.

20. Joseph Rosenbloom, *Consumer Complaint Guide* (New York: CCM Information Corporation, 1971).

21. John Dorfman, *A Consumer's Arsenal* (New York: Praeger, 1976).

22. John M. Striker and Andrew O. Shapiro, *Super Threats* (New York: Holt, Rinehart & Winston, 1977).

23. Douglas Matthews, *Sue the Bastards: The Victim's Handbook* (New York: Arbor House, 1973).

24. State of California Department of Consumer Affairs, *The Compleat California Consumer Guide* (Sacramento, 1976), p. ii.

4. HOW BUSINESS SAYS NO

1. Example from the complaint project staff member's personal experience.

2. *II. Hearings before National Commission on Product Safety* (Washington: Commerce Clearing House, 1968), p. 509.

3. This section and parts of other sections in this chapter draw upon a detailed analysis of business responses to groups of complaints that was carried out by Joyce Munns.

5. SHORTCOMINGS OF THIRD-PARTY COMPLAINT HANDLERS

1. This power analysis is based on Eric H. Steele, "Fraud, Dispute, and the Consumer: Responding to Consumer Complaints," *University of Pennsylvania Law Review* (1975), 123:1107, 1115. See also Frank E. A. Sander, "Varieties of Dispute Processing," *Federal Rules Decisions* (1976), 70:111, 114.

2. National Institute for Consumer Justice, "Staff Studies on Business Sponsored Mechanisms for Redress and Arbitration," p. 74. Mimeo on file at Center for Study of Responsive Law, Washington, D.C.

3. Benjamin Rosenthal, "Report on the Better Business Bureau," Mimeo on file at Center for Study of Responsive Law, Washington, D.C.

4. *Wall Street Journal*, Aug. 5, 1976, p. 1.

5. See Philip G. Schrag, *Counsel for the Deceived* (New York: Pantheon, 1972).

6. *New York Times*, July 12, 1977, p. 31.

7. *Ibid.*

8. American Bar Association Commission to Study the Federal Trade Commission, *Report of the ABA Commission to Study the Federal Trade Commission* (Chicago, 1969).

9. U.S. House of Representatives, Staff of House Committee on Banking, Currency, and Housing, *Do Financial Agencies Listen to Consumers? Staff Report of the Committee on Banking, Currency and Housing*, House of Representatives, 94th Cong., 2d sess. (1976), pp. 1–2.

10. Commonwealth of Massachusetts, Department of the Attorney General, *Consumer Protection Division Fiscal 1976 Report* (Boston: Commonwealth of Massachusetts, 1976), pp. 11–12.

11. U.S. Senate, Committee on Governmental Affairs, *Study on Federal Regulation*; vol. 3, *Public Participation in Regulatory Agency Proceedings*, 95th Cong., 1st sess. (1977), p. 90.

12. John H. Kazanjian, "Consumer Protection by State Attorneys General: A Time for Renewal," *Notre Dame Lawyer* (1973), 49:410.

13. U.S. House of Representatives, Committee on Banking, Currency and

Housing, *Do Financial Agencies Listen to Consumers?* 94th Cong., 2d sess., 1976.

14. TARP, *Consumer Complaint Handling in America: Summary of Findings and Recommendations*, (Washington, D.C.: Office of Consumer Affairs, 1978), pp. 60–84.

15. Eric H. Steele, "Fraud, Dispute, and the Consumer: Responding to Consumer Complaints," *University of Pennsylvania Law Review* (1975), 123:1150–55.

16. Albert O. Hirschman, *Exit, Voice and Loyalty: Responses to Decline in Firms, Organizations and States* (Cambridge: Harvard University Press, 1970).

6. SURVEYING CONSUMER TROUBLES AND OBSTACLES TO REDRESS

1. *Advertising Age*, Oct. 15, 1979, p. 20; Opinion Research Corporation, *Consumerism—A Special Report* (Princeton: Opinion Research Corporation, 1973), p. 8. This question does not ask about flaws or errors, but uses the strong words "cheated or deceived." An extreme question such as this, particularly since an affirmative answer may suggest to some that they are admitting a weakness, can be expected to produce a conservative estimate of the variable under consideration. See Steven L. Diamond, Scott Ward, and Ronald Faber; "Consumer Problems and Consumerism: Analysis of Calls to a Consumer Hot Line" (Dec. 1974). Unpublished paper on file at Marketing Science Institute and Center for Study of Responsive Law, Washington, D.C.

2. Letter from Ned Smith, Ford Motor Company, on file at Center for Study of Responsive Law, Washington, D.C.

3. Raymond C. Stokes, "Consumer Complaints and Consumer Dissatisfaction (Washington, D.C.: R. C. Stokes Associates, 1974), p. 11. Quoted in Charles R. Handy and Martin Pfaff, *Consumer Satisfaction with Food Products and Marketing Services* (Washington, D.C.: U.S. Department of Agriculture, Economic Research Service, 1975), p. 1.

4. TARP, *A National Survey of Complaint Handling Procedures Used by Consumers* (Washington, D.C.: Office of Consumer Affairs, 1976).

5. This calculation is based on usage rates for all third parties, as shown in the CSRL survey reported in this chapter.

6. "Legal Services and the Public," *Alternatives* (1976), 3:5.

7. Handy and Pfaff, *Consumer Satisfaction*.

8. Results of the CSRL survey have been published as a working paper, "Talking Back to Business," Arthur Best and Alan R. Andreasen (Washington, D.C.: Center for Study of Responsive Law, 1976) and in two articles: Best and Andreasen, "Consumer Response to Unsatisfactory Purchases: A Survey of Perceiving Defects, Voicing Complaints, and Obtaining Redress," *Law & Society Review* (1977), 11:701; Andreasen and Best, "Consumers Complain—Does Business Respond?" *Harvard Business Review* (1977),55(4):93. This chapter is largely an adaptation of the *Law & Society Review* article.

9. U.S. Department of Labor, Bureau of Labor Statistics, *Consumer Expenditure Survey Series: Interview Survey, 1972 and 1973*, Report 455-2 (1976), p. 4.

10. *Ibid.*

11. *Ibid.*, p. 5.

12. Occupational prestige was quantified with the 1960 Hodge-Siegel-Rossi prestige scores, as modified by the National Opinion Research Center, "National Data Program for the Social Sciences: Codebook for the Spring 1972 General Social Survey, 1972. Mimeo on file at Center for Study of Responsive Law, Washington, D.C.

13. Studies have examined only one product type or one or more serious complaints across various purchase categories. See J. P. Liefeld, H. C. Edgecombe, and Linda Wolfe, "Demographic Characteristics of Canadian Consumer Complainers," *Journal of Consumer Affairs* (1975), 9:73; Rex H. Warland, Robert O. Herrmann, and Jane Willits, "Dissatisfied Consumers: Who Gets Upset and Who Takes Action," *Journal of Consumer Affairs* (1975), 9:148; Handy and Pfaff, *Consumer Satisfaction.*

14. See Albert O. Hirschman, *Exit, Voice and Loyalty: Responses to Decline in Firms, Organizations, and States* (Cambridge: Harvard University Press, 1970).

15. The case studies themselves are not relied upon for exact projections of quantitative relationships in the complaint process. On this point, the following analysis by Earl Lomon Koos, in *Familes in Trouble* (New York: King's Crown Press, 1946), p. 2. is pertinent: "As Margaret Mead has pointed out, the social scientist often finds it necessary 'to illuminate rather than to demonstrate' a thesis. Demonstration requires generalization, and assured generalizations are impossible in a small number of cases possessing a large number of variables and sub-variables. Furthermore, since it is impossible to control the variables affecting family life as the physical scientist controls the conditions of his experiments, we are often unable to do more than illuminate our thesis."

16. See Marc Galanter, "Why the Haves Come Out Ahead: Speculation on the Limits of Legal Change," *Law & Society Review* (1974), 9:95.

7. CONSUMER INITIATIVES FOR IMPROVING TREATMENT OF COMPLAINTS: AT THE BUYER-SELLER STAGE AND BEYOND

1. Consumer Law Training Center, "The Consumer Law Training Center," 1975. Mimeo on file at Center for Study of Responsive Law, Washington, D.C.

2. *Wall Street Journal*, Feb. 10, 1978, p. 32.

3. Interview with Christine A. Bjorklund, Consumer Fraud Division, San Francisco Office of the District Attorney, May 26, 1977.

4. See U.S. Senate, *To Establish an Independent Consumer Agency: Hearings on S. 200 Before the Committee on Government Operations*, United States Senate, 94th Cong., 1st sess. (1975), p. 6. Statement of Senator Abraham Ribicoff.

5. See H. R. Lurie, "Consumer Complaints: A Proposed Federal Trade Commission Rule," *University of Michigan Journal of Law Reform* (1972), 5:426.

6. Such groups are proposed in Robert B. Leflar and Martin H. Rogol, "Consumer Participation in the Regulation of Publc Utilities: A Model Act," *Harvard Journal on Legislation* (1976), 13:235; and Arthur Best and Bernard L.

Brown, "Governmental Facilitation of Consumerism; A Proposal for Consumer Action Groups," *Temple Law Quarterly* (1977), 50:253.

7. See Best and Brown, "Governmental Facilitation of Consumerism."

8. *Federal Trade Commission v. Sperry & Hutchinson Co.*, 405 U.S. 233 (1972).

9. White collar criminals and business organizations have social positions that militate against such prosecutions. See Donald Black, *The Behavior of Law* (New York; Academic Press: 1976), p. 97.

8. MEDIATION

1. Whirlpool, Westinghouse, Ford, and Chrysler are among companies that have promoted complaint-handling techniques. Earl Johnson, Jr., Valerie Kantor, and Elizabeth Schwartz, *Outside the Courts* (Denver: National Center for State Courts, 1977), p. 66. General Motors, as well as Ford and Chrysler, is experimenting with new dispute settlement procedures. *Advertising Age*, March 12, 1979, p. 87.

2. New York City Department of Consumer Affairs, "Complaint Handling Study," Mimeo on file at Center for Study of Responsive Law, Washington, D.C.

3. *New York Times*, March 29, 1976, p. 31. Data for 1979 based on author's observations.

4. *Editor & Publisher*, Sept. 2, 1978, pp. 22–23 (for statistics).

5. Linda R. Singer, "Nonjudicial Dispute Resolution Systems: The Effects on Justice for the Poor," *Clearinghouse Review* (1979), 13:569, 579.

6. John H. Kazanjian, "Consumer Protection by State Attorneys General: A Time for Renewal," *Notre Dame Lawyer* (1973), 49:410, n. 84.

9. ARBITRATION

1. Earl Johnson, Jr., Valerie Kantor, and Elizabeth Schwartz, *Outside the Courts* (Denver: National Center for State Courts, 1977), p. 39.

2. National Institute for Consumer Justice, "Staff Studies on (1) Business-Sponsored Mechanisms for Redress; (2) Arbitration." 1972; pp. 89–90 (cited hereafter as NICJ Arbitration). Mimeo on file at Center for Study of Responsive Law, Washington, D.C.

3. Telephone interview with Michael Feit, former administrator of Albany pilot project, Aug. 8, 1976.

4. Telephone interview with Dean Determan, Council of Better Business Bureaus, Aug. 5, 1976.

5. *BNA Consumerism—New Developments for Business* (1977), 5:164.

6. *Ibid.*

7. John J. McGonagle, Jr., "Developments in Consumer Arbitration," *The Brief* (Winter 1974–75, pp. 82, 86–87.

8. NICJ Arbitration, p. 72.

9. Austin Sarat, "Alternatives in Dispute Processing," *Law & Society Review* (1975), 10:339.

10. Dean W. Determan, "The Arbitration of Small Claims," *Forum* (1975), 10:831, 836.

11. See "Does Consumer Arbitration Really Work?" *Changing Times* (1973), 27:19, 20.

12. Jean Carper, "You Can Get Your Money Back," *Readers Digest* (May 1976), pp. 106, 108.

13. *Ibid.*, p. 109.

14. Determan, "Arbitration," p. 836.

15. E. Johnson et al., *Outside the Courts*, p. 43.

16. Determan, "Arbitration," p. 839.

17. E. Johnson et al., *Outside the Courts*, p. 40.

18. The Los Angeles office was unable to furnish a reason for the termination of the requirement. Telephone interview with Ms. McNicholas, Consumer Arbitration Program of Los Angeles Better Business Bureau, Aug. 5, 1976.

19. Determan, "Arbitration," pp. 837, 839.

20. See Determan, "Arbitration," p. 837.

10. COURTS FOR CONSUMER CASES

1. See, for example, Roscoe Pound, *The Causes of Popular Dissatisfaction with the Administration of Justice* (1906; reprinted in *Federal Rules Decisions* (1964), 35:273; Edgar S. Cahn and Jean Camper Cahn, "What Price Justice? The Civilian Perspective Revisited," *Notre Dame Lawyer* (1966), 41:920, 950.

2. Barbara Yngvesson and Patricia Hennessey, "Small Claims, Complex Disputes: A Review of the Small Claims Literature," *Law & Society Review* (1975), 9:219, 221–23.

3. U.S. Senate, *Adequacy of Consumer Redress Mechanisms: Joint Hearings before the Subcommittee on Consumers of the Senate Committee on Commerce and the Subcommittee on the Representation of Citizens' Interest of the Senate Committee on the Judiciary*, 93d Cong., 1st sess. (1973), p. 5 (hereafter cited as *Adequacy of Consumer Redress Mechanisms*).

4. Interview with Jeffrey H. Joseph, Director, Government and Consumer Affairs, Chamber of Commerce of the United States, May 26, 1977.

5. U.S. Senate, *Consumer Controversies: Hearings on S. 2928 before the Subcommittee on Consumers of the Senate Committee on Commerce and the Subcommittee on Representation of Citizen Interests of the Senate Committee on the Judiciary*, 93d Cong., 2d sess. (1974) pp. 211–25.

6. Robert Beresford and A. Cooper, "A Neighborhood Court for Neighborhood Suits," *Judicature* (1977), 61:185.

7. Yngvesson and Hennessey, "Small Claims," p. 254.

8. Reginald Heber Smith, *Justice and the Poor*, (New York: Russell Sage Foundation, 1919).

9. Yngvesson and Hennessey, "Small Claims," p. 224.

10. *Ibid.*

11. National Institute for Consumer Justice, "Staff Studies on Small Claims Courts," 1972, p. 6 (cited hereafter as NICJ Small Claims Studies). Mimeo on file at Center for Study of Responsive Law, Washington, D.C.

12. *Ibid.*

13. *Consumer Reports*, Oct. 1971, pp. 629–31.

14. Douglas Matthews, *Sue the Bastards: A Victim's Handbook* (New York: Arbor House, 1973).

15. John C. Runhka, *Housing Justice in Small Claims Courts* (Williamsburg: National Center for State Courts, 1979).

16. Jeffrey H. Joseph and Barry A. Friedman, "Consumer Redress Through the Small Claims Court: A Proposed Model Consumer Justice Act," *Boston College Industrial and Commercial Law Review* (1977), 18:839, 841.

17. Senate Report No. 1164, 93d Cong., 2d sess. (1974), p. 4. The Senate Commerce Committee used this estimate in 1977. U.S. Senate, *Consumer Controversies Resolution Act: Hearing on S. 957 Before the Subcommittee for Consumers of the Senate Committee on Commerce, Science, and Transportation*, 95th Cong., 1st sess. (1977), p. 1.

18. *Adequacy of Consumer Redress Mechanisms*, pp. 26–27 (statement of John H. Weiss, Project Director, Small Claims Study Group).

19. Yngvesson and Hennessey, "Small Claims," p. 227.

20. *Ibid.*, p. 237.

21. "Comment," *Pepperdine Law Review* (1973), 1:71, 87.

22. Stephen Weller, John C. Ruhnka, and A. Martin, "Success in Small Claims: Is a Lawyer Really Necessary?" *Judicature* (1977), 61:176, 181.

23. John Montague Steadman and Richard S. Rosenstein, "Small Claims' Consumer Plaintiffs in the Philadelphia Municipal Court: An Empirical Study," *University of Pennsylvania Law Review* (1973), 121:1308, 1330–31.

24. Yngvesson and Hennessey, "Small Claims," p. 264.

25. Volunteers for this work came from a University of Pennsylvania undergraduate organization, the Pennsylvania Consumers Board.

26. E. g., N.Y. City Civil Court Act §1809 (McKinney Supp. 1977).

27. Weller et al., "Success in Small Claims," p. 178, n. 12.

28. Yngvesson and Hennessey, "Small Claims," pp. 243–46.

29. NICJ Small Claims Studies, pp. 140–45.

30. See David Caplovitz, *Consumers in Trouble* (New York: Free Press, 1974), pp. 134, 200.

31. *Consumer Reports*, October 1971, p. 628.

32. Yngvesson and Hennessey, "Small Claims," p. 243; "Comment," *Pepperdine Law Review* (1973), 1:85.

33. Robert Hollingsworth, William B. Feldman, and David C. Clark, "The Ohio Small Claims Court: An Empirical Study," *University of Cincinnati Law Review* (1973), 42:469, 513, where the authors report no judgments for defendants in 100 cases in Clermont county.

34. Special Committee on Consumer Protection, Community Service Society of New York, "Large Grievances About Small Claims" (New York, 1972), pp. 7–8 (hereafter cited as CSS, "Large Grievances").

35. Hollingsworth et al., "The Ohio Small Claims Court," p. 489.

36. NICJ Small Claims Studies, p. 134.

37. Yngvesson and Hennessey, "Small Claims," p. 222.

38. Weller et al., "Success in Small Claims," p. 178, n. 11.

39. Yngvesson and Hennessey, "Small Claims," pp. 250–51.

40. Weller et al., "Success in Small Claims," p. 182.

41. "The Persecution and Intimidation of the Low-Income Litigant as Performed by the Small Claims Courts in California," *Stanford Law Review* (1969), 21:1657, 1664.

42. *Adequacy of Consumer Redress Mechanisms.* pp. 30–31; CSS, "Large Grievances," p. 9.

43. CSS, "Large Grievances," pp. 17–23.

44. Yngvesson and Hennessey, "Small Claims," p. 265.

45. Beresford, "A Neighborhood Court."

46. Letter of Richard S. Friedman, Court Administrator, Toledo Municipal Court, reprinted in *Judicature* (1977), 61:1530.

47. Jack B. Weinstein and B. Zimmerman, "Let the People Observe Their Courts," *Judicature* (1977), 61:156, 157.

48. Beresford and Cooper, "A Neighborhood Court," p. 188.

49. N.Y. City Civil Court Act §1812 (McKinney Supp. 1977).

50. N.Y. City Civil Court Act §1811 (McKinney Supp. 1977).

51. Ohio Rev. Code Ann. §4509.31, et seq.

52. Maurice Rosenberg, "Devising Procedures that are Civil to Promote Justice that is Civilized," *Michigan Law Review* (1971), 69:797.

53. Frye, "NEISS: Medical Records as an Important Contribution to Consumer Product Safety," *Medical Record News* (April 1975), p. 23.

54. *National Law Journal*, Feb. 25, 1980, p. 8.

11. LOWER COST LEGAL SERVICE

1. Roscoe Pound, *The Causes of Popular Dissatisfaction with the Administration of Justice*, reprinted in *Federal Rules Decisions* (1964), 35:273, 290.

2. Barbara A. Curran, *The Legal Needs of the Public, Final Report* (Chicago: American Bar Foundation, 1977), pp. 159–62.

3. Quoted in Charles Leviton, "Automobile Club Activites: The Problem from the Standpoint of the Bar," *Law and Contemporary Problems* (1938), 5:11, 13.

4. *NAACP v. Button*, 371 U.S. 415 (1963); *Brotherhood of Ry. Trainmen v. Virginia ex. rel. Virginia State Bar*, 377 U.S. 1 (1964); *United Mine Workers v. Illinois State Bar Association*, 389 U.S. 217 (1967); *United Transportation Workers v. State Bar of Michigan*, 401 U.S. 576 (1971).

5. *United Transportation Workers v. State Bar of Michigan* 401 U.S. 576, 585–86 (1971).

6. Interview with Charles Baron, Resource Center for Consumers of Legal Services, January 8, 1976. See Employee Retirement Income Security Act of 1974, 29 U.S.C. 1001, §514(b) (2) (B).

7. S. Tischer, L. Bernabei, and M. Green, "Bringing the Bar to Justice," 1977, pp. 40–41. Mimeo on file at Center for Study of Responsive Law, Washington, D.C.

8. *Ibid.*

9. Barlow F. Christensen, *Lawyers For People of Moderate Means: Some Problems of the Availability of Legal Services* (Chicago: American Bar Foundation 1970), p. 340.

10. Interview with Charles Baron, note 6 above.

11. Lester Brickman, "Of Arterial Passageways Through the Legal Process: The Right of Universal Access to Courts and Lawyering Services." *New York University Law Review* (1973), 48:595.

12. U.S., Senate, *Prepaid Legal Services Plans: Hearings before the Subcommittee on Representation of Citizen Interests of the Committee on the Judiciary U.S. Senate*, 93d Cong., 2d sess. (1974), pp. 236a–236c.

13. Richard Scupi, "Legal Services Plan, Laborer's District 37, Council of Washington D.C. & Vicinity: A Progress Report After One Year of Operation, June 1, 1973–May 31, 1974," 1974, pp. 8–10. Mimeo on file at Center for Study of Responsive Law, Washington, D.C.

14. Interview with Charles Baron, note 6 above.

15. Tisher et al., "Bringing the Bar to Justice," pp. 46–47.

16. Interview with Lisa Schwartz, Resource Center for Legal Services, January 8, 1976.

17. "Student Legal Services of Indiana University, Third Annual Report," 1974, p. 9. Mimeo on file at Center for Study of Responsive Law, Washington, D.C.

18. Interview with Lisa Schwartz, note 16, above.

19. American Bar Association Special Committee on Prepaid Legal Services, *A Primer of Prepaid Legal Services* (Chicago: American Bar Association, 1976) pp. 19–20.

20. Preble Stolz, "Insurance for Legal Services: A Preliminary Study of Feasibility," *University of Chicago Law Review* (1968), 35:417, 422.

21. *Bates v. State Bar of Arizona*, 97 S. Ct. 2691 (1977).

22. Bureau of National Affairs, *Antitrust & Trade Regulation Report* (1978), no. 845, p. D-2.

23. *Advertising Age*, Nov. 12, 1979, p. 109.

24. *National Law Journal*, March 24, 1980, p. 2.

25. *New York Times*, Aug. 3, 1977, p. A.9.

26. Tisher et al., *Bringing the Bar to Justice*, n. 9, p. 45.

12. PRODUCT AND SERVICE RELIABILITY: A GOAL FOR CONSUMER PROTECTION

1. Robert S. Lynd, "The People as Consumers," *Recent Social Trends in the United States*, Report of the President's Research Committee on Social Trends (New York: McGraw-Hill, 1933).

2. See statistics collected in Sol Kroll, "Products Reliability: A Reasonable Expectation—The Ultimate Goal," *Drake Law Review* (1976), 25:828, 837.

3. James Andrew Hinds, Jr., "To Right Mass Wrongs: A Federal Class Action Act," *Harvard Journal on Legislation* (1976), 13:776, 812–16.

4. *Eisen v. Carlisle & Jacquelin*, 417 U.S. 156 (1974) imposes a requirement

that each reasonably identifiable class member receive notification of the lawsuit.

5. See, e.g., "Developments in the Law-Class Actions," *Harvard Law Review* (1976), 89:1318.

6. See Bureau of National Affairs, *Antitrust & Trade Regulation Report* (1977), no. 842, pp. F-1-16.

7. See, e.g., Hinds, "To Right Mass Wrongs."

8. See Robert B. Leflar and Martin H. Rogol, "Consumer Participation in the Regulation of Public Utilities: A Model Act," *Harvard Journal on Legislation* (1976), 13:235. Arthur Best and Bernard L. Brown, "Governmental Facilitation of Consumerism: A Proposal for Consumer Action Groups," *Temple Law Quarterly* (1977), 50:253.

9. Holt, C. J., in *Ashby v. White*, 2 Ld. Raym. 938, 955, 92 Eng. Rep. 126 (1703).

Index